MznLnx

Missing Links Exam Preps

Exam Prep for

Finite Mathematics and Calculus with Applications

Lial, Greenwell, Ritchey, 7th Edition

The MznLnx Exam Prep is your link from the texbook and lecture to your exams.
The MznLnx Exam Preps are unauthorized and comprehensive reviews of your textbooks.

All material provided by MznLnx and Rico Publications (c) 2010
Textbook publishers and textbook authors do not particpate in or contribute to these reviews.

MznLnx

Rico Publications

Exam Prep for Finite Mathematics and Calculus with Applications
7th Edition
Lial, Greenwell, Ritchey

Publisher: Raymond Houge
Assistant Editor: Michael Rouger
Text and Cover Designer: Lisa Buckner
Marketing Manager: Sara Swagger
Project Manager, Editorial Production: Jerry Emerson
Art Director: Vernon Lowerui

Product Manager: Dave Mason
Editorial Assitant: Rachel Guzmanji
Pedagogy: Debra Long
Cover Image: Jim Reed/Getty Images
Text and Cover Printer: City Printing, Inc.
Compositor: Media Mix, Inc.

(c) 2010 Rico Publications
ALL RIGHTS RESERVED. No part of this work covered by the copyright may be reproduced or used in any form or by an means--graphic, electronic, or mechanical, including photocopying, recording, taping, Web distribution, information storage, and retrieval systems, or in any other manner--without the written permission of the publisher.

Printed in the United States
ISBN:

For more information about our products, contact us at:
Dave.Mason@RicoPublications.com

For permission to use material from this text or product, submit a request online to:
Dave.Mason@RicoPublications.com

Contents

CHAPTER 1
LINEAR FUNCTIONS — 1

CHAPTER 2
SYSTEMS OF LINEAR EQUATIONS AND MATRICES — 14

CHAPTER 3
LINEAR PROGRAMMING: THE GRAPHICAL METHOD — 22

CHAPTER 4
LINEAR PROGRAMMING: THE SIMPLEX METHOD — 27

CHAPTER 5
MATHEMATICS OF FINANCE — 35

CHAPTER 6
LOGIC — 41

CHAPTER 7
SETS AND PROBABILITY — 46

CHAPTER 8
COUNTING PRINCIPLES; FURTHER PROBABILITY TOPICS — 54

CHAPTER 9
STATISTICS — 65

CHAPTER 10
NONLINEAR FUNCTIONS — 79

CHAPTER 11
THE DERIVATIVE — 98

CHAPTER 12
CALCULATING THE DERIVATIVE — 108

CHAPTER 13
GRAPHS AND THE DERIVATIVE — 118

CHAPTER 14
APPLICATIONS OF THE DERIVATIVE — 128

CHAPTER 15
INTEGRATION — 138

CHAPTER 16
FURTHER TECHNIQUES AND APPLICATIONS OF INTEGRATION — 154

CHAPTER 17
MULTIVARIABLE CALCULUS — 168

CHAPTER 18
PROBABILITY AND CALCULUS — 183

ANSWER KEY — 193

TO THE STUDENT

COMPREHENSIVE

The *MznLnx* Exam Prep series is designed to help you pass your exams. Editors at MznLnx review your textbooks and then prepare these practice exams to help you master the textbook material. Unlike study guides, workbooks, and practice tests provided by the texbook publisher and textbook authors, *MznLnx* gives you **all** of the material in each chapter in exam form, not just samples, so you can be sure to nail your exam.

MECHANICAL

The MznLnx Exam Prep series creates exams that will help you learn the subject matter as well as test you on your understanding. Each question is designed to help you master the concept. Just working through the exams, you gain an understanding of the subject--its a simple mechanical process that produces success.

INTEGRATED STUDY GUIDE AND REVIEW

MznLnx is not just a set of exams designed to test you, its also a comprehensive review of the subject content. Each exam question is also a review of the concept, making sure that you will get the answer correct without having to go to other sources of material. You learn as you go! Its the easiest way to pass an exam.

HUMOR

Studying can be tedious and dry. MznLnx's instructional design includes moderate humor within the exam questions on occassion, to break the tedium and revitalize the brain

Chapter 1. LINEAR FUNCTIONS

1. Exponentiation is a mathematical operation, written a^n, involving two numbers, the base a and the _____ n. When n is a positive integer, exponentiation corresponds to repeated multiplication:

$$a^n = \underbrace{a \times \cdots \times a}_{n},$$

just as multiplication by a positive integer corresponds to repeated addition:

$$a \times n = \underbrace{a + \cdots + a}_{n}.$$

The _____ is usually shown as a superscript to the right of the base. The exponentiation a^n can be read as: a raised to the n-th power, a raised to the power [of] n or possibly a raised to the _____ [of] n, or more briefly: a to the n-th power or a to the power [of] n, or even more briefly: a to the n.

- a. Exponent
- b. Exponential sum
- c. Exponentiating by squaring
- d. Exponential tree

2. _____ is the mathematical operation of scaling one number by another. It is one of the four basic operations in elementary arithmetic.

_____ is defined for whole numbers in terms of repeated addition; for example, 4 multiplied by 3 can be calculated by adding 3 copies of 4 together:

$$4 + 4 + 4 = 12.$$

_____ of rational numbers and real numbers is defined by systematic generalization of this basic idea.

- a. Highest common factor
- b. Least common multiple
- c. The number 0 is even.
- d. Multiplication

3. _____ is the likelihood or chance that something is the case or will happen. Theoretical _____ is used extensively in areas such as statistics, mathematics, science and philosophy to draw conclusions about the likelihood of potential events and the underlying mechanics of complex systems.

The word _____ does not have a consistent direct definition.

- a. Standardized moment
- b. Discrete random variable
- c. Statistical significance
- d. Probability

4. In probability theory and statistics, a _____ identifies either the probability of each value of an unidentified random variable, or the probability of the value falling within a particular interval. The probability function describes the range of possible values that a random variable can attain and the probability that the value of the random variable is within any subset of that range.

Chapter 1. LINEAR FUNCTIONS

When the random variable takes values in the set of real numbers, the _____ is completely described by the cumulative distribution function, whose value at each real x is the probability that the random variable is smaller than or equal to x.

- a. Normal distribution
- b. Statistical graphics
- c. Probability distribution
- d. Z-test

5. The word _____ means curving in or hollowed inward.
- a. Clipping
- b. Concavity
- c. Key server
- d. Harmonic series

6. In probability theory, a probability distribution is called _____ if its cumulative distribution function is _____. That is equivalent to saying that for random variables X with the distribution in question, Pr[X = a] = 0 for all real numbers a. If the distribution of X is _____ then X is called a _____ random variable.
- a. Continuous phase modulation
- b. Conull set
- c. Concatenated codes
- d. Continuous

7. In differential geometry, a discipline within mathematics, a _____ is a subset of the tangent bundle of a manifold satisfying certain properties. _____s are used to build up notions of integrability, and specifically of a foliation of a manifold
- a. Coherence
- b. Constraint
- c. Discontinuity
- d. Distribution

8. The _____ or Dirac's delta is a mathematical construct introduced by the British theoretical physicist Paul Dirac. Informally, it is a function representing an infinitely sharp peak bounding unit area: a function that has the value zero everywhere except at x = 0 where its value is infinitely large in such a way that its total integral is 1. It is a continuous analogue of the discrete Kronecker delta.
- a. Hyperfunction
- b. Weak derivative
- c. Schwartz kernel theorem
- d. Dirac delta

9. The mathematical concept of a _____ expresses the intuitive idea of deterministic dependence between two quantities, one of which is viewed as primary and the other as secondary. A _____ then is a way to associate a unique output for each input of a specified type, for example, a real number or an element of a given set.
- a. Coherent
- b. Going up
- c. Grill
- d. Function

10. The _____ are the set of numbers consisting of the natural numbers including 0 and their negatives. They are numbers that can be written without a fractional or decimal component, and fall within the set {... −2, −1, 0, 1, 2, ...}.
- a. A Mathematical Theory of Communication
- b. A posteriori
- c. A chemical equation
- d. Integers

11. In mathematics, a _____ is a set of real numbers with the property that any number that lies between two numbers in the set is also included in the set. For example, the set of all numbers x satisfying $0 \leq x \leq 1$ is an _____ which contains 0 and 1, as well as all numbers between them. Other examples of _____s are the set of all real numbers $\mathbb{R}$, the set of all positive real numbers, and the empty set.

Chapter 1. LINEAR FUNCTIONS

a. Interval
c. Ideal
b. Order
d. Annihilator

12. In mathematics, a _____ is an expression constructed from variables and constants, using the operations of addition, subtraction, multiplication, and constant non-negative whole number exponents. For example, $x^2 - 4x + 7$ is a _____, but $x^2 - 4/x + 7x^{3/2}$ is not, because its second term involves division by the variable x and also because its third term contains an exponent that is not a whole number.

_____s are one of the most important concepts in algebra and throughout mathematics and science.

a. Coimage
c. Semifield
b. Polynomial
d. Group extension

13. In probability theory and statistics, the _____ of a random variable, probability distribution averaging the squared distance of its possible values from the expected value. Whereas the mean is a way to describe the location of a distribution, the _____ is a way to capture its scale or degree of being spread out. The unit of _____ is the square of the unit of the original variable.

a. Kendall tau rank correlation coefficient
c. Probability distribution
b. Variance
d. Nonlinear regression

14. The x-axis is the horizontal axis of a two-dimensional plot in the _____, that is typically pointed to the right. Also known as a right-handed coordinate system.

a. 120-cell
c. 1-center problem
b. 2-3 heap
d. Cartesian coordinate system

15. A _____ is an abstract model that uses mathematical language to describe the behavior of a system. Eykhoff defined a _____ as 'a representation of the essential aspects of an existing system which presents knowledge of that system in usable form'.

a. Total least squares
c. Rata Die
b. Metaheuristic
d. Mathematical model

16. In quantum field theory and statistical mechanics in the thermodynamic limit, a system with a global symmetry can have more than one phase. For parameters where the symmetry is spontaneously broken, the system is said to be _____. When the global symmetry is unbroken the system is disordered.

a. Isoenthalpic-isobaric ensemble
c. Einstein relation
b. Ursell function
d. Ordered

17. In mathematics, an _____ is a collection of objects having two coordinates (or entries or projections), such that one can always uniquely determine the object, which is the first coordinate (or first entry or left projection) of the pair as well as the second coordinate (or second entry or right projection.) If the first coordinate is a and the second is b, the usual notation for an _____ is (a, b.) The pair is 'ordered' in that (a, b) differs from (b, a) unless a = b.

a. Ordered pair
c. A Mathematical Theory of Communication
b. A posteriori
d. A chemical equation

18. In mathematics, the _____ of a Euclidean space is a special point, usually denoted by the letter O, used as a fixed point of reference for the geometry of the surrounding space. In a Cartesian coordinate system, the _____ is the point where the axes of the system intersect. In Euclidean geometry, the _____ may be chosen freely as any convenient point of reference.

   a. Interval
   c. OMAC
   b. Autonomous system
   d. Origin

19. A _____, in mathematics, is a polynomial function of the form $f(x) = ax^2 + bx + c$, where $a \neq 0$. The graph of a _____ is a parabola whose major axis is parallel to the y-axis.

The expression $ax^2 + bx + c$ in the definition of a _____ is a polynomial of degree 2 or a 2nd degree polynomial, because the highest exponent of x is 2.

   a. Multivariate division algorithm
   c. Laguerre polynomials
   b. Discriminant
   d. Quadratic function

20. A _____ is a software program that facilitates symbolic mathematics. The core functionality of a CAS is manipulation of mathematical expressions in symbolic form.

The symbolic manipulations supported typically include

- simplification to the smallest possible expression or some standard form, including automatic simplification with assumptions and simplification with constraints
- substitution of symbolic, functors or numeric values for expressions
- change of form of expressions: expanding products and powers, partial and full factorization, rewriting as partial fractions, constraint satisfaction, rewriting trigonometric functions as exponentials, etc.
- partial and total differentiation
- symbolic constrained and unconstrained global optimization
- solution of linear and some non-linear equations over various domains
- solution of some differential and difference equations
- taking some limits
- some indefinite and definite integration, including multidimensional integrals
- integral transforms
- arbitrary-precision numeric operations
- Series operations such as expansion, summation and products
- matrix operations including products, inverses, etc.
- display of mathematical expressions in two-dimensional mathematical form, often using typesetting systems similar to TeX
- add-ons for use in applied mathematics such as physics packages for physical computation
- plotting graphs and parametric plots of functions in two and three dimensions, and animating them
- APIs for linking it on an external program such as a database, or using in a programming language to use the _____
- drawing charts and diagrams
- string manipulation such as matching and searching
- statistical computation
- Theorem proving and verification
- graphic production and editing such as CGI and signal processing as image processing
- sound synthesis

Many also include a programming language, allowing users to implement their own algorithms.

Some _____s focus on a specific area of application; these are typically developed in academia and are free.

a. Computer algebra system
c. 2-3 heap
b. 1-center problem
d. 120-cell

21. In ecology, predation describes a biological interaction where a _____ (an organism that is hunting) feeds on its prey, the organism that is attacked. _____s may or may not kill their prey prior to feeding on them, but the act of predation always results in the death of the prey. The other main category of consumption is detritivory, the consumption of dead organic material (detritus.)

Chapter 1. LINEAR FUNCTIONS

    a. 120-cell
    b. Predator
    c. 1-center problem
    d. Prey

22. The _____ is the horizontal axis of a two- dimensional plot in the Cartesian coordinate system, that is typically pointed to the right. Also known as a right-handed coordinate system.
    a. 1-center problem
    b. X-axis
    c. 120-cell
    d. 2-3 heap

23. The _____ is one of the coordinates of a point in a two or three-dimensional cartesian coordinate system, equal to the distance of a point from the y-axis in a 2D system, or from the plane of y and z axes in a 3D system, measured along a line parallel to the x axis.
    a. 120-cell
    b. 1-center problem
    c. 2-3 heap
    d. X-coordinate

24. In reference to a 2D and 3D plane, the _____ is the vertical height of a 2D or 3D object.
    a. 1-center problem
    b. Y-axis
    c. 120-cell
    d. 2-3 heap

25. The _____ is the distance between a point and an axis in the Cartesian Coordinate System.
    a. 120-cell
    b. Y-coordinate
    c. 2-3 heap
    d. 1-center problem

26. In mathematics, the _____ is an approach to finding a particular solution to certain inhomogeneous ordinary differential equations and recurrence relations. It is closely related to the annihilator method, but instead of using a particular kind of differential operator in order to find the best possible form of the particular solution, a 'guess' is made as to the appropriate form, which is then tested by differentiating the resulting equation. In this sense, the _____ is less formal but more intuitive than the annihilator method.
    a. Phase line
    b. Differential algebraic equations
    c. Linear differential equation
    d. Method of undetermined coefficients

27. A _____ consists of one quarter of the coordinate plane.
    a. 120-cell
    b. 1-center problem
    c. Quadrant
    d. 2-3 heap

28. _____ is used to describe the steepness, incline, gradient, or grade of a straight line. A higher _____ value indicates a steeper incline. The _____ is defined as the ratio of the 'rise' divided by the 'run' between two points on a line, or in other words, the ratio of the altitude change to the horizontal distance between any two points on the line.
    a. Slope
    b. Point plotting
    c. Cognitively Guided Instruction
    d. Number line

29. In mathematics, the concept of a _____ tries to capture the intuitive idea of a geometrical one-dimensional and continuous object. A simple example is the circle. In everyday use of the term '_____', a straight line is not curved, but in mathematical parlance _____s include straight lines and line segments.
    a. Quadrifolium
    b. Negative pedal curve
    c. Kappa curve
    d. Curve

Chapter 1. LINEAR FUNCTIONS

30. A _____ is an algebraic equation in which each term is either a constant or the product of a constant and a single variable. _____s can have one, two, three or more variables.

_____s occur with great regularity in applied mathematics.

a. Quartic equation
b. Quadratic equation
c. Difference of two squares
d. Linear equation

31. In mathematics, two quantities are called _____ if they vary in such a way that one of the quantities is a constant multiple of the other, or equivalently if they have a constant ratio.

a. 2-3 heap
b. Proportional
c. 1-center problem
d. 120-cell

32. _____ is a form where m is the slope of the line and b is the y-intercept, which is the y-coordinate of the point where the line crosses the y axis. This can be seen by letting x = 0, which immediately gives y = b.

a. Dynamical system
b. Commutative law
c. Separable extension
d. Slope-intercept form

33. The _____ expresses the fact that the difference in the y coordinate between two points on a line that is, y − y1 is proportional to the difference in the x coordinate that is, x − x1. The proportionality constant is m (the slope of the line.

a. Square function
b. Point-slope form
c. Rubin Causal Model
d. Cobb-Douglas

34. A _____ of a curve is the envelope of a family of congruent circles centered on the curve. It generalises the concept of _____ lines.

It is sometimes called the offset curve but the term 'offset' often refers also to translation.

a. Cissoid
b. Bifolium
c. Parallel
d. Cycloid

35. The existence and properties of _____ are the basis of Euclid's parallel postulate. _____ are two lines on the same plane that do not intersect even assuming that lines extend to infinity in either direction.

a. Vertical translation
b. Square wheel
c. Spidron
d. Parallel lines

36. In linear algebra, _____ is a version of Gaussian elimination that puts zeros both above and below each pivot element as it goes from the top row of the given matrix to the bottom. In other words, _____ brings a matrix to reduced row echelon form, whereas Gaussian elimination takes it only as far as row echelon form. Every matrix has a reduced row echelon form, and this algorithm is guaranteed to produce it.

a. Lax equivalence theorem
b. Gauss-Jordan elimination
c. Spheroidal wave functions
d. Conservation form

37. _____ and independent variables refer to values that change in relationship to each other. The _____ are those that are observed to change in response to the independent variables. The independent variables are those that are deliberately manipulated to invoke a change in the _____.

a. Steiner system
b. Round robin test
c. Yates analysis
d. Dependent variables

38. Dependent variables and _____ refer to values that change in relationship to each other. The dependent variables are those that are observed to change in response to the _____. The _____ are those that are deliberately manipulated to invoke a change in the dependent variables.
   a. Operational confound
   b. Experimental design diagram
   c. One-factor-at-a-time method
   d. Independent variables

39. In economics, the _____ can be defined as the graph depicting the relationship between the price of a certain commodity, and the amount of it that consumers are willing and able to purchase at that given price. The _____ for all consumers together follows from the _____ of every individual consumer: the individual demands at each price are added together.

   _____s are used to estimate behaviors in competitive markets, and are often combined with supply curves to estimate the equilibrium price and the equilibrium quantity of that market.

   a. Phillips curve
   b. Lorenz curve
   c. 1-center problem
   d. Demand curve

40. _____ is an economic model describing effects on price and quantity in a market. It predicts that in a competitive market, price will function to equalize the quantity demanded by consumers, and the quantity supplied by producers, resulting in an economic equilibrium of price and quantity. The model incorporates other factors changing equilibrium as a shift of demand and/or supply.
   a. 1-center problem
   b. Marginal rate of substitution
   c. Cross price elasticity of demand
   d. Supply and demand

41. In economics, business, retail, and accounting, a _____ is the value of money that has been used up to produce something, and hence is not available for use anymore. In business, the _____ may be one of acquisition, in which case the amount of money expended to acquire it is counted as _____. In this case, money is the input that is gone in order to acquire the thing.
   a. 1-center problem
   b. 2-3 heap
   c. 120-cell
   d. Cost

42. The method of _____ or ordinary _____ is used to solve overdetermined systems. _____ is often applied in statistical contexts, particularly regression analysis.

   _____ can be interpreted as a method of fitting data.

   a. Non-linear least squares
   b. Rata Die
   c. Least squares
   d. System equivalence

43. _____ is the change in total cost that arises when the quantity produced changes by one unit.
   a. Limiting
   b. Notation
   c. Differential Algebra
   d. Marginal cost

Chapter 1. LINEAR FUNCTIONS

44. In mathematics, an _____, or central tendency of a data set refers to a measure of the 'middle' or 'expected' value of the data set. There are many different descriptive statistics that can be chosen as a measurement of the central tendency of the data items.

An _____ is a single value that is meant to typify a list of values.

a. A chemical equation
b. A Mathematical Theory of Communication
c. A posteriori
d. Average

45. In economics, specifically cost accounting, the _____ is the point at which cost or expenses and revenue are equal: there is no net loss or gain, and one has 'broken even'. Therefore has not made a profit or a loss.

In the linear Cost-Volume-Profit Analysis model, the _____ can be directly computed in terms of Total Revenue and Total Costs as:

$$TR = TC$$
$$P \times X = TFC + V \times X$$
$$P \times X - V \times X = TFC$$
$$(P - V) \times X = TFC$$
$$X = \frac{TFC}{P - V}$$

where:

- TFC is Total Fixed Costs,
- P is Unit Sale Price, and
- V is Unit Variable Cost.

The _____ can alternatively be computed as the point where Contribution equals Fixed Costs.

The quantity $(P - V)$ is of interest in its own right, and is called the Unit Contribution Margin: it is the marginal profit per unit, or alternatively the portion of each sale that contributes to Fixed Costs. Thus the _____ can be more simply computed as the point where Total Contribution = Total Fixed Cost:

$$\text{Total Contribution} = \text{Total Fixed Costs}$$
$$\text{Unit Contribution} \times \text{Number of Units} = \text{Total Fixed Costs}$$
$$\text{Number of Units} = \frac{\text{Total Fixed Costs}}{\text{Unit Contribution}}$$

In currency units to reach break-even, one can use the above calculation and multiply by Price, or equivalently use the Contribution Margin Ratio to compute it as:

$$\text{Break-even(in Sales)} = \frac{\text{Fixed Costs}}{C/P}.$$

R=C Where R is revenue generated C is cost incurred.

a. 1-center problem
b. 120-cell
c. Break-even point
d. Small numbers game

46. In economics, the cross elasticity of demand and _____ measures the responsiveness of the quantity demanded of a good to a change in the price of another good.

It is measured as the percentage change in quantity demanded for the first good that occurs in response to a percentage change in price of the second good. For example, if, in response to a 10% increase in the price of fuel, the quantity of new cars that are fuel inefficient demanded decreased by 20%, the cross elasticity of demand would be -20%/10% = -2.

a. Supply and demand
b. Marginal rate of substitution
c. 1-center problem
d. Cross price elasticity of demand

47. In mathematics, a _____ is a system which is not linear. Less technically, a _____ is any problem where the variabl to be solved for cannot be written as a linear sum of independent components. A nonhomogenous system, which is linear apart from the presence of a function of the independent variables, is nonlinear according to a strict definition, but such systems are usually studied alongside linear systems, because they can be transformed to a linear system as long as a particular solution is known.

a. 1-center problem
b. George Dantzig
c. Metric system
d. Nonlinear system

48. In mathematics, the _____ or least common denominator is the least common multiple of the denominators of a set of vulgar fractions. It is the smallest positive integer that is a multiple of the denominators. For instance, the _____ of

$$\left\{\frac{5}{12}, \frac{11}{18}\right\}$$

is 36 because the least common multiple of 12 and 18 is 36.

a. Highest common factor
b. The number 0 is even.
c. Lowest common denominator
d. Subtrahend

49. _____ is the addition of a set of numbers; the result is their sum or total. An interim or present total of a _____ process is termed the running total. The 'numbers' to be summed may be natural numbers, complex numbers, matrices, or still more complicated objects.

a. Summation
b. 120-cell
c. 1-center problem
d. 2-3 heap

50. A _____ is a deliberate process for transforming one or more inputs into one or more results, with variable change.

The term is used in a variety of senses, from the very definite arithmetical using an algorithm to the vague heuristics of calculating a strategy in a competition or calculating the chance of a successful relationship between two people.

Multiplying 7 by 8 is a simple algorithmic _____.

Chapter 1. LINEAR FUNCTIONS

a. Mathematical maturity
b. Mathematical object
c. Mathematics Subject Classification
d. Calculation

51. _____ is a branch of mathematics which focuses on the study of matrices. Initially a sub-branch of linear algebra, it has grown to cover subjects related to graph theory, algebra, combinatorics, and statistics as well.

The term matrix was first coined in 1848 by J.J. Sylvester as a name of an array of numbers.

a. Pairing
b. Segre classification
c. Semi-simple operators
d. Matrix theory

52. In mathematics, a _____ is a constant multiplicative factor of a certain object. For example, in the expression $9x^2$, the _____ of x^2 is 9.

The object can be such things as a variable, a vector, a function, etc.

a. Fibonacci polynomials
b. Stability radius
c. Multivariate division algorithm
d. Coefficient

53. In probability theory and statistics, _____ indicates the strength and direction of a linear relationship between two random variables. That is in contrast with the usage of the term in colloquial speech, denoting any relationship, not necessarily linear. In general statistical usage, _____ or co-relation refers to the departure of two random variables from independence.

a. Correlation
b. Summary statistics
c. Random variables
d. Sample size

54. A _____ typically refers to a class of handheld calculators that are capable of plotting graphs, solving simultaneous equations, and performing numerous other tasks with variables. Most popular _____s are also programmable, allowing the user to create customized programs, typically for scientific/engineering and education applications. Due to their large displays intended for graphing, they can also accommodate several lines of text and calculations at a time.

a. Graphing calculator
b. Support vector machines
c. Bump mapping
d. Genus

Chapter 1. LINEAR FUNCTIONS

55. _____ or amortisation is the process of decreasing an amount over a period of time. The word comes from Middle English amortisen to kill, alienate in mortmain, from Anglo-French amorteser, alteration of amortir, from Vulgar Latin admortire to kill, from Latin ad- + mort-, mors death. Particular instances of the term include:

- _____, the allocation of a lump sum amount to different time periods, particularly for loans and other forms of finance, including related interest or other finance charges.
    - _____ schedule, a table detailing each periodic payment on a loan, as generated by an _____ calculator.
    - Negative _____, an _____ schedule where the loan amount actually increases through not paying the full interest
- Amortized analysis, analyzing the execution cost of algorithms over a sequence of operations.
- _____ of capital expenditures of certain assets under accounting rules, particularly intangible assets, in a manner analogous to depreciation.
- _____

_____ is also used in the context of zoning regulations and describes the time in which a property owner has to relocate when the property's use constitutes a preexisting nonconforming use under zoning regulations.

- Depreciation

a. ISAAC
c. Identity
b. Origin
d. Amortization

56. An _____ is a table detailing each periodic payment on a amortizing loan, as generated by an amortization calculator.

While a portion of every payment is applied towards both the interest and the principal balance of the loan, the exact amount applied to principal each time varies. An _____ reveals the specific monetary amount put towards interest, as well as the specific put towards the Principal balance, with each payment.

a. Accounts receivable
c. A Mathematical Theory of Communication
b. Amortization schedule
d. A chemical equation

57. A _____ is a device for performing mathematical calculations, distinguished from a computer by having a limited problem solving ability and an interface optimized for interactive calculation rather than programming. _____s can be hardware or software, and mechanical or electronic, and are often built into devices such as PDAs or mobile phones.

Modern electronic _____s are generally small, digital, and usually inexpensive.

a. 2-3 heap
c. Calculator
b. 120-cell
d. 1-center problem

58. _____ is a method of constructing new data points from a discrete set of known data points.

Chapter 1. LINEAR FUNCTIONS 13

a. Interpolation
c. Integration by substitution
b. Uniform convergence
d. Archimedes' use of infinitesimals

59. In mathematics, the _____ of a number to a given base is the power or exponent to which the base must be raised in order to produce the number.

For example, the _____ of 1000 to the base 10 is 3, because 3 is how many 10s one must multiply to get 1000: thus 10 × 10 × 10 = 1000; the base-2 _____ of 32 is 5 because 5 is how many 2s one must multiply to get 32: thus 2 × 2 × 2 × 2 × 2 = 32. In the language of exponents: 10^3 = 1000, so $\log_{10} 1000 = 3$, and 2^5 = 32, so $\log_2 32 = 5$.

a. 1-center problem
c. 2-3 heap
b. Logarithm
d. 120-cell

Chapter 2. SYSTEMS OF LINEAR EQUATIONS AND MATRICES

1. In the study of metric spaces in mathematics, there are various notions of two metrics on the same underlying space being 'the same', or _____.

In the following, M will denote a non-empty set and d_1 and d_2 will denote two metrics on M.

The two metrics d_1 and d_2 are said to be topologically _____ if they generate the same topology on M.

   a. Equivalent
   b. A chemical equation
   c. A posteriori
   d. A Mathematical Theory of Communication

2. In linear algebra, _____ is a version of Gaussian elimination that puts zeros both above and below each pivot element as it goes from the top row of the given matrix to the bottom. In other words, _____ brings a matrix to reduced row echelon form, whereas Gaussian elimination takes it only as far as row echelon form. Every matrix has a reduced row echelon form, and this algorithm is guaranteed to produce it.

   a. Lax equivalence theorem
   b. Conservation form
   c. Spheroidal wave functions
   d. Gauss-Jordan elimination

3. A _____ is a mathematical model of a system based on the use of a linear operator. _____s typically exhibit features and properties that are much simpler than the general, nonlinear case. As a mathematical abstraction or idealization, _____s find important applications in automatic control theory, signal processing, and telecommunications.

   a. Predispositioning Theory
   b. Hybrid system
   c. Percolation
   d. Linear system

4. A _____ is a software program that facilitates symbolic mathematics. The core functionality of a CAS is manipulation of mathematical expressions in symbolic form.

Chapter 2. SYSTEMS OF LINEAR EQUATIONS AND MATRICES

The symbolic manipulations supported typically include

- simplification to the smallest possible expression or some standard form, including automatic simplification with assumptions and simplification with constraints
- substitution of symbolic, functors or numeric values for expressions
- change of form of expressions: expanding products and powers, partial and full factorization, rewriting as partial fractions, constraint satisfaction, rewriting trigonometric functions as exponentials, etc.
- partial and total differentiation
- symbolic constrained and unconstrained global optimization
- solution of linear and some non-linear equations over various domains
- solution of some differential and difference equations
- taking some limits
- some indefinite and definite integration, including multidimensional integrals
- integral transforms
- arbitrary-precision numeric operations
- Series operations such as expansion, summation and products
- matrix operations including products, inverses, etc.
- display of mathematical expressions in two-dimensional mathematical form, often using typesetting systems similar to TeX
- add-ons for use in applied mathematics such as physics packages for physical computation
- plotting graphs and parametric plots of functions in two and three dimensions, and animating them
- APIs for linking it on an external program such as a database, or using in a programming language to use the _____
- drawing charts and diagrams
- string manipulation such as matching and searching
- statistical computation
- Theorem proving and verification
- graphic production and editing such as CGI and signal processing as image processing
- sound synthesis

Many also include a programming language, allowing users to implement their own algorithms.

Some _____s focus on a specific area of application; these are typically developed in academia and are free.

- a. 120-cell
- b. Computer algebra system
- c. 1-center problem
- d. 2-3 heap

5. In mathematics, an _____ or member of a set is any one of the distinct objects that make up that set.

Writing A = {1,2,3,4}, means that the _____s of the set A are the numbers 1, 2, 3 and 4. Groups of _____s of A, for example {1,2}, are subsets of A.

Chapter 2. SYSTEMS OF LINEAR EQUATIONS AND MATRICES

a. Ideal
b. Universal code
c. Order
d. Element

6. _____ is a branch of mathematics which focuses on the study of matrices. Initially a sub-branch of linear algebra, it has grown to cover subjects related to graph theory, algebra, combinatorics, and statistics as well.

The term matrix was first coined in 1848 by J.J. Sylvester as a name of an array of numbers.

a. Semi-simple operators
b. Pairing
c. Segre classification
d. Matrix theory

7. A _____ is a device for performing mathematical calculations, distinguished from a computer by having a limited problem solving ability and an interface optimized for interactive calculation rather than programming. _____s can be hardware or software, and mechanical or electronic, and are often built into devices such as PDAs or mobile phones.

Modern electronic _____s are generally small, digital, and usually inexpensive.

a. 120-cell
b. 2-3 heap
c. 1-center problem
d. Calculator

8. A _____ typically refers to a class of handheld calculators that are capable of plotting graphs, solving simultaneous equations, and performing numerous other tasks with variables. Most popular _____s are also programmable, allowing the user to create customized programs, typically for scientific/engineering and education applications. Due to their large displays intended for graphing, they can also accommodate several lines of text and calculations at a time.

a. Genus
b. Bump mapping
c. Graphing calculator
d. Support vector machines

9. The function $\log_b(x)$ depends on both b and x, but the term _____ (or logarithmic function) in standard usage refers to a function of the form $\log_b(x)$ in which the base b is fixed and so the only argument is x. Thus there is one _____ for each value of the base b (which must be positive and must differ from 1.) Viewed in this way, the base-b _____ is the inverse function of the exponential function b^x.

a. Logarithm function
b. 2-3 heap
c. 1-center problem
d. 120-cell

10. In probability theory, a probability distribution is called _____ if its cumulative distribution function is _____. That is equivalent to saying that for random variables X with the distribution in question, Pr[X = a] = 0 for all real numbers a. If the distribution of X is _____ then X is called a _____ random variable.

a. Conull set
b. Continuous phase modulation
c. Concatenated codes
d. Continuous

11. The mathematical concept of a _____ expresses the intuitive idea of deterministic dependence between two quantities, one of which is viewed as primary and the other as secondary. A _____ then is a way to associate a unique output for each input of a specified type, for example, a real number or an element of a given set.

a. Coherent
b. Grill
c. Function
d. Going up

Chapter 2. SYSTEMS OF LINEAR EQUATIONS AND MATRICES

12. In physics and in _____ calculus, a _____ is a concept characterized by a magnitude and a direction. A _____ can be thought of as an arrow in Euclidean space, drawn from an initial point A pointing to a terminal point B.
   a. Deviation
   b. Vector
   c. Constraint
   d. Dominance

13. In mathematics, _____ is one of the basic operations defining a vector space in linear algebra. Note that _____ is different from scalar product which is an inner product between two vectors.

   More specifically, if K is a field and V is a vector space over K, then _____ is a function from K × V to V.

   a. Jordan normal form
   b. Scalar multiplication
   c. Non-negative matrix factorization
   d. Frobenius normal form

14. In mathematics the _____ of a set which is equipped with the operation of addition is an element which, when added to any element x in the set, yields x. One of the most familiar additive identities is the number 0 from elementary mathematics, but additive identities occur in other mathematical structures where addition is defined, such as in groups and rings.

   - The _____ familiar from elementary mathematics is zero, denoted 0. For example,

   $5 + 0 = 5 = 0 + 5$.

   - In the natural numbers N and all of its supersets, the _____ is 0. Thus for any one of these numbers n,

   $n + 0 = n = 0 + n$.

   Let N be a set which is closed under the operation of addition, denoted +. An _____ for N is any element e such that for any element n in N,

   $e + n = n = n + e$.

   a. Unique factorization domain
   b. Unit ring
   c. Additive identity
   d. Algebraically independent

15. In mathematics, the _____ of a number n is the number that, when added to n, yields zero. The _____ of n is denoted −n. For example, 7 is −7, because $7 + (−7) = 0$, and the _____ of −0.3 is 0.3, because $−0.3 + 0.3 = 0$.
   a. Arity
   b. Associativity
   c. Algebraic structure
   d. Additive inverse

Chapter 2. SYSTEMS OF LINEAR EQUATIONS AND MATRICES

16. In mathematics, the term _____ has several different important meanings:

- An _____ is an equality that remains true regardless of the values of any variables that appear within it, to distinguish it from an equality which is true under more particular conditions. For this, the 'triple bar' symbol ≡ is sometimes used.
- In algebra, an _____ or _____ element of a set S with a binary operation Â· is an element e that, when combined with any element x of S, produces that same x. That is, eÂ·x = xÂ·e = x for all x in S.
    - The _____ function from a set S to itself, often denoted id or id$_S$, s the function such that i = x for all x in S. This function serves as the _____ element in the set of all functions from S to itself with respect to function composition.
    - In linear algebra, the _____ matrix of size n is the n-by-n square matrix with ones on the main diagonal and zeros elsewhere. This matrix serves as the _____ with respect to matrix multiplication.

A common example of the first meaning is the trigonometric _____

$$\sin^2 \theta + \cos^2 \theta = 1$$

which is true for all real values of θ, as opposed to

$$\cos \theta = 1,$$

which is true only for some values of θ, not all. For example, the latter equation is true when $\theta = 0$, false when $\theta = 2$

The concepts of 'additive _____' and 'multiplicative _____' are central to the Peano axioms. The number 0 is the 'additive _____' for integers, real numbers, and complex numbers. For the real numbers, for all $a \in \mathbb{R}$,

$$0 + a = a,$$

$$a + 0 = a, \text{ and}$$

$$0 + 0 = 0.$$

Similarly, The number 1 is the 'multiplicative _____' for integers, real numbers, and complex numbers.

a. Intersection
b. Action
c. ARIA
d. Identity

Chapter 2. SYSTEMS OF LINEAR EQUATIONS AND MATRICES

17. In mathematics, an _____ is a statement about the relative size or order of two objects, or about whether they are the same or not

- The notation a < b means that a is less than b.
- The notation a > b means that a is greater than b.
- The notation a ≠ b means that a is not equal to b, but does not say that one is bigger than the other or even that they can be compared in size.

In all these cases, a is not equal to b, hence, '_____'.

These relations are known as strict _____

- The notation a ≤ b means that a is less than or equal to b;
- The notation a ≥ b means that a is greater than or equal to b;

An additional use of the notation is to show that one quantity is much greater than another, normally by several orders of magnitude.

- The notation a << b means that a is much less than b.
- The notation a >> b means that a is much greater than b.

If the sense of the _____ is the same for all values of the variables for which its members are defined, then the _____ is called an 'absolute' or 'unconditional' _____. If the sense of an _____ holds only for certain values of the variables involved, but is reversed or destroyed for other values of the variables, it is called a conditional _____.

An _____ may appear unsolvable because it only states whether a number is larger or smaller than another number; but it is possible to apply the same operations for equalities to inequalities. For example, to find x for the _____ 10x > 23 one would divide 23 by 10.

a. A chemical equation
c. Inequality
b. A Mathematical Theory of Communication
d. A posteriori

18. In mathematics, a _____ is an expression constructed from variables and constants, using the operations of addition, subtraction, multiplication, and constant non-negative whole number exponents. For example, $x^2 - 4x + 7$ is a _____, but $x^2 - 4/x + 7x^{3/2}$ is not, because its second term involves division by the variable x and also because its third term contains an exponent that is not a whole number.

_____s are one of the most important concepts in algebra and throughout mathematics and science.

a. Group extension
c. Coimage
b. Semifield
d. Polynomial

Chapter 2. SYSTEMS OF LINEAR EQUATIONS AND MATRICES

19. A _____ is the transfer of an interest in property (or in law the equivalent - a charge) to a lender as a security for a debt - usually a loan of money. While a _____ in itself is not a debt, it is lender's security for a debt. It is a transfer of an interest in land (or the equivalent), from the owner to the _____ lender, on the condition that this interest will be returned to the owner of the real estate when the terms of the _____ have been satisfied or performed.
    a. 2-3 heap   b. 1-center problem
    c. 120-cell   d. Mortgage

20. _____ is the mathematical operation of scaling one number by another. It is one of the four basic operations in elementary arithmetic.

_____ is defined for whole numbers in terms of repeated addition; for example, 4 multiplied by 3 can be calculated by adding 3 copies of 4 together:

$$4 + 4 + 4 = 12.$$

_____ of rational numbers and real numbers is defined by systematic generalization of this basic idea.

    a. Highest common factor   b. Least common multiple
    c. The number 0 is even.   d. Multiplication

21. In elementary algebra, a _____ is a polynomial with two terms: the sum of two monomials. It is the simplest kind of polynomial except for a monomial.

The _____ $a^2 - b^2$ can be factored as the product of two other _____ s:

    $a^2 - b^2$.

The product of a pair of linear _____ s $ax + b$ and $cx + d$ is:

    $2 + x + bd$.

A _____ raised to the nth power, represented as

    n

can be expanded by means of the _____ theorem or, equivalently, using Pascal's triangle.

    a. Cylindrical algebraic decomposition   b. Rational root theorem
    c. Real structure   d. Binomial

22. In mathematics, a _____ is a rectangular table of elements, which may be numbers or, more generally, any abstract quantities that can be added and multiplied. Matrices are used to describe linear equations, keep track of the coefficients of linear transformations and to record data that depend on multiple parameters. Matrices are described by the field of _____ theory.

Chapter 2. SYSTEMS OF LINEAR EQUATIONS AND MATRICES

a. Double counting
b. Matrix
c. Compression
d. Coherent

23. In mathematics, a _____ for a number x, denoted by $1/x$ or x^{-1}, is a number which when multiplied by x yields the multiplicative identity, 1. The _____ of x is also called the reciprocal of x. The _____ of a fraction p/q is q/p.
   a. Hyperbolic function
   b. Golden function
   c. Multiplicative inverse
   d. Double exponential

24. In mathematics, a _____ is a constant multiplicative factor of a certain object. For example, in the expression $9x^2$, the _____ of x^2 is 9.

The object can be such things as a variable, a vector, a function, etc.

   a. Multivariate division algorithm
   b. Fibonacci polynomials
   c. Stability radius
   d. Coefficient

25. _____ is a phenomenon which arises in the region of a continuous phase transition. Originally reported by Thomas Andrews in 1869 for the liquid-gas transition in carbon dioxide, many other examples have been discovered since. The phenomenon is most commonly demonstrated in binary fluid mixtures, such as methanol and cyclohexane.
   a. Percolation threshold
   b. Critical opalescence
   c. Critical temperature
   d. Fermi point

26. In mathematics, _____ of order k of functions is an equivalence relation, corresponding to having the same value at a point P and also the same derivatives there, up to order k. The equivalence classes are generally called jets. The point of osculation is also called the double cusp.
   a. Dominance
   b. Critical point
   c. Characteristic
   d. Contact

Chapter 3. LINEAR PROGRAMMING: THE GRAPHICAL METHOD

1. In mathematics, an _____ is a statement about the relative size or order of two objects, or about whether they are the same or not

- The notation a < b means that a is less than b.
- The notation a > b means that a is greater than b.
- The notation a ≠ b means that a is not equal to b, but does not say that one is bigger than the other or even that they can be compared in size.

In all these cases, a is not equal to b, hence, '_____'.

These relations are known as strict _____

- The notation a ≤ b means that a is less than or equal to b;
- The notation a ≥ b means that a is greater than or equal to b;

An additional use of the notation is to show that one quantity is much greater than another, normally by several orders of magnitude.

- The notation a << b means that a is much less than b.
- The notation a >> b means that a is much greater than b.

If the sense of the _____ is the same for all values of the variables for which its members are defined, then the _____ is called an 'absolute' or 'unconditional' _____. If the sense of an _____ holds only for certain values of the variables involved, but is reversed or destroyed for other values of the variables, it is called a conditional _____.

An _____ may appear unsolvable because it only states whether a number is larger or smaller than another number; but it is possible to apply the same operations for equalities to inequalities. For example, to find x for the _____ 10x > 23 one would divide 23 by 10.

a. A Mathematical Theory of Communication
b. Inequality
c. A posteriori
d. A chemical equation

2. In mathematics, _____ is a technique for optimization of a linear objective function, subject to linear equality and linear inequality constraints. Informally, _____ determines the way to achieve the best outcome in a given mathematical model given some list of requirements represented as linear equations.

More formally, given a polytope, and a real-valued affine function

$$f(x_1, x_2, \ldots, x_n) = c_1 x_1 + c_2 x_2 + \cdots + c_n x_n + d$$

defined on this polytope, a _____ method will find a point in the polytope where this function has the smallest value.

Chapter 3. LINEAR PROGRAMMING: THE GRAPHICAL METHOD

    a. Lin-Kernighan
    c. Descent direction
    b. Linear programming
    d. Linear programming relaxation

3. The word _____ means curving in or hollowed inward.
   a. Harmonic series
   b. Key server
   c. Clipping
   d. Concavity

4. In the mathematical area of order theory, every partially ordered set P gives rise to a _____ partially ordered set which is often denoted by P^{op} or P^d. This _____ order P^{op} is defined to be the set with the inverse order. It is easy to see that this construction, which can be depicted by flipping the Hasse diagram for P upside down, will indeed yield a partially ordered set.
   a. Dual
   b. Christofides heuristics
   c. Contraction mapping
   d. Context-sensitive language

5. In topology, the _____ of a subset S of a topological space X is the set of points which can be approached both from S and from the outside of S. More formally, it is the set of points in the closure of S, not belonging to the interior of S. An element of the _____ of S is called a _____ point of S.
   a. Heap
   b. Bertrand paradox
   c. Character
   d. Boundary

6. In linear algebra, _____ is a version of Gaussian elimination that puts zeros both above and below each pivot element as it goes from the top row of the given matrix to the bottom. In other words, _____ brings a matrix to reduced row echelon form, whereas Gaussian elimination takes it only as far as row echelon form. Every matrix has a reduced row echelon form, and this algorithm is guaranteed to produce it.
   a. Gauss-Jordan elimination
   b. Lax equivalence theorem
   c. Conservation form
   d. Spheroidal wave functions

7. _____ is either of the two parts into which a plane divides the three-dimensional space. More generally, a _____ is either of the two parts into which a hyperplane divides an affine space.
   a. Simple polytope
   b. Pendent
   c. Half-space
   d. Parallelogram law

8. In mathematics, a _____ is a set of real numbers with the property that any number that lies between two numbers in the set is also included in the set. For example, the set of all numbers x satisfying $0 \leq x \leq 1$ is an _____ which contains 0 and 1, as well as all numbers between them. Other examples of _____s are the set of all real numbers $\mathbb{R}$, the set of all positive real numbers, and the empty set.
   a. Annihilator
   b. Order
   c. Ideal
   d. Interval

9. A _____ is a software program that facilitates symbolic mathematics. The core functionality of a CAS is manipulation of mathematical expressions in symbolic form.

24   *Chapter 3. LINEAR PROGRAMMING: THE GRAPHICAL METHOD*

The symbolic manipulations supported typically include

- simplification to the smallest possible expression or some standard form, including automatic simplification with assumptions and simplification with constraints
- substitution of symbolic, functors or numeric values for expressions
- change of form of expressions: expanding products and powers, partial and full factorization, rewriting as partial fractions, constraint satisfaction, rewriting trigonometric functions as exponentials, etc.
- partial and total differentiation
- symbolic constrained and unconstrained global optimization
- solution of linear and some non-linear equations over various domains
- solution of some differential and difference equations
- taking some limits
- some indefinite and definite integration, including multidimensional integrals
- integral transforms
- arbitrary-precision numeric operations
- Series operations such as expansion, summation and products
- matrix operations including products, inverses, etc.
- display of mathematical expressions in two-dimensional mathematical form, often using typesetting systems similar to TeX
- add-ons for use in applied mathematics such as physics packages for physical computation
- plotting graphs and parametric plots of functions in two and three dimensions, and animating them
- APIs for linking it on an external program such as a database, or using in a programming language to use the _____
- drawing charts and diagrams
- string manipulation such as matching and searching
- statistical computation
- Theorem proving and verification
- graphic production and editing such as CGI and signal processing as image processing
- sound synthesis

Many also include a programming language, allowing users to implement their own algorithms.

Some _____s focus on a specific area of application; these are typically developed in academia and are free.

a. 2-3 heap   b. 1-center problem
c. Computer algebra system   d. 120-cell

10.   In mathematics, a _____ is an expression constructed from variables and constants, using the operations of addition, subtraction, multiplication, and constant non-negative whole number exponents. For example, $x^2 - 4x + 7$ is a _____, but $x^2 - 4/x + 7x^{3/2}$ is not, because its second term involves division by the variable x and also because its third term contains an exponent that is not a whole number.

_____s are one of the most important concepts in algebra and throughout mathematics and science.

a. Semifield
c. Coimage
b. Polynomial
d. Group extension

11. An _____ is a tree data structure in which each internal node has up to eight children. _____s are most often used to partition a three dimensional space by recursively subdividing it into eight octants. _____s are the three-dimensional analog of quadtrees.
   a. Interval tree
   c. External node
   b. Octree
   d. Adaptive k-d tree

12. The mathematical concept of a _____ expresses the intuitive idea of deterministic dependence between two quantities, one of which is viewed as primary and the other as secondary. A _____ then is a way to associate a unique output for each input of a specified type, for example, a real number or an element of a given set.
   a. Coherent
   c. Going up
   b. Grill
   d. Function

13. A set S of real numbers is called _____ from above if there is a real number k such that k ≥ s for all s in S. The number k is called an upper bound of S. The terms _____ from below and lower bound are similarly defined.
   a. Derivative algebra
   c. Descent
   b. Harmonic series
   d. Bounded

14. In mathematics, a _____ is a statement that can be proved on the basis of explicitly stated or previously agreed assumptions.
   a. Logical value
   c. Disjunction introduction
   b. Theorem
   d. Boolean function

15. The _____ are the set of numbers consisting of the natural numbers including 0 and their negatives. They are numbers that can be written without a fractional or decimal component, and fall within the set {... −2, −1, 0, 1, 2, ...}.
   a. Integers
   c. A posteriori
   b. A Mathematical Theory of Communication
   d. A chemical equation

16. Exponentiation is a mathematical operation, written a^n, involving two numbers, the base a and the _____ n. When n is a positive integer, exponentiation corresponds to repeated multiplication:

$$a^n = \underbrace{a \times \cdots \times a}_{n},$$

just as multiplication by a positive integer corresponds to repeated addition:

$$a \times n = \underbrace{a + \cdots + a}_{n}.$$

The _____ is usually shown as a superscript to the right of the base. The exponentiation a^n can be read as: a raised to the n-th power, a raised to the power [of] n or possibly a raised to the _____ [of] n, or more briefly: a to the n-th power or a to the power [of] n, or even more briefly: a to the n.

a. Exponential tree
b. Exponent
c. Exponential sum
d. Exponentiating by squaring

Chapter 4. LINEAR PROGRAMMING: THE SIMPLEX METHOD

1. In geometry, a _____ or n-_____ is an n-dimensional analogue of a triangle. Specifically, a _____ is the convex hull of a set of affinely independent points in some Euclidean space of dimension n or higher.

   For example, a 0-_____ is a point, a 1-_____ is a line segment, a 2-_____ is a triangle, a 3-_____ is a tetrahedron, and a 4-_____ is a pentachoron.

   a. Simplex   b. Hypercell
   c. Demihypercubes   d. Polytetrahedron

2. In mathematical optimization theory, the simplex algorithm, created by the American mathematician George Dantzig in 1947, is a popular algorithm for numerical solution of the linear programming problem. The journal Computing in Science and Engineering listed it as one of the top 10 algorithms of the century.

   An unrelated, but similarly named method is the Nelder-Mead method or downhill _____ due to Nelder ' Mead and is a numerical method for optimising many-dimensional unconstrained problems, belonging to the more general class of search algorithms.

   a. Hill climbing   b. Fibonacci search
   c. Differential evolution   d. Simplex method

3. _____, also sometimes known as standard form or as exponential notation, is a way of writing numbers that accommodates values too large or small to be conveniently written in standard decimal notation. _____ has a number of useful properties and is often favored by scientists, mathematicians and engineers, who work with such numbers.

   In _____, numbers are written in the form:

   $$a \times 10^b$$

   a. 1-center problem   b. Scientific notation
   c. Radix point   d. Leading zero

4. _____ is an economics theory, that refers to individuals or societies gaining the maximum amount out of the resources they have available to them. The theory proposed by most economists is that _____ refers to the _____ of profit.

   As some economists have begun to find out, this theory does not hold true for all people and cultures.

   a. Composite   b. Homogeneity
   c. Maximization   d. Boundary

5. In Linear programming a _____ is a variable which is added to a constraint to turn the inequality into an equation. This is required to turn an inequality into an equality where a linear combination of variables is less than or equal to a given constant in the former. As with the other variables in the augmented constraints, the _____ cannot take on negative values, as the Simplex algorithm requires them to be positive or zero.

a. Bellman equation	b. Slack variable
c. Shekel function	d. Shape optimization

6. In mathematical optimization theory, the _____, created by the North American mathematician George Dantzig in 1947, is a popular technique for numerical solution of the linear programming problem.

a. Feit–Thompson theorem	b. Sociable number
c. Partition	d. Simplex algorithm

7. In mathematics, an _____ or member of a set is any one of the distinct objects that make up that set.

Writing A = {1,2,3,4}, means that the _____s of the set A are the numbers 1, 2, 3 and 4. Groups of _____s of A, for example {1,2}, are subsets of A.

a. Order	b. Universal code
c. Element	d. Ideal

8. In linear algebra, _____ is a version of Gaussian elimination that puts zeros both above and below each pivot element as it goes from the top row of the given matrix to the bottom. In other words, _____ brings a matrix to reduced row echelon form, whereas Gaussian elimination takes it only as far as row echelon form. Every matrix has a reduced row echelon form, and this algorithm is guaranteed to produce it.

a. Conservation form	b. Lax equivalence theorem
c. Spheroidal wave functions	d. Gauss-Jordan elimination

9. In mathematics, _____ is a technique for optimization of a linear objective function, subject to linear equality and linear inequality constraints. Informally, _____ determines the way to achieve the best outcome in a given mathematical model given some list of requirements represented as linear equations.

More formally, given a polytope, and a real-valued affine function

$$f(x_1, x_2, \ldots, x_n) = c_1 x_1 + c_2 x_2 + \cdots + c_n x_n + d$$

defined on this polytope, a _____ method will find a point in the polytope where this function has the smallest value.

a. Linear programming relaxation	b. Lin-Kernighan
c. Descent direction	d. Linear programming

10. _____ is the study of how the variation in the output of a mathematical model can be apportioned, qualitatively or quantitatively, to different sources of variation in the input of a model.

In more general terms uncertainty and sensitivity analyses investigate the robustness of a study when the study includes some form of mathematical modelling. While uncertainty analysis studies the overall uncertainty in the conclusions of the study, _____ tries to identify what source of uncertainty weights more on the study's conclusions.

Chapter 4. LINEAR PROGRAMMING: THE SIMPLEX METHOD

a. 120-cell
c. 2-3 heap
b. 1-center problem
d. Sensitivity analysis

11. A _____ is a device for performing mathematical calculations, distinguished from a computer by having a limited problem solving ability and an interface optimized for interactive calculation rather than programming. _____s can be hardware or software, and mechanical or electronic, and are often built into devices such as PDAs or mobile phones.

Modern electronic _____s are generally small, digital, and usually inexpensive.

a. 2-3 heap
c. 1-center problem
b. 120-cell
d. Calculator

12. In the mathematical area of order theory, every partially ordered set P gives rise to a _____ partially ordered set which is often denoted by P^{op} or P^d. This _____ order P^{op} is defined to be the set with the inverse order. It is easy to see that this construction, which can be depicted by flipping the Hasse diagram for P upside down, will indeed yield a partially ordered set.

a. Christofides heuristics
c. Contraction mapping
b. Context-sensitive language
d. Dual

13. A _____ typically refers to a class of handheld calculators that are capable of plotting graphs, solving simultaneous equations, and performing numerous other tasks with variables. Most popular _____s are also programmable, allowing the user to create customized programs, typically for scientific/engineering and education applications. Due to their large displays intended for graphing, they can also accommodate several lines of text and calculations at a time.

a. Support vector machines
c. Bump mapping
b. Genus
d. Graphing calculator

14. _____ is a branch of mathematics which focuses on the study of matrices. Initially a sub-branch of linear algebra, it has grown to cover subjects related to graph theory, algebra, combinatorics, and statistics as well.

The term matrix was first coined in 1848 by J.J. Sylvester as a name of an array of numbers.

a. Pairing
c. Segre classification
b. Matrix theory
d. Semi-simple operators

15. In linear algebra, the _____ of a matrix A is another matrix A^T created by any one of the following equivalent actions:

- write the rows of A as the columns of A^T
- write the columns of A as the rows of A^T
- reflect A by its main diagonal to obtain A^T

Formally, the _____ of an m × n matrix A is the n × m matrix

$$\mathbf{A}^T_{ij} = \mathbf{A}_{ji} \text{ for } 1 \leq i \leq n, 1 \leq j \leq m.$$

- $\begin{bmatrix} 1 & 2 \\ 3 & 4 \end{bmatrix}^T = \begin{bmatrix} 1 & 3 \\ 2 & 4 \end{bmatrix}.$

- $\begin{bmatrix} 1 & 2 \\ 3 & 4 \\ 5 & 6 \end{bmatrix}^T = \begin{bmatrix} 1 & 3 & 5 \\ 2 & 4 & 6 \end{bmatrix}.$

For matrices A, B and scalar c we have the following properties of _____:

1. $\left(\mathbf{A}^T\right)^T = \mathbf{A}$

    Taking the _____ is an involution.

- $(\mathbf{A} + \mathbf{B})^T = \mathbf{A}^T + \mathbf{B}^T$

    The _____ respects addition.

- $(\mathbf{AB})^T = \mathbf{B}^T \mathbf{A}^T$

    Note that the order of the factors reverses. From this one can deduce that a square matrix A is invertible if and only if A^T is invertible, and in this case we have^T =$^{-1}$. It is relatively easy to extend this result to the general case of multiple matrices, where we find that^T = $Z^T Y^T X^T ... C^T B^T A^T$.

- $(c\mathbf{A})^T = c\mathbf{A}^T$

    The _____ of a scalar is the same scalar. Together with, this states that the _____ is a linear map from the space of m × n matrices to the space of all n × m matrices.

- $\det(\mathbf{A}^T) = \det(\mathbf{A})$

    The determinant of a matrix is the same as that of its _____.

- The dot product of two column vectors a and b can be computed as

Chapter 4. LINEAR PROGRAMMING: THE SIMPLEX METHOD

$$\mathbf{a} \cdot \mathbf{b} = \mathbf{a}^T \mathbf{b},$$

which is written as $a_i b^i$ in Einstein notation.

- If A has only real entries, then $A^T A$ is a positive-semidefinite matrix.
- $(\mathbf{A}^T)^{-1} = (\mathbf{A}^{-1})^T$

    The _____ of an invertible matrix is also invertible, and its inverse is the _____ of the inverse of the original matrix.

- If A is a square matrix, then its eigenvalues are equal to the eigenvalues of its _____.

A square matrix whose _____ is equal to itself is called a symmetric matrix; that is, A is symmetric if

$$\mathbf{A}^T = \mathbf{A}.$$

A square matrix whose _____ is also its inverse is called an orthogonal matrix; that is, G is orthogonal if

$$\mathbf{G}\mathbf{G}^T = \mathbf{G}^T\mathbf{G} = \mathbf{I}_n,$$ the identity matrix.

A square matrix whose _____ is equal to its negative is called skew-symmetric matrix; that is, A is skew-symmetric if

$$\mathbf{A}^T = -\mathbf{A}.$$

The conjugate _____ of the complex matrix A, written as A^*, is obtained by taking the _____ of A and the complex conjugate of each entry:

$$\mathbf{A}^* = (\overline{\mathbf{A}})^T = \overline{(\mathbf{A}^T)}.$$

If f: V→W is a linear map between vector spaces V and W with nondegenerate bilinear forms, we define the _____ of f to be the linear map ${}^t f$: W→V, determined by

$$B_V(v, {}^t f(w)) = B_W(f(v), w) \quad \forall\, v \in V, w \in W.$$

Here, B_V and B_W are the bilinear forms on V and W respectively. The matrix of the _____ of a map is the transposed matrix only if the bases are orthonormal with respect to their bilinear forms.

Over a complex vector space, one often works with sesquilinear forms instead of bilinear.

a. Tridiagonal matrix
b. Cartan matrix
c. Polynomial matrix
d. Transpose

16. In the geometry of the projective plane, _____ refers to geometric transformations that replace points by lines and lines by points while preserving incidence properties among the transformed objects. The existence of such transformations leads to a general principle, that any theorem about incidences between points and lines in the projective plane may be transformed into another theorem about lines and points, by a substitution of the appropriate words.

_____ in the projective plane is a special case of _____ for projective spaces, transformations that interchange

dimension + codimension.

a. Decidable
b. Blocking
c. Disk
d. Duality

17. In mathematics, a _____ is a statement that can be proved on the basis of explicitly stated or previously agreed assumptions.
   a. Boolean function
   b. Disjunction introduction
   c. Theorem
   d. Logical value

18. An _____ is a tree data structure in which each internal node has up to eight children. _____s are most often used to partition a three dimensional space by recursively subdividing it into eight octants. _____s are the three-dimensional analog of quadtrees.
   a. External node
   b. Octree
   c. Interval tree
   d. Adaptive k-d tree

19. The mathematical concept of a _____ expresses the intuitive idea of deterministic dependence between two quantities, one of which is viewed as primary and the other as secondary. A _____ then is a way to associate a unique output for each input of a specified type, for example, a real number or an element of a given set.
   a. Grill
   b. Going up
   c. Coherent
   d. Function

20. In economics, business, retail, and accounting, a _____ is the value of money that has been used up to produce something, and hence is not available for use anymore. In business, the _____ may be one of acquisition, in which case the amount of money expended to acquire it is counted as _____. In this case, money is the input that is gone in order to acquire the thing.
   a. Cost
   b. 120-cell
   c. 1-center problem
   d. 2-3 heap

21. In Linear programming a _____ is a variable which is subtracted from a constraint to turn the inequality into an equation.

This is required to turn an inequality into an equality where a linear combination of variables is greater than or equal to a given constant in the former. As with the other variables in the augmented constraints, the _____ cannot take on negative values, as the Simplex algorithm requires them to be positive or zero.

Chapter 4. LINEAR PROGRAMMING: THE SIMPLEX METHOD

    a. Global optimum
    b. Surplus variable
    c. Successive linear programming
    d. Quantum annealing

22. In mathematics, a _____ is a condition that a solution to an optimization problem must satisfy. There are two types of _____s: equality _____s and inequality _____s. The set of solutions that satisfy all _____s is called the feasible set.
    a. Foci
    b. Concurrent
    c. Decidable
    d. Constraint

23. A _____ is a software program that facilitates symbolic mathematics. The core functionality of a CAS is manipulation of mathematical expressions in symbolic form.

The symbolic manipulations supported typically include

- simplification to the smallest possible expression or some standard form, including automatic simplification with assumptions and simplification with constraints
- substitution of symbolic, functors or numeric values for expressions
- change of form of expressions: expanding products and powers, partial and full factorization, rewriting as partial fractions, constraint satisfaction, rewriting trigonometric functions as exponentials, etc.
- partial and total differentiation
- symbolic constrained and unconstrained global optimization
- solution of linear and some non-linear equations over various domains
- solution of some differential and difference equations
- taking some limits
- some indefinite and definite integration, including multidimensional integrals
- integral transforms
- arbitrary-precision numeric operations
- Series operations such as expansion, summation and products
- matrix operations including products, inverses, etc.
- display of mathematical expressions in two-dimensional mathematical form, often using typesetting systems similar to TeX
- add-ons for use in applied mathematics such as physics packages for physical computation
- plotting graphs and parametric plots of functions in two and three dimensions, and animating them
- APIs for linking it on an external program such as a database, or using in a programming language to use the _____
- drawing charts and diagrams
- string manipulation such as matching and searching
- statistical computation
- Theorem proving and verification
- graphic production and editing such as CGI and signal processing as image processing
- sound synthesis

Many also include a programming language, allowing users to implement their own algorithms.

Chapter 4. LINEAR PROGRAMMING: THE SIMPLEX METHOD

Some _____s focus on a specific area of application; these are typically developed in academia and are free.

a. 120-cell
c. 2-3 heap
b. 1-center problem
d. Computer algebra system

24. The _____ are the set of numbers consisting of the natural numbers including 0 and their negatives. They are numbers that can be written without a fractional or decimal component, and fall within the set {... −2, −1, 0, 1, 2, ...}.

a. A chemical equation
c. A Mathematical Theory of Communication
b. A posteriori
d. Integers

25. Exponentiation is a mathematical operation, written a^n, involving two numbers, the base a and the _____ n. When n is a positive integer, exponentiation corresponds to repeated multiplication:

$$a^n = \underbrace{a \times \cdots \times a}_{n},$$

just as multiplication by a positive integer corresponds to repeated addition:

$$a \times n = \underbrace{a + \cdots + a}_{n}.$$

The _____ is usually shown as a superscript to the right of the base. The exponentiation a^n can be read as: a raised to the n-th power, a raised to the power [of] n or possibly a raised to the _____ [of] n, or more briefly: a to the n-th power or a to the power [of] n, or even more briefly: a to the n.

a. Exponent
c. Exponentiating by squaring
b. Exponential sum
d. Exponential tree

Chapter 5. MATHEMATICS OF FINANCE

1. _____ is a fee, paid on borrowed capital. Assets lent include money, shares, consumer goods through hire purchase, major assets such as aircraft, and even entire factories in finance lease arrangements. The _____ is calculated upon the value of the assets in the same manner as upon money.

   a. A Mathematical Theory of Communication
   b. Interest
   c. Interest expense
   d. Interest sensitivity gap

2. In mathematics, a _____ is a natural number which has exactly two distinct natural number divisors: 1 and itself. An infinitude of _____s exists, as demonstrated by Euclid around 300 BC. The first twenty-five _____s are:

   2, 3, 5, 7, 11, 13, 17, 19, 23, 29, 31, 37, 41, 43, 47, 53, 59, 61, 67, 71, 73, 79, 83, 89, 97.

   a. Prime number
   b. Pronic number
   c. Highly composite number
   d. Perrin number

3. In abstract algebra, a module S over a ring R is called _____ or irreducible if it is not the zero module 0 and if its only submodules are 0 and S. Understanding the _____ modules over a ring is usually helpful because these modules form the 'building blocks' of all other modules in a certain sense.

   Abelian groups are the same as Z-modules.

   a. Simple
   b. Harmonic series
   c. Basis
   d. Derivation

4. In computational complexity theory, an algorithm is said to take _____ if the asymptotic upper bound for the time it requires is proportional to the size of the input, which is usually denoted n.

   Informally spoken, the running time increases linearly with the size of the input. For example, a procedure that adds up all elements of a list requires time proportional to the length of the list.

   a. Constructible function
   b. Truth table reduction
   c. Time-constructible function
   d. Linear time

5. _____ or amortisation is the process of decreasing an amount over a period of time. The word comes from Middle English amortisen to kill, alienate in mortmain, from Anglo-French amorteser, alteration of amortir, from Vulgar Latin admortire to kill, from Latin ad- + mort-, mors death. Particular instances of the term include:

   - _____, the allocation of a lump sum amount to different time periods, particularly for loans and other forms of finance, including related interest or other finance charges.
     - _____ schedule, a table detailing each periodic payment on a loan, as generated by an _____ calculator.
     - Negative _____, an _____ schedule where the loan amount actually increases through not paying the full interest
   - Amortized analysis, analyzing the execution cost of algorithms over a sequence of operations.
   - _____ of capital expenditures of certain assets under accounting rules, particularly intangible assets, in a manner analogous to depreciation.
   - _____

36 Chapter 5. MATHEMATICS OF FINANCE

_____ is also used in the context of zoning regulations and describes the time in which a property owner has to relocate when the property's use constitutes a preexisting nonconforming use under zoning regulations.

- Depreciation

a. Identity
b. Origin
c. Amortization
d. ISAAC

6. In mathematics, a _____ is an expression constructed from variables and constants, using the operations of addition, subtraction, multiplication, and constant non-negative whole number exponents. For example, $x^2 - 4x + 7$ is a _____, but $x^2 - 4/x + 7x^{3/2}$ is not, because its second term involves division by the variable x and also because its third term contains an exponent that is not a whole number.

_____s are one of the most important concepts in algebra and throughout mathematics and science.

a. Coimage
b. Group extension
c. Semifield
d. Polynomial

7. In vascular plants, the _____ is the organ of a plant body that typically lies below the surface of the soil. This is not always the case, however, since a _____ can also be aerial (that is, growing above the ground) or aerating (that is, growing up above the ground or especially above water.) Furthermore, a stem normally occurring below ground is not exceptional either

a. 120-cell
b. 1-center problem
c. 2-3 heap
d. Root

8. _____ involves reducing the number of significant digits in a number. The result of _____ is a 'shorter' number having fewer non-zero digits yet similar in magnitude. The result is less precise but easier to use.

a. Rounding
b. Shabakh
c. Sudan function
d. Hyper operator

9. _____ is the concept of adding accumulated interest back to the principal, so that interest is earned on interest from that moment on. The act of declaring interest to be principal is called compounding. A loan, for example, may have its interest compounded every month: in this case, a loan with $100 principal and 1% interest per month would have a balance of $101 at the end of the first month.

a. Net interest margin securities
b. Retained interest
c. Compound interest
d. Net interest margin

10. In probability theory, a probability distribution is called _____ if its cumulative distribution function is _____. That is equivalent to saying that for random variables X with the distribution in question, Pr[X = a] = 0 for all real numbers a. If the distribution of X is _____ then X is called a _____ random variable.

a. Conull set
b. Continuous phase modulation
c. Concatenated codes
d. Continuous

11. In calculus, the _____ is a formula for the derivative of the composite of two functions.

Chapter 5. MATHEMATICS OF FINANCE

In intuitive terms, if a variable, y, depends on a second variable, u, which in turn depends on a third variable, x, then the rate of change of y with respect to x can be computed as the rate of change of y with respect to u multiplied by the rate of change of u with respect to x. Schematically,

$$\frac{dy}{dx} = \frac{dy}{du} \cdot \frac{du}{dx}.$$

For an explanation of notation used in this section, see Function composition.

The _____ states that, under appropriate conditions,

$$(f \circ g)'(x) = f'(g(x))g'(x),$$

which in short form is written as

$$(f \circ g)' = f' \circ g \cdot g'.$$

Alternatively, in the Leibniz notation, the _____ is

$$\frac{dy}{dx} = \frac{dy}{du} \cdot \frac{du}{dx}.$$

In integration, the counterpart to the _____ is the substitution rule.

a. 120-cell
c. 1-center problem
b. Product rule
d. Chain rule

12. In mathematics and in the sciences, a _____ (plural: _____e, formulæ or _____s) is a concise way of expressing information symbolically (as in a mathematical or chemical _____), or a general relationship between quantities. One of many famous _____e is Albert Einstein's E = mc² (see special relativity

In mathematics, a _____ is a key to solve an equation with variables. For example, the problem of determining the volume of a sphere is one that requires a significant amount of integral calculus to solve.

a. Formula
c. 1-center problem
b. 120-cell
d. 2-3 heap

13. In mathematics, a _____ is a number that can be expressed as an integral of an algebraic function over an algebraic domain. Kontsevich and Zagier define a _____ as a complex number whose real and imaginary parts are values of absolutely convergent integrals of rational functions with rational coefficients, over domains in given by polynomial inequalities with rational coefficients.

Chapter 5. MATHEMATICS OF FINANCE

   a. Boussinesq approximation
   c. Closeness

   b. Period
   d. Disk

14. _____ is a quantity expressing the two-dimensional size of a defined part of a surface, typically a region bounded by a closed curve. The term surface _____ refers to the total _____ of the exposed surface of a 3-dimensional solid, such as the sum of the _____s of the exposed sides of a polyhedron. _____ is an important invariant in the differential geometry of surfaces.
   a. A Mathematical Theory of Communication
   c. A posteriori

   b. A chemical equation
   d. Area

15. A _____ is a deliberate process for transforming one or more inputs into one or more results, with variable change.

The term is used in a variety of senses, from the very definite arithmetical using an algorithm to the vague heuristics of calculating a strategy in a competition or calculating the chance of a successful relationship between two people.

Multiplying 7 by 8 is a simple algorithmic _____.

   a. Mathematics Subject Classification
   c. Mathematical object

   b. Calculation
   d. Mathematical maturity

16. _____ is usually defined as the activity of using and developing computer technology, computer hardware and software. It is the computer-specific part of information technology. Computer science (or _____ science) is the study and the science of the theoretical foundations of information and computation and their implementation and application in computer systems.
   a. Deterministic finite state machine
   c. Computing

   b. Parallel Random Access Machine
   d. Probabilistic Turing Machine

17. In mathematics, the _____ or least common denominator is the least common multiple of the denominators of a set of vulgar fractions. It is the smallest positive integer that is a multiple of the denominators. For instance, the _____ of

$$\left\{\frac{5}{12}, \frac{11}{18}\right\}$$

is 36 because the least common multiple of 12 and 18 is 36.

   a. Highest common factor
   c. The number 0 is even.

   b. Subtrahend
   d. Lowest common denominator

18. In linear algebra, _____ is a version of Gaussian elimination that puts zeros both above and below each pivot element as it goes from the top row of the given matrix to the bottom. In other words, _____ brings a matrix to reduced row echelon form, whereas Gaussian elimination takes it only as far as row echelon form. Every matrix has a reduced row echelon form, and this algorithm is guaranteed to produce it.

Chapter 5. MATHEMATICS OF FINANCE 39

    a. Spheroidal wave functions   b. Conservation form
    c. Lax equivalence theorem   d. Gauss-Jordan elimination

19. An _____ is a table detailing each periodic payment on a amortizing loan, as generated by an amortization calculator.

While a portion of every payment is applied towards both the interest and the principal balance of the loan, the exact amount applied to principal each time varies. An _____ reveals the specific monetary amount put towards interest, as well as the specific put towards the Principal balance, with each payment.

    a. A Mathematical Theory of Communication   b. Accounts receivable
    c. A chemical equation   d. Amortization schedule

20. This article gives two concrete _____s of the central limit theorem. Both involve the sum of independent and identically-distributed random variables and show how the probability distribution of the sum approaches the normal distribution as the number of terms in the sum increases.

The first _____ involves a continuous probability distribution, for which the random variables have a probability density function.

    a. Empirical processes   b. Independent,
    c. Urn problem   d. Illustration

21. A _____ typically refers to a class of handheld calculators that are capable of plotting graphs, solving simultaneous equations, and performing numerous other tasks with variables. Most popular _____s are also programmable, allowing the user to create customized programs, typically for scientific/engineering and education applications. Due to their large displays intended for graphing, they can also accommodate several lines of text and calculations at a time.
    a. Bump mapping   b. Genus
    c. Support vector machines   d. Graphing calculator

22. A _____ is a device for performing mathematical calculations, distinguished from a computer by having a limited problem solving ability and an interface optimized for interactive calculation rather than programming. _____s can be hardware or software, and mechanical or electronic, and are often built into devices such as PDAs or mobile phones.

Modern electronic _____s are generally small, digital, and usually inexpensive.

    a. 120-cell   b. 1-center problem
    c. 2-3 heap   d. Calculator

23. In mathematics, the _____ is an approach to finding a particular solution to certain inhomogeneous ordinary differential equations and recurrence relations. It is closely related to the annihilator method, but instead of using a particular kind of differential operator in order to find the best possible form of the particular solution, a 'guess' is made as to the appropriate form, which is then tested by differentiating the resulting equation. In this sense, the _____ is less formal but more intuitive than the annihilator method.

a. Linear differential equation
b. Phase line
c. Differential algebraic equations
d. Method of undetermined coefficients

Chapter 6. LOGIC

1. _____ is the study of the principles of valid demonstration and inference. _____ is a branch of philosophy, a part of the classical trivium of grammar, _____, and rhetoric. of λογικÏŒς, 'possessed of reason, intellectual, dialectical, argumentative', from λÏŒγος logos, 'word, thought, idea, argument, account, reason, or principle'.
    a. Counterpart theory
    b. Logic
    c. Satisfiability
    d. Boolean function

2. In logic, two sentences (either in a formal language or a natural language) may be joined by means of a _____ to form a compound sentence. The truth-value of the compound is uniquely determined by the truth-values of the simpler sentences. The _____ therefore represents a function, and since the value of the compound sentence is a truth-value, it is called a truth-function and the _____ is called a 'truth-functional connective'.
    a. Fallacies of definition
    b. Logical connective
    c. Set theory
    d. Satisfiability

3. In logic and mathematics, _____ or not is an operation on logical values, for example, the logical value of a proposition, that sends true to false and false to true. Intuitively, the _____ of a proposition holds exactly when that proposition does not hold. In grammar, nor is an adverb which acts as a coordinating conjunction.
    a. Negation
    b. 1-center problem
    c. Syntax
    d. Sentence diagram

4. In elementary algebra, a _____ is a polynomial consisting of three terms; in other words, a _____ is the sum of three monomials. It can be factored using simple steps

In linguistics, a _____ is a fixed expression which is made from three words; e.g. 'lights, camera, action', 'signed, sealed, delivered'.

    a. Trinomial
    b. Relation algebra
    c. Symmetric difference
    d. Recurrence relation

5. A _____ is a mathematical table used in logic -- specifically in connection with Boolean algebra, boolean functions, and propositional calculus -- to compute the functional values of logical expressions on each of their functional arguments, that is, on each combination of values taken by their logical variables. In particular, _____s can be used to tell whether a propositional expression is true for all legitimate input values, that is, logically valid.

The pattern of reasoning that the _____ tabulates was Frege's, Peirce's, and Schröder's by 1880.

    a. 1-center problem
    b. Truth table
    c. 120-cell
    d. 2-3 heap

6. In logic and mathematics, or, also known as logical _____ or inclusive _____ is a logical operator that results in true whenever one or more of its operands are true. In grammar, or is a coordinating conjunction. In ordinary language 'or' rather has the meaning of exclusive _____.
    a. Disjunction
    b. Triquetra
    c. Cube
    d. Zero-point energy

7. In mathematics, a _____ can mean either an element of the set {1, 2, 3, ...} or an element of the set {0, 1, 2, 3, ...}. The latter is especially preferred in mathematical logic, set theory, and computer science.

_____s have two main purposes: they can be used for counting, and they can be used for ordering.

    a. Suslin cardinal
    b. Natural number
    c. Strong partition cardinal
    d. Cardinal numbers

8. Induction or _____, sometimes called inductive logic, is the process of reasoning in which the premises of an argument are believed to support the conclusion but do not entail it;. Induction is a form of reasoning that makes generalizations based on individual instances. It is used to ascribe properties or relations to types based on an observation instance; or to formulate laws based on limited observations of recurring phenomenal patterns.

    a. Idempotency of entailment
    b. Inductive reasoning
    c. Intuitionistic logic
    d. Affine logic

9. In the study of metric spaces in mathematics, there are various notions of two metrics on the same underlying space being 'the same', or _____.

In the following, M will denote a non-empty set and d_1 and d_2 will denote two metrics on M.

The two metrics d_1 and d_2 are said to be topologically _____ if they generate the same topology on M.

    a. A posteriori
    b. A chemical equation
    c. A Mathematical Theory of Communication
    d. Equivalent

10. In mathematics, the _____ of a ring R, often denoted cha, is defined to be the smallest number of times one must add the ring's multiplicative identity element to itself to get the additive identity element; the ring is said to have _____ zero if this repeated sum never reaches the additive identity. That is, cha is the smallest positive number n such that

$$\underbrace{1 + \cdots + 1}_{n \text{ summands}} = 0$$

if such a number n exists, and 0 otherwise. The _____ may also be taken to be the exponent of the ring's additive group, that is, the smallest positive n such that

$$\underbrace{a + \cdots + a}_{n \text{ summands}} = 0$$

for every element a of the ring.

    a. Characteristic
    b. Coherent
    c. Disk
    d. Class

11. _____, an American electronic engineer and mathematician, is 'the father of information theory'.

Shannon is famous for having founded information theory with one landmark paper published in 1948. But he is also credited with founding both digital computer and digital circuit design theory in 1937, when, as a 21-year-old master's student at MIT, he wrote a thesis demonstrating that electrical application of Boolean algebra could construct and resolve any logical, numerical relationship.

a. Adi Shamir
b. Agnes Meyer Driscoll
c. Claude Elwood Shannon
d. Abraham Sinkov

12.   A _____ of a curve is the envelope of a family of congruent circles centered on the curve. It generalises the concept of _____ lines.

It is sometimes called the offset curve but the term 'offset' often refers also to translation.

a. Parallel
b. Cycloid
c. Bifolium
d. Cissoid

13.   In mathematics, a _____ is often represented as the sum of a sequence of terms. That is, a _____ is represented as a list of numbers with addition operations between them, for example this arithmetic sequence:

   1 + 2 + 3 + 4 + 5 + ... + 99 + 100

In most cases of interest the terms of the sequence are produced according to a certain rule, such as by a formula, by an algorithm, by a sequence of measurements, or even by a random number generator.

a. Concavity
b. Contact
c. Series
d. Blind

14.   In the geometry of the projective plane, _____ refers to geometric transformations that replace points by lines and lines by points while preserving incidence properties among the transformed objects. The existence of such transformations leads to a general principle, that any theorem about incidences between points and lines in the projective plane may be transformed into another theorem about lines and points, by a substitution of the appropriate words.

_____ in the projective plane is a special case of _____ for projective spaces, transformations that interchange

   dimension + codimension.

a. Blocking
b. Decidable
c. Disk
d. Duality

15.   In propositional logic, contraposition is a logical relationship between two statements of material implication. A proposition Q is materially implied by a proposition P when the following relationship holds:

$(P \rightarrow Q)$

In vernacular terms, this states 'If P then Q', or, 'If Socrates is a man then Socrates is human.' In a conditional such as this, P is called the antecedent and Q the consequent. One statement is the _____ of the other just when its antecedent is the negated consequent of the other, and vice-versa.

- a. Control chart
- b. Contrapositive
- c. Contour map
- d. Continuous signal

16. In mathematics, the _____ of a number n is the number that, when added to n, yields zero. The _____ of n is denoted −n. For example, 7 is −7, because 7 + (−7) = 0, and the _____ of −0.3 is 0.3, because −0.3 + 0.3 = 0.
    - a. Arity
    - b. Algebraic structure
    - c. Associativity
    - d. Additive inverse

17. In mathematics, a _____ is a set of real numbers with the property that any number that lies between two numbers in the set is also included in the set. For example, the set of all numbers x satisfying $0 \leq x \leq 1$ is an _____ which contains 0 and 1, as well as all numbers between them. Other examples of _____s are the set of all real numbers $\mathbb{R}$, the set of all positive real numbers, and the empty set.
    - a. Annihilator
    - b. Ideal
    - c. Interval
    - d. Order

18. _____ is the notation in which permitted values for a variable are expressed as ranging over a certain interval; "5 < x < 9" is an example of the application of _____.
    - a. A Mathematical Theory of Communication
    - b. Implicit differentiation
    - c. Interval notation
    - d. Infinity

19. In psychology, _____ has two distinct fields of application. The first involves test _____, a concept that has evolved with the field of psychometrics but which textbooks still commonly gloss over in explaining that it is the degree to which a test measures what it was designed to measure. The second involves research design.
    - a. Model theory
    - b. Validity
    - c. Finitism
    - d. Modal logic

20. A _____ is a 2D geometric symbolic representation of information according to some visualization technique. Sometimes, the technique uses a 3D visualization which is then projected onto the 2D surface. The word graph is sometimes used as a synonym for _____.
    - a. 120-cell
    - b. 1-center problem
    - c. Diagram
    - d. 2-3 heap

21. A _____ undone, which forms a cube _____ cube; a type of _____

A _____ is a problem or enigma that challenges ingenuity. In a basic _____ one is intended to piece together objects (_____ pieces) in a logical way in order to come up with the desired shape, picture or solution. _____s are often contrived as a form of entertainment, but they can also stem from serious mathematical or logistical problems -- in such cases, their successful resolution can be a significant contribution to mathematical research .

   a. Visible
   c. The Doctrine of Chances
   b. Puzzle
   d. The Code Book

Chapter 7. SETS AND PROBABILITY

1. In mathematics, an _____ or member of a set is any one of the distinct objects that make up that set.

Writing A = {1,2,3,4}, means that the _____s of the set A are the numbers 1, 2, 3 and 4. Groups of _____s of A, for example {1,2}, are subsets of A.

   a. Order
   b. Universal code
   c. Ideal
   d. Element

2. In discrete mathematics and predominantly in set theory, a _____ is a concept used in comparisons of sets to refer to the unique values of one set in relation to another. The terms 'absolute' and 'relative' _____ refer to more specific applications of the concept, with universal _____s referring to elements unique to the universal set and the latter referring to the unique elements of one set in relation to another. In this image, the universal set is represented by the border of the image, and the set A as a disc.

   a. Complement
   b. Derivative algebra
   c. Kernel
   d. Huge

3. In mathematics, especially in set theory, a set A is a _____ of a set B if A is 'contained' inside B. Notice that A and B may coincide. The relationship of one set being a _____ of another is called inclusion.

   a. Horizontal line test
   b. Set of all sets
   c. Cartesian product
   d. Subset

4. In mathematics, and more specifically set theory, the _____ is the unique set having no members. Some axiomatic set theories assure that the _____ exists by including an axiom of _____; in other theories, its existence can be deduced. Many possible properties of sets are trivially true for the _____.

   a. Inverse function
   b. Empty function
   c. A Mathematical Theory of Communication
   d. Empty set

5. In set theory, a _____ is a partially ordered set such that for each $t \in T$, the set $\{s \in T : s < t\}$ is well-ordered by the relation <. For each $t \in T$, the order type of $\{s \in T : s < t\}$ is called the height of t. The height of T itself is the least ordinal greater than the height of each element of T.

   a. Tree
   b. Set-theoretic topology
   c. Definable numbers
   d. Transitive reduction

6. A _____ is a 2D geometric symbolic representation of information according to some visualization technique. Sometimes, the technique uses a 3D visualization which is then projected onto the 2D surface. The word graph is sometimes used as a synonym for _____.

   a. 120-cell
   b. 1-center problem
   c. 2-3 heap
   d. Diagram

7. _____ or set diagrams are diagrams that show all hypothetically possible logical relations between a finite collection of sets. _____ were invented around 1880 by John Venn. They are used in many fields, including set theory, probability, logic, statistics, and computer science.

   a. 120-cell
   b. 1-center problem
   c. 2-3 heap
   d. Venn diagrams

8. A _____ is a software program that facilitates symbolic mathematics. The core functionality of a CAS is manipulation of mathematical expressions in symbolic form.

Chapter 7. SETS AND PROBABILITY

The symbolic manipulations supported typically include

- simplification to the smallest possible expression or some standard form, including automatic simplification with assumptions and simplification with constraints
- substitution of symbolic, functors or numeric values for expressions
- change of form of expressions: expanding products and powers, partial and full factorization, rewriting as partial fractions, constraint satisfaction, rewriting trigonometric functions as exponentials, etc.
- partial and total differentiation
- symbolic constrained and unconstrained global optimization
- solution of linear and some non-linear equations over various domains
- solution of some differential and difference equations
- taking some limits
- some indefinite and definite integration, including multidimensional integrals
- integral transforms
- arbitrary-precision numeric operations
- Series operations such as expansion, summation and products
- matrix operations including products, inverses, etc.
- display of mathematical expressions in two-dimensional mathematical form, often using typesetting systems similar to TeX
- add-ons for use in applied mathematics such as physics packages for physical computation
- plotting graphs and parametric plots of functions in two and three dimensions, and animating them
- APIs for linking it on an external program such as a database, or using in a programming language to use the _____
- drawing charts and diagrams
- string manipulation such as matching and searching
- statistical computation
- Theorem proving and verification
- graphic production and editing such as CGI and signal processing as image processing
- sound synthesis

Many also include a programming language, allowing users to implement their own algorithms.

Some _____ s focus on a specific area of application; these are typically developed in academia and are free.

  a. 1-center problem
  c. 120-cell

  b. Computer algebra system
  d. 2-3 heap

9. In probability theory, an _____ is a set of outcomes to which a probability is assigned. Typically, when the sample space is finite, any subset of the sample space is an _____. However, this approach does not work well in cases where the sample space is infinite, most notably when the outcome is a real number.
  a. Audio compression
  c. Information set

  b. Event
  d. Equaliser

Chapter 7. SETS AND PROBABILITY

10. In mathematics, the _____ of two sets A and B is the set that contains all elements of A that also belong to B, but no other elements.

For explanation of the symbols used in this article, refer to the table of mathematical symbols.

The _____ of A and B

The _____ of A and B is written 'A ∩ B'. Formally:

x is an element of A ∩ B if and only if
- x is an element of A and
- x is an element of B.

For example:
- The _____ of the sets {1, 2, 3} and {2, 3, 4} is {2, 3}.
- The number 9 is not in the _____ of the set of prime numbers {2, 3, 5, 7, 11, â€¦} and the set of odd numbers {1, 3, 5, 7, 9, 11, â€¦}.

If the _____ of two sets A and B is empty, that is they have no elements in common, then they are said to be disjoint, denoted: A ∩ B = Ø. For example the sets {1, 2} and {3, 4} are disjoint, written
{1, 2} ∩ {3, 4} = Ø.

- a. Intersection
- b. Advice
- c. Order
- d. Erlang

11. In mathematics, two sets are said to be disjoint if they have no element in common. For example, {1, 2, 3} and {4, 5, 6} are _____.

Formally, two sets A and B are disjoint if their intersection is the empty set.
wikimedia.org/math/b/3/5/b35d3befc06b831ff4d6cd63bf922efb.png">

This definition extends to any collection of sets.

- a. Subset
- b. Preimage
- c. Horizontal line test
- d. Disjoint sets

12. In set theory, the term _____ refers to a set operation used in the convergence of set elements to form a resultant set containing the elements of both sets. As a simple example, a _____ of two disjoint sets, which do not have elements in common results in a set containing all elements from both sets. A Venn diagram representing the _____ of sets A and B.
- a. Introduction
- b. Event
- c. UES
- d. Union

Chapter 7. SETS AND PROBABILITY

13. In game theory, an _____ is a set of moves or strategies taken by the players, or their payoffs resulting from the actions or strategies taken by all players. The two are complementary in that given knowledge of the set of strategies of all players, the final state of the game is known, as are any relevant payoffs. In a game where chance or a random event is involved, the _____ is not known from only the set of strategies, but is only realized when the random even are realized.
    a. Algebraic
    b. Equaliser
    c. Autonomous system
    d. Outcome

14. In statistics, a _____ is a subset of a population. Typically, the population is very large, making a census or a complete enumeration of all the values in the population impractical or impossible. The _____ represents a subset of manageable size.
    a. Duality
    b. Boussinesq approximation
    c. Dispersion
    d. Sample

15. In probability theory, the _____ or universal _____, often denoted S, Ω of an experiment or random trial is the set of all possible outcomes. For example, if the experiment is tossing a coin, the _____ is the set {head, tail}. For tossing a single six-sided die, the _____ is {1, 2, 3, 4, 5, 6}.
    a. Martingale central limit theorem
    b. Markov chain
    c. Marginal distribution
    d. Sample space

16. In mathematics, the concept of a _____ tries to capture the intuitive idea of a geometrical one-dimensional and continuous object. A simple example is the circle. In everyday use of the term '_____', a straight line is not curved, but in mathematical parlance _____s include straight lines and line segments.
    a. Quadrifolium
    b. Curve
    c. Negative pedal curve
    d. Kappa curve

17. In scientific inquiry, an _____ is a method of investigating particular types of research questions or solving particular types of problems. The _____ is a cornerstone in the empirical approach to acquiring deeper knowledge about the world and is used in both natural sciences as well as in social sciences. An _____ is defined, in science, as a method of investigating less known fields, solving practical problems and proving theoretical assumptions.
    a. A Mathematical Theory of Communication
    b. Experiment
    c. A chemical equation
    d. A posteriori

18. In simple terms, two events are _____ if they cannot occur at the same time.

    In logic, two _____ propositions are propositions that logically cannot both be true. To say that more than two propositions are _____ may, depending on context mean that no two of them can both be true, or only that they cannot all be true.

    a. Philosophy
    b. Philosophy of mathematics
    c. Mutually exclusive
    d. Determinism

19. In mathematics, a _____ is a statement that can be proved on the basis of explicitly stated or previously agreed assumptions.
    a. Disjunction introduction
    b. Boolean function
    c. Logical value
    d. Theorem

Chapter 7. SETS AND PROBABILITY

20. In the mathematics of probability, an _____ is an event x with a probability Pr of zero, or Pr(x) = 0.

An _____ is not the same as the stronger concept of logical impossibility. For any continuous probability distribution the probability of any single elementary event is 0, yet the event is not logically impossible as an event outside the distribution.

- a. Impossible event
- b. A posteriori
- c. A Mathematical Theory of Communication
- d. A chemical equation

21. In abstract algebra, a module S over a ring R is called _____ or irreducible if it is not the zero module 0 and if its only submodules are 0 and S. Understanding the _____ modules over a ring is usually helpful because these modules form the 'building blocks' of all other modules in a certain sense.

Abelian groups are the same as Z-modules.

- a. Derivation
- b. Harmonic series
- c. Simple
- d. Basis

22. _____ is the likelihood or chance that something is the case or will happen. Theoretical _____ is used extensively in areas such as statistics, mathematics, science and philosophy to draw conclusions about the likelihood of potential events and the underlying mechanics of complex systems.

The word _____ does not have a consistent direct definition.

- a. Statistical significance
- b. Discrete random variable
- c. Standardized moment
- d. Probability

23. In vascular plants, the _____ is the organ of a plant body that typically lies below the surface of the soil. This is not always the case, however, since a _____ can also be aerial (that is, growing above the ground) or aerating (that is, growing up above the ground or especially above water.) Furthermore, a stem normally occurring below ground is not exceptional either

- a. 120-cell
- b. 2-3 heap
- c. 1-center problem
- d. Root

24. In probability theory and statistics the _____ in favour of an event or a proposition are the quantity p /, where p is the probability of the event or proposition. The _____ against the same event are / p. For example, if you chose a random day of the week, then the _____ that you would choose a Sunday would be 1/6, not 1/7.

- a. Event
- b. Anscombe transform
- c. Estimation of covariance matrices
- d. Odds

25. The word _____ denotes information gained by means of observation, experience as opposed to theoretical. A central concept in science and the scientific method is that all evidence must be _____ that is, dependent on evidence or consequences that are observable by the senses. It is usually differentiated from the philosophic usage of empiricism by the use of the adjective '_____' or the adverb 'empirically.' '_____' as an adjective or adverb is used in conjunction with both the natural and social sciences, and refers to the use of working hypotheses that are testable using observation or experiment.

Chapter 7. SETS AND PROBABILITY

a. A Mathematical Theory of Communication
b. A chemical equation
c. A posteriori
d. Empirical

26. In mathematics, differential rings, differential fields and differential algebras are rings, fields and algebras equipped with a _____, which is a unary function satisfying the Leibniz product law. A natural example of a differential field is the field of rational functions over the complex numbers in one variable, C

A differential ring is a ring R equipped with one or more _____s

$$\partial : R \to R$$

such that each _____ satisfies the Leibniz product rule

$$\partial(r_1 r_2) = (\partial r_1) r_2 + r_1 (\partial r_2),$$

for every $r_1, r_2 \in R$.

a. Derivation
b. Cusp
c. Leibniz formula
d. Discontinuity

27. In differential geometry, a discipline within mathematics, a _____ is a subset of the tangent bundle of a manifold satisfying certain properties. _____s are used to build up notions of integrability, and specifically of a foliation of a manifold
a. Coherence
b. Constraint
c. Discontinuity
d. Distribution

28. The _____ or Dirac's delta is a mathematical construct introduced by the British theoretical physicist Paul Dirac. Informally, it is a function representing an infinitely sharp peak bounding unit area: a function that has the value zero everywhere except at x = 0 where its value is infinitely large in such a way that its total integral is 1. It is a continuous analogue of the discrete Kronecker delta.
a. Schwartz kernel theorem
b. Dirac delta
c. Hyperfunction
d. Weak derivative

29. In probability theory and statistics, a _____ identifies either the probability of each value of an unidentified random variable, or the probability of the value falling within a particular interval. The probability function describes the range of possible values that a random variable can attain and the probability that the value of the random variable is within any subset of that range.

When the random variable takes values in the set of real numbers, the _____ is completely described by the cumulative distribution function, whose value at each real x is the probability that the random variable is smaller than or equal to x.

a. Statistical graphics
b. Z-test
c. Normal distribution
d. Probability distribution

52 Chapter 7. SETS AND PROBABILITY

30. In elementary algebra, a _____ is a polynomial with two terms: the sum of two monomials. It is the simplest kind of polynomial except for a monomial.

The _____ $a^2 - b^2$ can be factored as the product of two other _____s:

$a^2 - b^2$.

The product of a pair of linear _____s $ax + b$ and $cx + d$ is:

$2 + x + bd$.

A _____ raised to the nth power, represented as

n

can be expanded by means of the _____ theorem or, equivalently, using Pascal's triangle.

a. Rational root theorem
c. Cylindrical algebraic decomposition
b. Real structure
d. Binomial

31. _____ typically deals with the probability of several successive decisions, each of which has two possible outcomes.

The probability of an event can be expressed as a _____ if its outcomes can be broken down into two probabilities p and q, where p and q are complementary For example, tossing a coin can be either heads or tails, each which have a probability of 0.5. Rolling a four on a six-sided die can be expressed as the probability of getting a 4 or the probability of rolling something else.

a. Markov chain
c. Marginal distribution
b. Quantile
d. Binomial probability

32. In probability theory, a probability distribution is called _____ if its cumulative distribution function is _____. That is equivalent to saying that for random variables X with the distribution in question, Pr[X = a] = 0 for all real numbers a. If the distribution of X is _____ then X is called a _____ random variable.

a. Continuous phase modulation
c. Conull set
b. Continuous
d. Concatenated codes

33. _____ is the probability of some event A, given the occurrence of some other event B. _____ is written P[A | B], and is read 'the probability of A, given B'.

Joint probability is the probability of two events in conjunction. That is, it is the probability of both events together. The joint probability of A and B is written $P(A \cap B)$ or $P(A, B)$.

Chapter 7. SETS AND PROBABILITY

a. Sample space
b. Quantile
c. Renewal theory
d. Conditional probability

34. The _____ governs the differentiation of products of differentiable functions.
   a. Reciprocal Rule
   b. 1-center problem
   c. 120-cell
   d. Product rule

35. A _____ is an abstract model that uses mathematical language to describe the behavior of a system. Eykhoff defined a _____ as 'a representation of the essential aspects of an existing system which presents knowledge of that system in usable form'.
   a. Mathematical model
   b. Metaheuristic
   c. Rata Die
   d. Total least squares

36. In ecology, predation describes a biological interaction where a _____ (an organism that is hunting) feeds on its prey, the organism that is attacked. _____s may or may not kill their prey prior to feeding on them, but the act of predation always results in the death of the prey. The other main category of consumption is detritivory, the consumption of dead organic material (detritus.)
   a. Prey
   b. 1-center problem
   c. 120-cell
   d. Predator

Chapter 8. COUNTING PRINCIPLES; FURTHER PROBABILITY TOPICS

1. A _____ is the transfer of an interest in property (or in law the equivalent - a charge) to a lender as a security for a debt - usually a loan of money. While a _____ in itself is not a debt, it is lender's security for a debt. It is a transfer of an interest in land (or the equivalent), from the owner to the _____ lender, on the condition that this interest will be returned to the owner of the real estate when the terms of the _____ have been satisfied or performed.

   a. Mortgage
   b. 1-center problem
   c. 120-cell
   d. 2-3 heap

2. _____ is the mathematical operation of scaling one number by another. It is one of the four basic operations in elementary arithmetic.

   _____ is defined for whole numbers in terms of repeated addition; for example, 4 multiplied by 3 can be calculated by adding 3 copies of 4 together:

   $$4 + 4 + 4 = 12.$$

   _____ of rational numbers and real numbers is defined by systematic generalization of this basic idea.

   a. Least common multiple
   b. Highest common factor
   c. The number 0 is even.
   d. Multiplication

3. In elementary algebra, a _____ is a polynomial with two terms: the sum of two monomials. It is the simplest kind of polynomial except for a monomial.

   The _____ $a^2 - b^2$ can be factored as the product of two other _____ s:

   $a^2 - b^2$.

   The product of a pair of linear _____ s a x + b and c x + d is:

   2 +x + bd.

   A _____ raised to the nth power, represented as

   n

   can be expanded by means of the _____ theorem or, equivalently, using Pascal's triangle.

   a. Real structure
   b. Cylindrical algebraic decomposition
   c. Rational root theorem
   d. Binomial

4. _____ is a branch of mathematics which focuses on the study of matrices. Initially a sub-branch of linear algebra, it has grown to cover subjects related to graph theory, algebra, combinatorics, and statistics as well.

   The term matrix was first coined in 1848 by J.J. Sylvester as a name of an array of numbers.

Chapter 8. COUNTING PRINCIPLES; FURTHER PROBABILITY TOPICS

a. Matrix theory
b. Semi-simple operators
c. Segre classification
d. Pairing

5. In mathematics, a _____ is an expression constructed from variables and constants, using the operations of addition, subtraction, multiplication, and constant non-negative whole number exponents. For example, $x^2 - 4x + 7$ is a _____, but $x^2 - 4/x + 7x^{3/2}$ is not, because its second term involves division by the variable x and also because its third term contains an exponent that is not a whole number.

_____s are one of the most important concepts in algebra and throughout mathematics and science.

a. Group extension
b. Semifield
c. Polynomial
d. Coimage

6. In mathematics, a _____ can mean either an element of the set {1, 2, 3, ...} or an element of the set {0, 1, 2, 3, ...}. The latter is especially preferred in mathematical logic, set theory, and computer science.

_____s have two main purposes: they can be used for counting, and they can be used for ordering.

a. Suslin cardinal
b. Cardinal numbers
c. Strong partition cardinal
d. Natural number

7. In mathematics, the _____ of a non-negative integer n, denoted by n!, is the product of all positive integers less than or equal to n. For example,

$$5! = 1 \times 2 \times 3 \times 4 \times 5 = 120$$

and
$$6! = 1 \times 2 \times 3 \times 4 \times 5 \times 6 = 720$$

The notation n! was introduced by Christian Kramp in 1808.

The _____ function is formally defined by

$$n! = \prod_{k=1}^{n} k \qquad \forall n \in \mathbb{N}.$$

The above definition incorporates the instance

$$0! = 1$$

as an instance of the fact that the product of no numbers at all is 1.

a. Plane partition
b. Partition of a set
c. Symbolic combinatorics
d. Factorial

8. In mathematics, in the realm of group theory, a group is said to be _____ if it equals its own commutator subgroup if the group has no nontrivial abelian quotients.

The smallest _____ group is the alternating group A_5. More generally, any non-abelian simple group is _____ since the commutator subgroup is a normal subgroup with abelian quotient.

a. Quaternion group
b. Group of Lie type
c. Free product
d. Perfect

9. In several fields of mathematics the term _____ is used with different but closely related meanings. They all relate to the notion of mapping the elements of a set to other elements of the same set, i.e., exchanging elements of a set.

The general concept of _____ can be defined more formally in different contexts:

In combinatorics, a _____ is usually understood to be a sequence containing each element from a finite set once, and only once.

a. Cyclic permutation
b. Linearly independent
c. Tensor product
d. Permutation

10. In mathematics, a _____ is a statement that can be proved on the basis of explicitly stated or previously agreed assumptions.
a. Boolean function
b. Logical value
c. Disjunction introduction
d. Theorem

11. In linear algebra, _____ is a version of Gaussian elimination that puts zeros both above and below each pivot element as it goes from the top row of the given matrix to the bottom. In other words, _____ brings a matrix to reduced row echelon form, whereas Gaussian elimination takes it only as far as row echelon form. Every matrix has a reduced row echelon form, and this algorithm is guaranteed to produce it.
a. Lax equivalence theorem
b. Conservation form
c. Spheroidal wave functions
d. Gauss-Jordan elimination

12. In combinatorial mathematics, a _____ is an un-ordered collection of distinct elements, usually of a prescribed size and taken from a given set. Given such a set S, a _____ of elements of S is just a subset of S, where as always forsets the order of the elements is not taken into account. Also, as always forsets, no elements can be repeated more than once in a _____; this is often referred to as a 'collection without repetition'.
a. Sparsity
b. Combination
c. Heawood number
d. Fill-in

Chapter 8. COUNTING PRINCIPLES; FURTHER PROBABILITY TOPICS 57

13. A _____ typically refers to a class of handheld calculators that are capable of plotting graphs, solving simultaneous equations, and performing numerous other tasks with variables. Most popular _____s are also programmable, allowing the user to create customized programs, typically for scientific/engineering and education applications. Due to their large displays intended for graphing, they can also accommodate several lines of text and calculations at a time.
   a. Graphing calculator
   b. Support vector machines
   c. Bump mapping
   d. Genus

14. _____ or amortisation is the process of decreasing an amount over a period of time. The word comes from Middle English amortisen to kill, alienate in mortmain, from Anglo-French amorteser, alteration of amortir, from Vulgar Latin admortire to kill, from Latin ad- + mort-, mors death. Particular instances of the term include:

   - _____, the allocation of a lump sum amount to different time periods, particularly for loans and other forms of finance, including related interest or other finance charges.
     - _____ schedule, a table detailing each periodic payment on a loan, as generated by an _____ calculator.
     - Negative _____, an _____ schedule where the loan amount actually increases through not paying the full interest
   - Amortized analysis, analyzing the execution cost of algorithms over a sequence of operations.
   - _____ of capital expenditures of certain assets under accounting rules, particularly intangible assets, in a manner analogous to depreciation.
   - _____

_____ is also used in the context of zoning regulations and describes the time in which a property owner has to relocate when the property's use constitutes a preexisting nonconforming use under zoning regulations.

   - Depreciation

   a. Origin
   b. Amortization
   c. ISAAC
   d. Identity

15. An _____ is a table detailing each periodic payment on a amortizing loan, as generated by an amortization calculator.

While a portion of every payment is applied towards both the interest and the principal balance of the loan, the exact amount applied to principal each time varies. An _____ reveals the specific monetary amount put towards interest, as well as the specific put towards the Principal balance, with each payment.

   a. Amortization schedule
   b. A Mathematical Theory of Communication
   c. Accounts receivable
   d. A chemical equation

16. _____ is a quantity expressing the two-dimensional size of a defined part of a surface, typically a region bounded by a closed curve. The term surface _____ refers to the total _____ of the exposed surface of a 3-dimensional solid, such as the sum of the _____s of the exposed sides of a polyhedron. _____ is an important invariant in the differential geometry of surfaces.

a. A chemical equation
c. A Mathematical Theory of Communication
b. A posteriori
d. Area

17. A _____ is a device for performing mathematical calculations, distinguished from a computer by having a limited problem solving ability and an interface optimized for interactive calculation rather than programming. _____s can be hardware or software, and mechanical or electronic, and are often built into devices such as PDAs or mobile phones.

Modern electronic _____s are generally small, digital, and usually inexpensive.

a. 1-center problem
c. 2-3 heap
b. Calculator
d. 120-cell

18. _____ is usually defined as the activity of using and developing computer technology, computer hardware and software. It is the computer-specific part of information technology. Computer science (or _____ science) is the study and the science of the theoretical foundations of information and computation and their implementation and application in computer systems.

a. Deterministic finite state machine
c. Probabilistic Turing Machine
b. Parallel Random Access Machine
d. Computing

19. In mathematics and in the sciences, a _____ (plural: _____e, formulæ or _____s) is a concise way of expressing information symbolically (as in a mathematical or chemical _____), or a general relationship between quantities. One of many famous _____e is Albert Einstein's $E = mc^2$ (see special relativity

In mathematics, a _____ is a key to solve an equation with variables. For example, the problem of determining the volume of a sphere is one that requires a significant amount of integral calculus to solve.

a. 120-cell
c. 2-3 heap
b. 1-center problem
d. Formula

20. _____ is the likelihood or chance that something is the case or will happen. Theoretical _____ is used extensively in areas such as statistics, mathematics, science and philosophy to draw conclusions about the likelihood of potential events and the underlying mechanics of complex systems.

The word _____ does not have a consistent direct definition.

a. Standardized moment
c. Probability
b. Discrete random variable
d. Statistical significance

21. In set theory, a _____ is a partially ordered set such that for each t ∈ T, the set {s ∈ T : s < t} is well-ordered by the relation <. For each t ∈ T, the order type of {s ∈ T : s < t} is called the height of t. The height of T itself is the least ordinal greater than the height of each element of T.

a. Definable numbers
c. Transitive reduction
b. Set-theoretic topology
d. Tree

22. A _____ is a software program that facilitates symbolic mathematics. The core functionality of a CAS is manipulation of mathematical expressions in symbolic form.

Chapter 8. COUNTING PRINCIPLES; FURTHER PROBABILITY TOPICS

The symbolic manipulations supported typically include

- simplification to the smallest possible expression or some standard form, including automatic simplification with assumptions and simplification with constraints
- substitution of symbolic, functors or numeric values for expressions
- change of form of expressions: expanding products and powers, partial and full factorization, rewriting as partial fractions, constraint satisfaction, rewriting trigonometric functions as exponentials, etc.
- partial and total differentiation
- symbolic constrained and unconstrained global optimization
- solution of linear and some non-linear equations over various domains
- solution of some differential and difference equations
- taking some limits
- some indefinite and definite integration, including multidimensional integrals
- integral transforms
- arbitrary-precision numeric operations
- Series operations such as expansion, summation and products
- matrix operations including products, inverses, etc.
- display of mathematical expressions in two-dimensional mathematical form, often using typesetting systems similar to TeX
- add-ons for use in applied mathematics such as physics packages for physical computation
- plotting graphs and parametric plots of functions in two and three dimensions, and animating them
- APIs for linking it on an external program such as a database, or using in a programming language to use the _____
- drawing charts and diagrams
- string manipulation such as matching and searching
- statistical computation
- Theorem proving and verification
- graphic production and editing such as CGI and signal processing as image processing
- sound synthesis

Many also include a programming language, allowing users to implement their own algorithms.

Some _____s focus on a specific area of application; these are typically developed in academia and are free.

a. 1-center problem
c. 2-3 heap
b. 120-cell
d. Computer algebra system

23. A _____ is a 2D geometric symbolic representation of information according to some visualization technique. Sometimes, the technique uses a 3D visualization which is then projected onto the 2D surface. The word graph is sometimes used as a synonym for _____.

a. Diagram
c. 1-center problem
b. 120-cell
d. 2-3 heap

Chapter 8. COUNTING PRINCIPLES; FURTHER PROBABILITY TOPICS

24. Introduction

In the theory of probability and statistics, a _____ is an experiment whose outcome is random and can be either of two possible outcomes, 'success' and 'failure'.

In practice it refers to a single experiment which can have one of two possible outcomes. These events can be phrased into 'yes or no' questions:

- Did the coin land heads?
- Was the newborn child a girl?
- Were a person's eyes green?
- Did a mosquito die after the area was sprayed with insecticide?
- Did a potential customer decide to buy a product?
- Did a citizen vote for a specific candidate?
- Did an employee vote pro-union?

Therefore success and failure are labels for outcomes, and should not be construed literally. Examples of _____s include

- Flipping a coin. In this context, obverse conventionally denotes success and reverse denotes failure. A fair coin has the probability of success 0.5 by definition.
- Rolling a die, where a six is 'success' and everything else a 'failure'.
- In conducting a political opinion poll, choosing a voter at random to ascertain whether that voter will vote 'yes' in an upcoming referendum.

Mathematically, a _____ can be described by a sample space Ω consisting of two values, s for 'success' and f for 'failure'. Therefore the sample space is $\Omega = \{s, f\}$.

a. Point process
b. Marginal distribution
c. Law of total cumulance
d. Bernoulli trial

25. In scientific inquiry, an _____ is a method of investigating particular types of research questions or solving particular types of problems. The _____ is a cornerstone in the empirical approach to acquiring deeper knowledge about the world and is used in both natural sciences as well as in social sciences. An _____ is defined, in science, as a method of investigating less known fields, solving practical problems and proving theoretical assumptions.

a. A Mathematical Theory of Communication
b. A chemical equation
c. A posteriori
d. Experiment

26. A _____ is one of the basic shapes of geometry: a polygon with three corners or vertices and three sides or edges which are line segments. A _____ with vertices A, B, and C is denoted ABC.

In Euclidean geometry any three non-collinear points determine a unique _____ and a unique plane.

a. Fuhrmann circle
b. Kepler triangle
c. Triangle
d. 1-center problem

27. In differential geometry, a discipline within mathematics, a _____ is a subset of the tangent bundle of a manifold satisfying certain properties. _____s are used to build up notions of integrability, and specifically of a foliation of a manifold
    a. Constraint
    b. Coherence
    c. Discontinuity
    d. Distribution

28. The _____ or Dirac's delta is a mathematical construct introduced by the British theoretical physicist Paul Dirac. Informally, it is a function representing an infinitely sharp peak bounding unit area: a function that has the value zero everywhere except at x = 0 where its value is infinitely large in such a way that its total integral is 1. It is a continuous analogue of the discrete Kronecker delta.
    a. Schwartz kernel theorem
    b. Weak derivative
    c. Hyperfunction
    d. Dirac delta

29. In probability theory and statistics, the _____ of a random variable is the integral of the random variable with respect to its probability measure. For discrete random variables this is equivalent to the probability-weighted sum of the possible values, and for continuous random variables with a density function it is the probability density -weighted integral of the possible values.

    The _____ may be intuitively understood by the law of large numbers: The _____, when it exists, is almost surely the limit of the sample mean as sample size grows to infinity.

    a. Expected value
    b. Illustration
    c. Event
    d. Infinitely divisible distribution

30. In probability theory and statistics, a _____ identifies either the probability of each value of an unidentified random variable, or the probability of the value falling within a particular interval. The probability function describes the range of possible values that a random variable can attain and the probability that the value of the random variable is within any subset of that range.

    When the random variable takes values in the set of real numbers, the _____ is completely described by the cumulative distribution function, whose value at each real x is the probability that the random variable is smaller than or equal to x.

    a. Probability distribution
    b. Statistical graphics
    c. Z-test
    d. Normal distribution

31. In mathematics, _____ are used in the study of chance and probability. They were developed to assist in the analysis of games of chance, stochastic events, and the results of scientific experiments by capturing only the mathematical properties necessary to answer probabilistic questions. Further formalizations have firmly grounded the entity in the theoretical domains of mathematics by making use of measure theory.
    a. Median polish
    b. Random variables
    c. Statistical dispersion
    d. Statistics

Chapter 8. COUNTING PRINCIPLES; FURTHER PROBABILITY TOPICS

32. _____ typically deals with the probability of several successive decisions, each of which has two possible outcomes.

The probability of an event can be expressed as a _____ if its outcomes can be broken down into two probabilities p and q, where p and q are complementary For example, tossing a coin can be either heads or tails, each which have a probability of 0.5. Rolling a four on a six-sided die can be expressed as the probability of getting a 4 or the probability of rolling something else.

- a. Marginal distribution
- b. Markov chain
- c. Quantile
- d. Binomial probability

33. In probability theory, a probability distribution is called _____ if its cumulative distribution function is _____. That is equivalent to saying that for random variables X with the distribution in question, Pr[X = a] = 0 for all real numbers a. If the distribution of X is _____ then X is called a _____ random variable.
- a. Conull set
- b. Continuous phase modulation
- c. Concatenated codes
- d. Continuous

34. In statistics, a _____ is a graphical display of tabulated frequencies, shown as bars. It shows what proportion of cases fall into each of several categories. A _____ differs from a bar chart in that it is the area of the bar that denotes the value, not the height as in bar charts, a crucial distinction when the categories are not of uniform width.
- a. First-hitting-time models
- b. Histogram
- c. Standardized moment
- d. Probability distribution

35. In mathematics, a _____ is a system which is not linear. Less technically, a _____ is any problem where the variabl to be solved for cannot be written as a linear sum of independent components. A nonhomogenous system, which is linear apart from the presence of a function of the independent variables, is nonlinear according to a strict definition, but such systems are usually studied alongside linear systems, because they can be transformed to a linear system as long as a particular solution is known.
- a. 1-center problem
- b. George Dantzig
- c. Metric system
- d. Nonlinear system

36. In mathematics, an _____, or central tendency of a data set refers to a measure of the 'middle' or 'expected' value of the data set. There are many different descriptive statistics that can be chosen as a measurement of the central tendency of the data items.

An _____ is a single value that is meant to typify a list of values.

- a. A posteriori
- b. A chemical equation
- c. A Mathematical Theory of Communication
- d. Average

37. The mathematical concept of a _____ expresses the intuitive idea of deterministic dependence between two quantities, one of which is viewed as primary and the other as secondary. A _____ then is a way to associate a unique output for each input of a specified type, for example, a real number or an element of a given set.
- a. Grill
- b. Coherent
- c. Going up
- d. Function

Chapter 8. COUNTING PRINCIPLES; FURTHER PROBABILITY TOPICS

38. _____ is a temperature scale that is named after the German physicist Daniel Gabriel _____, who proposed it in 1724.

In this scale, the freezing point of water is 32 degrees _____ and the boiling point 212 °F, placing the boiling and freezing points of water exactly 180 degrees apart. A degree on the _____ scale is 1/180th part of the interval between the ice point and the boiling point.

a. 120-cell
b. 2-3 heap
c. 1-center problem
d. Fahrenheit

39. A _____ is a structured activity, usually undertaken for enjoyment and sometimes also used as an educational tool. _____s are distinct from work, which is usually carried out for remuneration, and from art, which is more concerned with the expression of ideas. However, the distinction is not clear-cut, and many _____s are also considered to be work (such as professional players of spectator sports/_____s) or art (such as jigsaw puzzles or _____s involving an artistic layout such as Mah-jongg solitaire.)

a. 120-cell
b. 1-center problem
c. 2-3 heap
d. Game

40. _____ can be regarded as an outcome of mental processes leading to the selection of a course of action among several alternatives. Every _____ process produces a final choice. The output can be an action or an opinion of choice.

a. 1-center problem
b. Decision making
c. 120-cell
d. 2-3 heap

41. In mathematics, the _____ is when a number is squared and is then subtracted from another squared number. It refers to the identity

$$a^2 - b^2 = (a + b)(a - b)$$

from elementary algebra.

The proof is straightforward, starting from the RHS: apply the distributive law to get a sum of four terms, and set

$$ba - ab = 0$$

as an application of the commutative law.

a. Quartic equation
b. Quadratic equation
c. Linear equation
d. Difference of two squares

42. In elementary algebra, a _____ is a polynomial consisting of three terms; in other words, a _____ is the sum of three monomials. It can be factored using simple steps

In linguistics, a _____ is a fixed expression which is made from three words; e.g. 'lights, camera, action', 'signed, sealed, delivered'.

a. Relation algebra
b. Symmetric difference
c. Recurrence relation
d. Trinomial

Chapter 9. STATISTICS

1. In differential geometry, a discipline within mathematics, a _____ is a subset of the tangent bundle of a manifold satisfying certain properties. _____s are used to build up notions of integrability, and specifically of a foliation of a manifold
   - a. Distribution
   - b. Coherence
   - c. Discontinuity
   - d. Constraint

2. The _____ or Dirac's delta is a mathematical construct introduced by the British theoretical physicist Paul Dirac. Informally, it is a function representing an infinitely sharp peak bounding unit area: a function that has the value zero everywhere except at x = 0 where its value is infinitely large in such a way that its total integral is 1. It is a continuous analogue of the discrete Kronecker delta.
   - a. Dirac delta
   - b. Weak derivative
   - c. Schwartz kernel theorem
   - d. Hyperfunction

3. A sample is a subject chosen from a population for investigation. A _____ is one chosen by a method involving an unpredictable component. Random sampling can also refer to taking a number of independent observations from the same probability distribution, without involving any real population.
   - a. Randomized response
   - b. Selection bias
   - c. Systematic sampling
   - d. Random sample

4. A _____ is the result of applying a function to a set of data.

More formally, statistical theory defines a _____ as a function of a sample where the function itself is independent of the sample's distribution: the term is used both for the function and for the value of the function on a given sample.

A _____ is distinct from an unknown statistical parameter, which is not computable from a sample.

   - a. Statistic
   - b. Parameter space
   - c. Loss function
   - d. Spatial dependence

5. _____ is a mathematical science pertaining to the collection, analysis, interpretation or explanation, and presentation of data. It also provides tools for prediction and forecasting based on data. It is applicable to a wide variety of academic disciplines, from the natural and social sciences to the humanities, government and business.
   - a. Percentile rank
   - b. Statistics
   - c. Probability distribution
   - d. Regression toward the mean

6. In elementary algebra, a _____ is a polynomial with two terms: the sum of two monomials. It is the simplest kind of polynomial except for a monomial.

The _____ $a^2 - b^2$ can be factored as the product of two other _____s:

$a^2 - b^2$.

The product of a pair of linear _____s a x + b and c x + d is:

2 +x + bd.

A _____ raised to the nth power, represented as

n

can be expanded by means of the _____ theorem or, equivalently, using Pascal's triangle.

a. Real structure
b. Binomial
c. Rational root theorem
d. Cylindrical algebraic decomposition

7. In statistics the _____ of an event i is the number n_i of times the event occurred in the experiment or the study. These frequencies are often graphically represented in histograms.

We speak of absolute frequencies, when the counts n_i themselves are given and of

$$f_i = \frac{n_i}{N} = \frac{n_i}{\sum_i n_i}$$

Taking the f_i for all i and tabulating or plotting them leads to a _____ distribution.

a. Frequency
b. Robinson-Dadson curves
c. Subharmonic
d. Digital room correction

8. In statistics, a _____ is a list of the values that a variable takes in a sample. It is usually a list, ordered by quantity, showing the number of times each value appears. For example, if 100 people rate a five-point Likert scale assessing their agreement with a statement on a scale on which 1 denotes strong agreement and 5 strong disagreement, the _____ of their responses might look like:

This simple tabulation has two drawbacks.

a. Covariance
b. Percentile
c. Frequency Distribution
d. Confounding

9. In statistics, a _____ is a subset of a population. Typically, the population is very large, making a census or a complete enumeration of all the values in the population impractical or impossible. The _____ represents a subset of manageable size.

a. Boussinesq approximation
b. Duality
c. Sample
d. Dispersion

Chapter 9. STATISTICS

10. In statistics, a _____ is a graphical display of tabulated frequencies, shown as bars. It shows what proportion of cases fall into each of several categories. A _____ differs from a bar chart in that it is the area of the bar that denotes the value, not the height as in bar charts, a crucial distinction when the categories are not of uniform width.

   a. First-hitting-time models   b. Probability distribution
   c. Standardized moment   d. Histogram

11. In mathematics, an _____ is a statement about the relative size or order of two objects, or about whether they are the same or not

- The notation a < b means that a is less than b.
- The notation a > b means that a is greater than b.
- The notation a ≠ b means that a is not equal to b, but does not say that one is bigger than the other or even that they can be compared in size.

In all these cases, a is not equal to b, hence, '_____'.

These relations are known as strict _____

- The notation a ≤ b means that a is less than or equal to b;
- The notation a ≥ b means that a is greater than or equal to b;

An additional use of the notation is to show that one quantity is much greater than another, normally by several orders of magnitude.

- The notation a << b means that a is much less than b.
- The notation a >> b means that a is much greater than b.

If the sense of the _____ is the same for all values of the variables for which its members are defined, then the _____ is called an 'absolute' or 'unconditional' _____. If the sense of an _____ holds only for certain values of the variables involved, but is reversed or destroyed for other values of the variables, it is called a conditional _____.

An _____ may appear unsolvable because it only states whether a number is larger or smaller than another number; but it is possible to apply the same operations for equalities to inequalities. For example, to find x for the _____ 10x > 23 one would divide 23 by 10.

   a. A posteriori   b. A Mathematical Theory of Communication
   c. Inequality   d. A chemical equation

12. In geometry a _____ is traditionally a plane figure that is bounded by a closed path or circuit, composed of a finite sequence of straight line segments. These segments are called its edges or sides, and the points where two edges meet are the _____'s vertices or corners. The interior of the _____ is sometimes called its body.

   a. Polygon   b. Regular polygon
   c. Parallelogon   d. Polygonal curve

Chapter 9. STATISTICS

13. _____ are used in computer graphics to compose images that are three-dimensional in appearance. Usually triangular, _____ arise when an object's surface is modeled, vertices are selected, and the object is rendered in a wire frame model. This is quicker to display than a shaded model; thus the _____ are a stage in computer animation.
   a. Polygons
   b. Heptadecagon
   c. Triskaidecagon
   d. Visibility polygon

14. In mathematics, an average, or _____ of a data set refers to a measure of the 'middle' or 'expected' value of the data set. There are many different descriptive statistics that can be chosen as a measurement of the _____ of the data items.

An average is a single value that is meant to typify a list of values.

   a. Trimean
   b. Quartile
   c. Mean reciprocal rank
   d. Central tendency

15. In linear algebra, _____ is a version of Gaussian elimination that puts zeros both above and below each pivot element as it goes from the top row of the given matrix to the bottom. In other words, _____ brings a matrix to reduced row echelon form, whereas Gaussian elimination takes it only as far as row echelon form. Every matrix has a reduced row echelon form, and this algorithm is guaranteed to produce it.
   a. Spheroidal wave functions
   b. Conservation form
   c. Lax equivalence theorem
   d. Gauss-Jordan elimination

16. In statistics, _____ has two related meanings:

   - the arithmetic _____.
   - the expected value of a random variable, which is also called the population _____.

It is sometimes stated that the '_____' _____s average. This is incorrect if '_____' is taken in the specific sense of 'arithmetic _____' as there are different types of averages: the _____, median, and mode. For instance, average house prices almost always use the median value for the average.

For a real-valued random variable X, the _____ is the expectation of X.

   a. Probability
   b. Statistical population
   c. Mean
   d. Proportional hazards model

17. _____ is the addition of a set of numbers; the result is their sum or total. An interim or present total of a _____ process is termed the running total. The 'numbers' to be summed may be natural numbers, complex numbers, matrices, or still more complicated objects.
   a. 2-3 heap
   b. 1-center problem
   c. 120-cell
   d. Summation

18. In probability theory and statistics, the _____ is the discrete probability distribution of the number of successes in a sequence of n independent yes/no experiments, each of which yields success with probability p. Such a success/failure experiment is also called a Bernoulli experiment or Bernoulli trial. In fact, when n = 1, the _____ is a Bernoulli distribution.

a. Biostatistics
b. Binomial distribution
c. Coefficient of variation
d. Median

19. _____ is a branch of mathematics which focuses on the study of matrices. Initially a sub-branch of linear algebra, it has grown to cover subjects related to graph theory, algebra, combinatorics, and statistics as well.

The term matrix was first coined in 1848 by J.J. Sylvester as a name of an array of numbers.

a. Matrix theory
b. Pairing
c. Semi-simple operators
d. Segre classification

20. In mathematics the concept of a _____ generalizes notions such as 'length', 'area', and 'volume'. Informally, given some base set, a '_____' is any consistent assignment of 'sizes' to the subsets of the base set. Depending on the application, the 'size' of a subset may be interpreted as its physical size, the amount of something that lies within the subset, or the probability that some random process will yield a result within the subset.

a. Measure
b. Cusp
c. Lattice
d. Congruent

21. In mathematics, a _____ is an expression constructed from variables and constants, using the operations of addition, subtraction, multiplication, and constant non-negative whole number exponents. For example, $x^2 - 4x + 7$ is a _____, but $x^2 - 4/x + 7x^{3/2}$ is not, because its second term involves division by the variable x and also because its third term contains an exponent that is not a whole number.

_____s are one of the most important concepts in algebra and throughout mathematics and science.

a. Semifield
b. Group extension
c. Coimage
d. Polynomial

22. In mathematics, a _____ is a set of real numbers with the property that any number that lies between two numbers in the set is also included in the set. For example, the set of all numbers x satisfying $0 \leq x \leq 1$ is an _____ which contains 0 and 1, as well as all numbers between them. Other examples of _____s are the set of all real numbers $\mathbb{R}$, the set of all positive real numbers, and the empty set.

a. Order
b. Annihilator
c. Ideal
d. Interval

23. In geometry, a _____ of a triangle is a line segment joining a vertex to the midpoint of the opposing side. Every triangle has exactly three _____s; one running from each vertex to the opposite side.

The three _____s are concurrent at a point known as the triangle's centroid, or center of mass of the triangle.

a. Statistical significance
b. Correlation
c. Percentile rank
d. Median

24. _____ and sample covariance are statistics computed from a collection of data, thought of as being random.

Chapter 9. STATISTICS

Given a random sample $\mathbf{x}_1, \ldots, \mathbf{x}_N$ from an n-dimensional random variable $\mathbf{X}$, the _____ is

$$\bar{\mathbf{x}} = \frac{1}{N} \sum_{k=1}^{N} \mathbf{x}_k.$$

In coordinates, writing the vectors as columns,

$$\mathbf{x}_k = \begin{bmatrix} x_{1k} \\ \vdots \\ x_{nk} \end{bmatrix}, \quad \bar{\mathbf{x}} = \begin{bmatrix} \bar{x}_1 \\ \vdots \\ \bar{x}_n \end{bmatrix},$$

the entries of the _____ are

$$\bar{x}_i = \frac{1}{N} \sum_{k=1}^{N} x_{ik}, \quad i = 1, \ldots, n.$$

The sample covariance of $\mathbf{x}_1, \ldots, \mathbf{x}_N$ is the n-by-n matrix $\mathbf{Q} = [q_{ij}]$ with the entries given by

$$q_{ij} = \frac{1}{N-1} \sum_{k=1}^{N} (x_{ik} - \bar{x}_i)(x_{jk} - \bar{x}_j)$$

The _____ and the sample covariance matrix are unbiased estimates of the mean and the covariance matrix of the random variable $\mathbf{X}$. The reason why the sample covariance matrix has $N - 1$ in the denominator rather than N is essentially that the population mean E is not known and is replaced by the _____ $\bar{x}$.

a. Mathematical statistics
b. Covariance
c. Skewness
d. Sample mean

25. In statistics, the _____ is the value that occurs the most frequently in a data set or a probability distribution. In some fields, notably education, sample data are often called scores, and the sample _____ is known as the modal score.

Like the statistical mean and the median, the _____ is a way of capturing important information about a random variable or a population in a single quantity.

a. Function
b. Deltoid
c. Field
d. Mode

Chapter 9. STATISTICS

26. In descriptive statistics, the _____ is the length of the smallest interval which contains all the data. It is calculated by subtracting the smallest observations from the greatest and provides an indication of statistical dispersion.

It is measured in the same units as the data.

a. Range
c. Kernel

b. Class
d. Bandwidth

27. In mathematics, the _____ of a real number is its numerical value without regard to its sign. So, for example, 3 is the _____ of both 3 and −3.

The _____ of a number a is denoted by $|a|$.

Generalizations of the _____ for real numbers occur in a wide variety of mathematical settings.

a. A Mathematical Theory of Communication
c. A chemical equation

b. Area hyperbolic functions
d. Absolute value

28. In mathematics and statistics, _____ is a measure of difference for interval and ratio variables between the observed value and the mean. The sign of _____, either positive or negative, indicates whether the observation is larger than or smaller than the mean. The magnitude of the value reports how different an observation is from the mean.

a. Functional
c. Conchoid

b. Filter
d. Deviation

29. In probability theory and statistics, the definition of variance is either the expected value, or average of _____ from the mean. Computations for analysis of variance involve the partitioning of a sum of _____. An understanding of the complex computations involved is greatly enhanced by a detailed study of the statistical value:

$$E(X^2).$$

It is well-known that for a random variable X with mean μ and variance σ²:

$$\sigma^2 = E(X^2) - \mu^2$$

Therefore

$$E(X^2) = \sigma^2 + \mu^2.$$

From the above, the following are readly derived:

$$E\left(\sum (X^2)\right) = n\sigma^2 + n\mu^2$$

$$E\left(\left(\sum X\right)^2\right) = n\sigma^2 + n^2\mu^2$$

The sum of _____ needed to calculate variance is most easily calculated as

$$S = \sum x^2 - \left(\sum x\right)^2 / n$$

From the two derived expectations above the expected value of this sum is

$$E(S) = n\sigma^2 + n\mu^2 - (n\sigma^2 + n^2\mu^2)/n$$

which implies

$$E(S) = (n-1)\sigma^2.$$

This effectively proves the use of the divisor in the calculation of an unbiased sample estimate of σ^2

In the situation where data is available for k different treatment groups having size n_i where i varies from 1 to k, then it is assumed that the expected mean of each group is

$$E(\mu_i) = \mu + T_i$$

and the variance of each treatment group is unchanged from the population variance σ^2.

a. Squared deviations
c. Moment about the mean
b. Qualitative variation
d. Minimum mean square error

30. In probability and statistics, the _____ is a measure of the dispersion of a collection of numbers. It can apply to a probability distribution, a random variable, a population or a data set. The _____ is usually denoted with the letter σ.
a. Null hypothesis
c. Statistical population
b. Standard deviation
d. Failure rate

Chapter 9. STATISTICS

31. In mathematics, a _____ of a number x is a number r such that r^2 = x, or, in other words, a number r whose square is x. Every non-negative real number x has a unique non-negative _____, called the principal _____, which is denoted with a radical symbol as $\sqrt{x}$, or, using exponent notation, as $x^{1/2}$. For example, the principal _____ of 9 is 3, denoted $\sqrt{9}$ = 3, because 3^2 = 3 × 3 = 9.

    a. Square root
    b. Hyperbolic functions
    c. Double exponential
    d. Multiplicative inverse

32. In probability theory and statistics, the _____ of a random variable, probability distribution averaging the squared distance of its possible values from the expected value. Whereas the mean is a way to describe the location of a distribution, the _____ is a way to capture its scale or degree of being spread out. The unit of _____ is the square of the unit of the original variable.

    a. Nonlinear regression
    b. Kendall tau rank correlation coefficient
    c. Probability distribution
    d. Variance

33. In mathematics and in the sciences, a _____ (plural: _____e, formulæ or _____s) is a concise way of expressing information symbolically (as in a mathematical or chemical _____), or a general relationship between quantities. One of many famous _____e is Albert Einstein's E = mc^2 (see special relativity

In mathematics, a _____ is a key to solve an equation with variables. For example, the problem of determining the volume of a sphere is one that requires a significant amount of integral calculus to solve.

    a. 1-center problem
    b. 120-cell
    c. 2-3 heap
    d. Formula

34. In vascular plants, the _____ is the organ of a plant body that typically lies below the surface of the soil. This is not always the case, however, since a _____ can also be aerial (that is, growing above the ground) or aerating (that is, growing up above the ground or especially above water.) Furthermore, a stem normally occurring below ground is not exceptional either

    a. 1-center problem
    b. 2-3 heap
    c. Root
    d. 120-cell

35. A _____ is a deliberate process for transforming one or more inputs into one or more results, with variable change.

The term is used in a variety of senses, from the very definite arithmetical using an algorithm to the vague heuristics of calculating a strategy in a competition or calculating the chance of a successful relationship between two people.

Multiplying 7 by 8 is a simple algorithmic _____.

    a. Calculation
    b. Mathematical object
    c. Mathematical maturity
    d. Mathematics Subject Classification

Chapter 9. STATISTICS

36. In mathematics, _____ are used in the study of chance and probability. They were developed to assist in the analysis of games of chance, stochastic events, and the results of scientific experiments by capturing only the mathematical properties necessary to answer probabilistic questions. Further formalizations have firmly grounded the entity in the theoretical domains of mathematics by making use of measure theory.
   a. Statistics
   b. Statistical dispersion
   c. Random variables
   d. Median polish

37. In probability theory, a probability distribution is called _____ if its cumulative distribution function is _____. That is equivalent to saying that for random variables X with the distribution in question, Pr[X = a] = 0 for all real numbers a. If the distribution of X is _____ then X is called a _____ random variable.
   a. Continuous
   b. Continuous phase modulation
   c. Concatenated codes
   d. Conull set

38. _____ is an effective method of monitoring a process through the use of control charts. Control charts enable the use of objective criteria for distinguishing background variation from events of significance based on statistical techniques. Much of its power lies in the ability to monitor both process center and its variation about that center.
   a. Quality control
   b. Statistical process control
   c. 120-cell
   d. 1-center problem

39. The word _____ denotes information gained by means of observation, experience as opposed to theoretical. A central concept in science and the scientific method is that all evidence must be _____ that is, dependent on evidence or consequences that are observable by the senses. It is usually differentiated from the philosophic usage of empiricism by the use of the adjective '_____' or the adverb 'empirically.' '_____' as an adjective or adverb is used in conjunction with both the natural and social sciences, and refers to the use of working hypotheses that are testable using observation or experiment.
   a. A Mathematical Theory of Communication
   b. A posteriori
   c. A chemical equation
   d. Empirical

40. _____ is the likelihood or chance that something is the case or will happen. Theoretical _____ is used extensively in areas such as statistics, mathematics, science and philosophy to draw conclusions about the likelihood of potential events and the underlying mechanics of complex systems.

The word _____ does not have a consistent direct definition.

   a. Discrete random variable
   b. Probability
   c. Standardized moment
   d. Statistical significance

41. In probability theory and statistics, a _____ identifies either the probability of each value of an unidentified random variable, or the probability of the value falling within a particular interval. The probability function describes the range of possible values that a random variable can attain and the probability that the value of the random variable is within any subset of that range.

When the random variable takes values in the set of real numbers, the _____ is completely described by the cumulative distribution function, whose value at each real x is the probability that the random variable is smaller than or equal to x.

a. Z-test
b. Normal distribution
c. Statistical graphics
d. Probability distribution

42. In mathematics, differential rings, differential fields and differential algebras are rings, fields and algebras equipped with a _____, which is a unary function satisfying the Leibniz product law. A natural example of a differential field is the field of rational functions over the complex numbers in one variable, C

A differential ring is a ring R equipped with one or more _____ s

$$\partial : R \to R$$

such that each _____ satisfies the Leibniz product rule

$$\partial(r_1 r_2) = (\partial r_1)r_2 + r_1(\partial r_2),$$

for every $r_1, r_2 \in R$.

a. Leibniz formula
b. Cusp
c. Discontinuity
d. Derivation

43. In mathematics, specifically in combinatorial commutative algebra, a convex lattice polytope P is called _____ if it has the following property: given any positive integer n, every lattice point of the dilation nP, obtained from P by scaling its vertices by the factor n and taking the convex hull of the resulting points, can be written as the sum of exactly n lattice points in P. This property plays an important role in the theory of toric varieties, where it corresponds to projective normality of the toric variety determined by P.

The simplex in R^k with the vertices at the origin and along the unit coordinate vectors is _____.

a. Polytetrahedron
b. Hypercube
c. Demihypercubes
d. Normal

44. The _____ is an important family of continuous probability distributions, applicable in many fields. Each member of the family may be defined by two parameters, location and scale: the mean and variance respectively. The standard _____ is the _____ with a mean of zero and a variance of one.

a. Percentile rank
b. Coefficient of variation
c. Null hypothesis
d. Normal Distribution

45. In mathematics, a _____ is a statement that can be proved on the basis of explicitly stated or previously agreed assumptions.

a. Disjunction introduction
b. Boolean function
c. Theorem
d. Logical value

Chapter 9. STATISTICS

46. _____ is a quantity expressing the two-dimensional size of a defined part of a surface, typically a region bounded by a closed curve. The term surface _____ refers to the total _____ of the exposed surface of a 3-dimensional solid, such as the sum of the _____s of the exposed sides of a polyhedron. _____ is an important invariant in the differential geometry of surfaces.
   a. A chemical equation
   b. A Mathematical Theory of Communication
   c. Area
   d. A posteriori

47. In mathematics, the concept of a _____ tries to capture the intuitive idea of a geometrical one-dimensional and continuous object. A simple example is the circle. In everyday use of the term '_____', a straight line is not curved, but in mathematical parlance _____s include straight lines and line segments.
   a. Negative pedal curve
   b. Kappa curve
   c. Curve
   d. Quadrifolium

48. _____ is a dimensionless quantity derived by subtracting the population mean from an individual raw score and then dividing the difference by the population standard deviation.
   a. 2-3 heap
   b. 1-center problem
   c. Z-score
   d. 120-cell

49. In statistics, a standard score is a dimensionless quantity derived by subtracting the population mean from an individual raw score and then dividing the difference by the population standard deviation. This conversion process is called standardizing or normalizing.

Standard scores are also called z-values, _____, normal scores, and standardized variables.

   a. Converge absolutely
   b. CIE 1931 XYZ color space
   c. Z-scores
   d. Bernstein inequalities

50. _____ is a branch of mathematics that includes the study of limits, derivatives, integrals, and infinite series, and constitutes a major part of modern university education. Historically, it has been referred to as 'the _____ of infinitesimals', or 'infinitesimal _____'. Most basically, _____ is the study of change, in the same way that geometry is the study of space.
   a. Hyperbolic angle
   b. Partial sum
   c. Test for Divergence
   d. Calculus

51. The _____ specifies the relationship between the two central operations of calculus, differentiation and integration.

The first part of the theorem, sometimes called the first _____, shows that an indefinite integration can be reversed by a differentiation.

The second part, sometimes called the second _____, allows one to compute the definite integral of a function by using any one of its infinitely many antiderivatives.

   a. Hyperbolic angle
   b. Standard part function
   c. Maxima and minima
   d. Fundamental Theorem of Calculus

Chapter 9. STATISTICS

52. Introduction

In the theory of probability and statistics, a _____ is an experiment whose outcome is random and can be either of two possible outcomes, 'success' and 'failure'.

In practice it refers to a single experiment which can have one of two possible outcomes. These events can be phrased into 'yes or no' questions:

- Did the coin land heads?
- Was the newborn child a girl?
- Were a person's eyes green?
- Did a mosquito die after the area was sprayed with insecticide?
- Did a potential customer decide to buy a product?
- Did a citizen vote for a specific candidate?
- Did an employee vote pro-union?

Therefore success and failure are labels for outcomes, and should not be construed literally. Examples of _____s include

- Flipping a coin. In this context, obverse conventionally denotes success and reverse denotes failure. A fair coin has the probability of success 0.5 by definition.
- Rolling a die, where a six is 'success' and everything else a 'failure'.
- In conducting a political opinion poll, choosing a voter at random to ascertain whether that voter will vote 'yes' in an upcoming referendum.

Mathematically, a _____ can be described by a sample space Ω consisting of two values, s for 'success' and f for 'failure'. Therefore the sample space is $\Omega = \{s, f\}$.

a. Marginal distribution
b. Point process
c. Law of total cumulance
d. Bernoulli trial

53. _____ typically deals with the probability of several successive decisions, each of which has two possible outcomes.

The probability of an event can be expressed as a _____ if its outcomes can be broken down into two probabilities p and q, where p and q are complementary For example, tossing a coin can be either heads or tails, each which have a probability of 0.5. Rolling a four on a six-sided die can be expressed as the probability of getting a 4 or the probability of rolling something else.

a. Markov chain
b. Binomial probability
c. Quantile
d. Marginal distribution

54. A _____ is a software program that facilitates symbolic mathematics. The core functionality of a CAS is manipulation of mathematical expressions in symbolic form.

Chapter 9. STATISTICS

The symbolic manipulations supported typically include

- simplification to the smallest possible expression or some standard form, including automatic simplification with assumptions and simplification with constraints
- substitution of symbolic, functors or numeric values for expressions
- change of form of expressions: expanding products and powers, partial and full factorization, rewriting as partial fractions, constraint satisfaction, rewriting trigonometric functions as exponentials, etc.
- partial and total differentiation
- symbolic constrained and unconstrained global optimization
- solution of linear and some non-linear equations over various domains
- solution of some differential and difference equations
- taking some limits
- some indefinite and definite integration, including multidimensional integrals
- integral transforms
- arbitrary-precision numeric operations
- Series operations such as expansion, summation and products
- matrix operations including products, inverses, etc.
- display of mathematical expressions in two-dimensional mathematical form, often using typesetting systems similar to TeX
- add-ons for use in applied mathematics such as physics packages for physical computation
- plotting graphs and parametric plots of functions in two and three dimensions, and animating them
- APIs for linking it on an external program such as a database, or using in a programming language to use the _____
- drawing charts and diagrams
- string manipulation such as matching and searching
- statistical computation
- Theorem proving and verification
- graphic production and editing such as CGI and signal processing as image processing
- sound synthesis

Many also include a programming language, allowing users to implement their own algorithms.

Some _____s focus on a specific area of application; these are typically developed in academia and are free.

a. 120-cell
b. 2-3 heap
c. 1-center problem
d. Computer algebra system

Chapter 10. NONLINEAR FUNCTIONS

1. In economics, business, retail, and accounting, a _____ is the value of money that has been used up to produce something, and hence is not available for use anymore. In business, the _____ may be one of acquisition, in which case the amount of money expended to acquire it is counted as _____. In this case, money is the input that is gone in order to acquire the thing.

   a. 2-3 heap
   c. 120-cell
   b. 1-center problem
   d. Cost

2. In economics, the cross elasticity of demand and _____ measures the responsiveness of the quantity demanded of a good to a change in the price of another good.

   It is measured as the percentage change in quantity demanded for the first good that occurs in response to a percentage change in price of the second good. For example, if, in response to a 10% increase in the price of fuel, the quantity of new cars that are fuel inefficient demanded decreased by 20%, the cross elasticity of demand would be -20%/10% = -2.

   a. 1-center problem
   c. Marginal rate of substitution
   b. Supply and demand
   d. Cross price elasticity of demand

3. In mathematics, a _____ is a system which is not linear. Less technically, a _____ is any problem where the variabl to be solved for cannot be written as a linear sum of independent components. A nonhomogenous system, which is linear apart from the presence of a function of the independent variables, is nonlinear according to a strict definition, but such systems are usually studied alongside linear systems, because they can be transformed to a linear system as long as a particular solution is known.

   a. George Dantzig
   c. 1-center problem
   b. Metric system
   d. Nonlinear system

4. In mathematics, an _____, or central tendency of a data set refers to a measure of the 'middle' or 'expected' value of the data set. There are many different descriptive statistics that can be chosen as a measurement of the central tendency of the data items.

   An _____ is a single value that is meant to typify a list of values.

   a. A posteriori
   c. A chemical equation
   b. Average
   d. A Mathematical Theory of Communication

5. The mathematical concept of a _____ expresses the intuitive idea of deterministic dependence between two quantities, one of which is viewed as primary and the other as secondary. A _____ then is a way to associate a unique output for each input of a specified type, for example, a real number or an element of a given set.

   a. Going up
   c. Coherent
   b. Grill
   d. Function

6. _____ and independent variables refer to values that change in relationship to each other. The _____ are those that are observed to change in response to the independent variables. The independent variables are those that are deliberately manipulated to invoke a change in the _____.

   a. Steiner system
   c. Yates analysis
   b. Dependent variables
   d. Round robin test

Chapter 10. NONLINEAR FUNCTIONS

7. In mathematics, especially in the area of abstract algebra known as ring theory, a _____ is a ring with 0 ≠ 1 such that ab = 0 implies that either a = 0 or b = 0. That is, it is a nontrivial ring without left or right zero divisors. A commutative _____ is called an integral _____.
   - a. Left primitive ring
   - b. Simple ring
   - c. Modular representation theory
   - d. Domain

8. Dependent variables and _____ refer to values that change in relationship to each other. The dependent variables are those that are observed to change in response to the _____. The _____ are those that are deliberately manipulated to invoke a change in the dependent variables.
   - a. Operational confound
   - b. Experimental design diagram
   - c. One-factor-at-a-time method
   - d. Independent variables

9. In descriptive statistics, the _____ is the length of the smallest interval which contains all the data. It is calculated by subtracting the smallest observations from the greatest and provides an indication of statistical dispersion.

   It is measured in the same units as the data.
   - a. Class
   - b. Bandwidth
   - c. Kernel
   - d. Range

10. _____ is a branch of mathematics which focuses on the study of matrices. Initially a sub-branch of linear algebra, it has grown to cover subjects related to graph theory, algebra, combinatorics, and statistics as well.

    The term matrix was first coined in 1848 by J.J. Sylvester as a name of an array of numbers.
    - a. Pairing
    - b. Matrix theory
    - c. Semi-simple operators
    - d. Segre classification

11. A _____ is the transfer of an interest in property (or in law the equivalent - a charge) to a lender as a security for a debt - usually a loan of money. While a _____ in itself is not a debt, it is lender's security for a debt. It is a transfer of an interest in land (or the equivalent), from the owner to the _____ lender, on the condition that this interest will be returned to the owner of the real estate when the terms of the _____ have been satisfied or performed.
    - a. Mortgage
    - b. 120-cell
    - c. 2-3 heap
    - d. 1-center problem

12. _____ is the mathematical operation of scaling one number by another. It is one of the four basic operations in elementary arithmetic.

    _____ is defined for whole numbers in terms of repeated addition; for example, 4 multiplied by 3 can be calculated by adding 3 copies of 4 together:

    $$4 + 4 + 4 = 12.$$

    _____ of rational numbers and real numbers is defined by systematic generalization of this basic idea.

Chapter 10. NONLINEAR FUNCTIONS

a. Highest common factor
c. Least common multiple
b. Multiplication
d. The number 0 is even.

13. In elementary algebra, a _____ is a polynomial with two terms: the sum of two monomials. It is the simplest kind of polynomial except for a monomial.

The _____ $a^2 - b^2$ can be factored as the product of two other _____s:

$a^2 - b^2$.

The product of a pair of linear _____s a x + b and c x + d is:

2 +x + bd.

A _____ raised to the nth power, represented as

n

can be expanded by means of the _____ theorem or, equivalently, using Pascal's triangle.

a. Real structure
c. Rational root theorem
b. Cylindrical algebraic decomposition
d. Binomial

14. In mathematics, a _____ is a function whose values do not vary and thus are constant. For example, if we have the function f→ B is a _____ if f
a. Squeeze mapping
c. Linear operator
b. Point reflection
d. Constant function

15. _____ is a fundamental construction of differential calculus and admits many possible generalizations within the fields of mathematical analysis, combinatorics, algebra, and geometry.

In real, complex, and functional analysis, _____s are generalized to functions of several real or complex variables and functions between topological vector spaces. An important case is the variational _____ in the calculus of variations.

a. Lin-Tsien equation
c. Metric derivative
b. Functional derivative
d. Derivative

16. In mathematics, an _____ is a statement about the relative size or order of two objects, or about whether they are the same or not

- The notation a < b means that a is less than b.
- The notation a > b means that a is greater than b.
- The notation a ≠ b means that a is not equal to b, but does not say that one is bigger than the other or even that they can be compared in size.

In all these cases, a is not equal to b, hence, '_____'.

These relations are known as strict _____

- The notation a ≤ b means that a is less than or equal to b;
- The notation a ≥ b means that a is greater than or equal to b;

An additional use of the notation is to show that one quantity is much greater than another, normally by several orders of magnitude.

- The notation a << b means that a is much less than b.
- The notation a >> b means that a is much greater than b.

If the sense of the _____ is the same for all values of the variables for which its members are defined, then the _____ is called an 'absolute' or 'unconditional' _____. If the sense of an _____ holds only for certain values of the variables involved, but is reversed or destroyed for other values of the variables, it is called a conditional _____.

An _____ may appear unsolvable because it only states whether a number is larger or smaller than another number; but it is possible to apply the same operations for equalities to inequalities. For example, to find x for the _____ 10x > 23 one would divide 23 by 10.

a. A Mathematical Theory of Communication
c. A posteriori
b. A chemical equation
d. Inequality

17. A _____ typically refers to a class of handheld calculators that are capable of plotting graphs, solving simultaneous equations, and performing numerous other tasks with variables. Most popular _____s are also programmable, allowing the user to create customized programs, typically for scientific/engineering and education applications. Due to their large displays intended for graphing, they can also accommodate several lines of text and calculations at a time.
a. Bump mapping
c. Support vector machines
b. Genus
d. Graphing calculator

18. In mathematics, a _____ is a polynomial equation of the second degree. The general form is

$$ax^2 + bx + c = 0,$$

where a ≠ 0.

The letters a, b, and c are called coefficients: the quadratic coefficient a is the coefficient of x^2, the linear coefficient b is the coefficient of x, and c is the constant coefficient, also called the free term or constant term.

a. Linear equation
b. Difference of two squares
c. Quartic equation
d. Quadratic equation

19. A quadratic equation with real solutions, called roots, which may be real or complex, is given by the _____ : $x = \frac{-b \pm \sqrt{b^2 - 4ac}}{2a}$.

a. Quotient
b. Parametric continuity
c. Quadratic formula
d. Differential Algebra

20. _____ or amortisation is the process of decreasing an amount over a period of time. The word comes from Middle English amortisen to kill, alienate in mortmain, from Anglo-French amorteser, alteration of amortir, from Vulgar Latin admortire to kill, from Latin ad- + mort-, mors death. Particular instances of the term include:

- _____, the allocation of a lump sum amount to different time periods, particularly for loans and other forms of finance, including related interest or other finance charges.
    - _____ schedule, a table detailing each periodic payment on a loan, as generated by an _____ calculator.
    - Negative _____, an _____ schedule where the loan amount actually increases through not paying the full interest
- Amortized analysis, analyzing the execution cost of algorithms over a sequence of operations.
- _____ of capital expenditures of certain assets under accounting rules, particularly intangible assets, in a manner analogous to depreciation.
- _____

_____ is also used in the context of zoning regulations and describes the time in which a property owner has to relocate when the property's use constitutes a preexisting nonconforming use under zoning regulations.

- Depreciation

a. ISAAC
b. Origin
c. Identity
d. Amortization

21. An _____ is a table detailing each periodic payment on a amortizing loan, as generated by an amortization calculator.

While a portion of every payment is applied towards both the interest and the principal balance of the loan, the exact amount applied to principal each time varies. An _____ reveals the specific monetary amount put towards interest, as well as the specific put towards the Principal balance, with each payment.

Chapter 10. NONLINEAR FUNCTIONS

a. A Mathematical Theory of Communication
b. A chemical equation
c. Accounts receivable
d. Amortization schedule

22. A _____ is a device for performing mathematical calculations, distinguished from a computer by having a limited problem solving ability and an interface optimized for interactive calculation rather than programming. _____s can be hardware or software, and mechanical or electronic, and are often built into devices such as PDAs or mobile phones.

Modern electronic _____s are generally small, digital, and usually inexpensive.

a. Calculator
b. 2-3 heap
c. 120-cell
d. 1-center problem

23. In mathematics and in the sciences, a _____ (plural: _____e, formulæ or _____s) is a concise way of expressing information symbolically (as in a mathematical or chemical _____), or a general relationship between quantities. One of many famous _____e is Albert Einstein's E = mc² (see special relativity

In mathematics, a _____ is a key to solve an equation with variables. For example, the problem of determining the volume of a sphere is one that requires a significant amount of integral calculus to solve.

a. 1-center problem
b. 120-cell
c. Formula
d. 2-3 heap

24. In linear algebra, _____ is a version of Gaussian elimination that puts zeros both above and below each pivot element as it goes from the top row of the given matrix to the bottom. In other words, _____ brings a matrix to reduced row echelon form, whereas Gaussian elimination takes it only as far as row echelon form. Every matrix has a reduced row echelon form, and this algorithm is guaranteed to produce it.

a. Lax equivalence theorem
b. Conservation form
c. Spheroidal wave functions
d. Gauss-Jordan elimination

25. In mathematics, the _____ is a conic section, the intersection of a right circular conical surface and a plane parallel to a generating straight line of that surface. Given a point and a line that lie in a plane, the locus of points in that plane that are equidistant to them is a _____.

A particular case arises when the plane is tangent to the conical surface of a circle.

a. Parabola
b. Matrix representation of conic sections
c. Directrix
d. Dandelin sphere

26. A _____, in mathematics, is a polynomial function of the form $f(x) = ax^2 + bx + c$, where $a \neq 0$. The graph of a _____ is a parabola whose major axis is parallel to the y-axis.

The expression ax² + bx + c in the definition of a _____ is a polynomial of degree 2 or a 2nd degree polynomial, because the highest exponent of x is 2.

Chapter 10. NONLINEAR FUNCTIONS 85

a. Laguerre polynomials
b. Multivariate division algorithm
c. Quadratic function
d. Discriminant

27. In geometry, a _____ is a special kind of point, usually a corner of a polygon, polyhedron, or higher dimensional polytope. In the geometry of curves a _____ is a point of where the first derivative of curvature is zero. In graph theory, a _____ is the fundamental unit out of which graphs are formed
a. Vertex
b. Crib
c. Dini
d. Duality

28. A _____ is a software program that facilitates symbolic mathematics. The core functionality of a CAS is manipulation of mathematical expressions in symbolic form.

The symbolic manipulations supported typically include

- simplification to the smallest possible expression or some standard form, including automatic simplification with assumptions and simplification with constraints
- substitution of symbolic, functors or numeric values for expressions
- change of form of expressions: expanding products and powers, partial and full factorization, rewriting as partial fractions, constraint satisfaction, rewriting trigonometric functions as exponentials, etc.
- partial and total differentiation
- symbolic constrained and unconstrained global optimization
- solution of linear and some non-linear equations over various domains
- solution of some differential and difference equations
- taking some limits
- some indefinite and definite integration, including multidimensional integrals
- integral transforms
- arbitrary-precision numeric operations
- Series operations such as expansion, summation and products
- matrix operations including products, inverses, etc.
- display of mathematical expressions in two-dimensional mathematical form, often using typesetting systems similar to TeX
- add-ons for use in applied mathematics such as physics packages for physical computation
- plotting graphs and parametric plots of functions in two and three dimensions, and animating them
- APIs for linking it on an external program such as a database, or using in a programming language to use the _____
- drawing charts and diagrams
- string manipulation such as matching and searching
- statistical computation
- Theorem proving and verification
- graphic production and editing such as CGI and signal processing as image processing
- sound synthesis

Many also include a programming language, allowing users to implement their own algorithms.

Some _____s focus on a specific area of application; these are typically developed in academia and are free.

   a. Computer algebra system
   b. 2-3 heap
   c. 1-center problem
   d. 120-cell

29. _____ is a quantity expressing the two-dimensional size of a defined part of a surface, typically a region bounded by a closed curve. The term surface _____ refers to the total _____ of the exposed surface of a 3-dimensional solid, such as the sum of the _____s of the exposed sides of a polyhedron. _____ is an important invariant in the differential geometry of surfaces.
   a. A chemical equation
   b. A Mathematical Theory of Communication
   c. A posteriori
   d. Area

30. The word _____ means curving in or hollowed inward.
   a. Concavity
   b. Harmonic series
   c. Clipping
   d. Key server

31. _____ is the interpreting of the meaning of a text and the subsequent production of an equivalent text, likewise called a '_____,' that communicates the same message in another language. The text to be translated is called the 'source text,' and the language that it is to be translated into is called the 'target language'; the final product is sometimes called the 'target text.'

_____ must take into account constraints that include context, the rules of grammar of the two languages, their writing conventions, and their idioms. A common misconception is that there exists a simple word-for-word correspondence between any two languages, and that _____ is a straightforward mechanical process; such a word-for-word _____, however, cannot take into account context, grammar, conventions, and idioms.

   a. 120-cell
   b. 2-3 heap
   c. 1-center problem
   d. Translation

32. In function graphing, a _____ is a related graph which, for every point (x, y); has a y value which differs from another graph, by exactly some constant c. For example, the antiderivatives of a family are _____s of each other.
   a. Complementary angles
   b. Parallel postulate
   c. Central angle
   d. Vertical translation

33. _____ is an algebraic technique used to solve quadratic equations, in analytic geometry for determining the shapes of graphs, and in calculus for computing integrals. The essential objective is to reduce a quadratic polynomial in a variable in an equation or expression to a squared polynomial of linear order. This can reduce an equation or integral to one that is more easily solved or evaluated.
   a. Relation algebra
   b. Monomial basis
   c. Permanent of a matrix
   d. Completing the square

34. The _____ is one of the coordinates of a point in a two or three-dimensional cartesian coordinate system, equal to the distance of a point from the y-axis in a 2D system, or from the plane of y and z axes in a 3D system, measured along a line parallel to the x axis.

Chapter 10. NONLINEAR FUNCTIONS

   a. 120-cell
   b. X-coordinate
   c. 1-center problem
   d. 2-3 heap

35. The _____ fallacy is an informal fallacy. It ascribes cause where none exists. The flaw is failing to account for natural fluctuations.
   a. Differential
   b. Degrees of freedom
   c. Regression
   d. Depth

36. In mathematics, _____ are used in the study of chance and probability. They were developed to assist in the analysis of games of chance, stochastic events, and the results of scientific experiments by capturing only the mathematical properties necessary to answer probabilistic questions. Further formalizations have firmly grounded the entity in the theoretical domains of mathematics by making use of measure theory.
   a. Statistics
   b. Median polish
   c. Statistical dispersion
   d. Random variables

37. In mathematics, a _____ is a constant multiplicative factor of a certain object. For example, in the expression $9x^2$, the _____ of x^2 is 9.

The object can be such things as a variable, a vector, a function, etc.

   a. Multivariate division algorithm
   b. Fibonacci polynomials
   c. Stability radius
   d. Coefficient

38. In mathematics, a _____ is an expression constructed from variables and constants, using the operations of addition, subtraction, multiplication, and constant non-negative whole number exponents. For example, $x^2 - 4x + 7$ is a _____, but $x^2 - 4/x + 7x^{3/2}$ is not, because its second term involves division by the variable x and also because its third term contains an exponent that is not a whole number.

_____s are one of the most important concepts in algebra and throughout mathematics and science.

   a. Coimage
   b. Polynomial
   c. Semifield
   d. Group extension

39. In probability theory, a probability distribution is called _____ if its cumulative distribution function is _____. That is equivalent to saying that for random variables X with the distribution in question, Pr[X = a] = 0 for all real numbers a. If the distribution of X is _____ then X is called a _____ random variable.
   a. Continuous phase modulation
   b. Concatenated codes
   c. Conull set
   d. Continuous

40. In vascular plants, the _____ is the organ of a plant body that typically lies below the surface of the soil. This is not always the case, however, since a _____ can also be aerial (that is, growing above the ground) or aerating (that is, growing up above the ground or especially above water.) Furthermore, a stem normally occurring below ground is not exceptional either
   a. 120-cell
   b. 2-3 heap
   c. 1-center problem
   d. Root

41. In mathematics, the _____s may be described informally in several different ways. The _____s include both rational numbers, such as 42 and −23/129, and irrational numbers, such as pi and the square root of two; or, a _____ can be given by an infinite decimal representation, such as 2.4871773339...., where the digits continue in some way; or, the _____s may be thought of as points on an infinitely long number line.

These descriptions of the _____s, while intuitively accessible, are not sufficiently rigorous for the purposes of pure mathematics.

a. Real number
b. Tally marks
c. Minkowski distance
d. Pre-algebra

42. _____ is a term in mathematics. It can refer to:

- a _____ line, in geometry
- the trigonometric function called _____
- the _____ method, a root-finding algorithm in numerical analysis

a. Solvable
b. Large set
c. Separable
d. Secant

43. In mathematics, a _____ is any function which can be written as the ratio of two polynomial functions. _____ of degree 2 :

$$y = \frac{x^2 - 3x - 2}{x^2 - 4}$$

In the case of one variable, x, a _____ is a function of the form

$$f(x) = \frac{P(x)}{Q(x)}$$

where P and Q are polynomial function in x and Q is not the zero polynomial. The domain of f is the set of all points x for which the denominator Q

a. 120-cell
b. Legendre rational functions
c. Rational function
d. 1-center problem

44. Exponentiation is a mathematical operation, written a^n, involving two numbers, the base a and the _____ n. When n is a positive integer, exponentiation corresponds to repeated multiplication:

$$a^n = \underbrace{a \times \cdots \times a}_{n},$$

Chapter 10. NONLINEAR FUNCTIONS

just as multiplication by a positive integer corresponds to repeated addition:

$$a \times n = \underbrace{a + \cdots + a}_{n}.$$

The _____ is usually shown as a superscript to the right of the base. The exponentiation a^n can be read as: a raised to the n-th power, a raised to the power [of] n or possibly a raised to the _____ [of] n, or more briefly: a to the n-th power or a to the power [of] n, or even more briefly: a to the n.

a. Exponent
c. Exponentiating by squaring
b. Exponential tree
d. Exponential sum

45. In trigonometry, the _____ is a function defined as $\tan x = \sin x / \cos x$. The function is so-named because it can be defined as the length of a certain segment of a _____ (in the geometric sense) to the unit circle. In plane geometry, a line is _____ to a curve, at some point, if both line and curve pass through the point with the same direction.

a. Hopf conjectures
c. Projective connection
b. Conformal geometry
d. Tangent

46. In geometry, the _____ to a curve at a given point is the straight line that 'just touches' the curve at that point. As it passes through the point of tangency, the _____ is 'going in the same direction' as the curve, and in this sense it is the best straight-line approximation to the curve at that point. The same definition applies to space curves and curves in n-dimensional Euclidean space.

a. Four-vertex theorem
c. Darboux frame
b. Chern-Weil theory
d. Tangent line

47. An _____ of a real-valued function y = f(x) is a curve which describes the behavior of f as either x or y tends to infinity.

In other words, as one moves along the graph of f(x) in some direction, the distance between it and the _____ eventually becomes smaller than any distance that one may specify.

If a curve A has the curve B as an _____, one says that A is asymptotic to B. Similarly B is asymptotic to A, so A and B are called asymptotic.

a. Improper integral
c. Isoperimetric dimension
b. Infinite product
d. Asymptote

48. Suppose f is a function. Then the line y = a is a _____ for f if

$$\lim_{x \to \infty} f(x) = a \text{ or } \lim_{x \to -\infty} f(x) = a.$$

Intuitively, this means that f(x) can be made as close as desired to a by making x big enough. How big is big enough depends on how close one wishes to make f(x) to a.

Chapter 10. NONLINEAR FUNCTIONS

a. 2-3 heap
b. 1-center problem
c. 120-cell
d. Horizontal asymptote

49. _____ is a term that refers both to:

- a formal discipline used to help appraise, or assess, the case for a project or proposal, which itself is a process known as project appraisal; and
- an informal approach to making decisions of any kind.

Under both definitions the process involves, whether explicitly or implicitly, weighing the total expected costs against the total expected benefits of one or more actions in order to choose the best or most profitable option. The formal process is often referred to as CBA, or _____ in the United States.

Closely related, but slightly different, formal techniques include cost-effectiveness analysis and benefit effectiveness analysis. Social Return on Investment analysis builds upon the logic of _____, but differs in that it is explicitly designed to inform the practical decision-making of enterprise managers and investors focused on optimising their social and environmental impacts.

a. Championship mobilization
b. Decision analysis
c. Reactive decision making
d. Cost-benefit analysis

50. In ecology, predation describes a biological interaction where a _____ (an organism that is hunting) feeds on its prey, the organism that is attacked. _____s may or may not kill their prey prior to feeding on them, but the act of predation always results in the death of the prey. The other main category of consumption is detritivory, the consumption of dead organic material (detritus.)

a. 120-cell
b. Predator
c. Prey
d. 1-center problem

51. In economics, _____ is equal to total cost divided by the number of goods produced Quantity-Q. It is also equal to the sum of average variable costs total variable costs divided by Q plus average fixed costs total fixed costs divided by Q. _____s may be dependent on the time period considered increasing production may be expensive or impossible in the short term, for example. _____s affect the supply curve and are a fundamental component of supply and demand.

a. Extreme value theorem
b. Uncertainty quantification
c. Equity
d. Average cost

52. In economics, the _____ is used to illustrate the idea that increases in the rate of taxation do not necessarily increase tax revenue.. Increasing taxes beyond the peak of the curve point will decrease tax revenue. The _____ was popularized by Arthur Laffer in the 1980s.

a. 2-3 heap
b. Laffer curve
c. 1-center problem
d. 120-cell

53. In mathematics, the concept of a _____ tries to capture the intuitive idea of a geometrical one-dimensional and continuous object. A simple example is the circle. In everyday use of the term '_____', a straight line is not curved, but in mathematical parlance _____s include straight lines and line segments.

Chapter 10. NONLINEAR FUNCTIONS

a. Negative pedal curve
b. Kappa curve
c. Quadrifolium
d. Curve

54. The _____ is a function in mathematics. The application of this function to a value x is written as ex. Equivalently, this can be written in the form e^x, where e is a mathematical constant, the base of the natural logarithm, which equals approximately 2.718281828, and is also known as Euler's number.

a. Area hyperbolic functions
b. Exponential Function
c. A chemical equation
d. A Mathematical Theory of Communication

55. _____ is a temperature scale that is named after the German physicist Daniel Gabriel _____, who proposed it in 1724.

In this scale, the freezing point of water is 32 degrees _____ and the boiling point 212 °F, placing the boiling and freezing points of water exactly 180 degrees apart. A degree on the _____ scale is 1/180th part of the interval between the ice point and the boiling point.

a. 1-center problem
b. Fahrenheit
c. 2-3 heap
d. 120-cell

56. A _____ is a structured activity, usually undertaken for enjoyment and sometimes also used as an educational tool. _____s are distinct from work, which is usually carried out for remuneration, and from art, which is more concerned with the expression of ideas. However, the distinction is not clear-cut, and many _____s are also considered to be work (such as professional players of spectator sports/_____s) or art (such as jigsaw puzzles or _____s involving an artistic layout such as Mah-jongg solitaire.)

a. Game
b. 2-3 heap
c. 1-center problem
d. 120-cell

57. In mathematics, the _____ is when a number is squared and is then subtracted from another squared number. It refers to the identity

$$a^2 - b^2 = (a+b)(a-b)$$

from elementary algebra.

The proof is straightforward, starting from the RHS: apply the distributive law to get a sum of four terms, and set

$$ba - ab = 0$$

as an application of the commutative law.

a. Quadratic equation
b. Linear equation
c. Quartic equation
d. Difference of two squares

Chapter 10. NONLINEAR FUNCTIONS

58. In probability theory and statistics, the _____ of a random variable is the integral of the random variable with respect to its probability measure. For discrete random variables this is equivalent to the probability-weighted sum of the possible values, and for continuous random variables with a density function it is the probability density -weighted integral of the possible values.

The _____ may be intuitively understood by the law of large numbers: The _____, when it exists, is almost surely the limit of the sample mean as sample size grows to infinity.

- a. Expected value
- b. Event
- c. Illustration
- d. Infinitely divisible distribution

59. In mathematics, in the realm of group theory, a group is said to be _____ if it equals its own commutator subgroup if the group has no nontrivial abelian quotients.

The smallest _____ group is the alternating group A_5. More generally, any non-abelian simple group is _____ since the commutator subgroup is a normal subgroup with abelian quotient.

- a. Free product
- b. Perfect
- c. Quaternion group
- d. Group of Lie type

60. In elementary algebra, a _____ is a polynomial consisting of three terms; in other words, a _____ is the sum of three monomials. It can be factored using simple steps

In linguistics, a _____ is a fixed expression which is made from three words; e.g. 'lights, camera, action', 'signed, sealed, delivered'.

- a. Recurrence relation
- b. Relation algebra
- c. Trinomial
- d. Symmetric difference

61. _____ is the concept of adding accumulated interest back to the principal, so that interest is earned on interest from that moment on. The act of declaring interest to be principal is called compounding. A loan, for example, may have its interest compounded every month: in this case, a loan with $100 principal and 1% interest per month would have a balance of $101 at the end of the first month.

- a. Net interest margin
- b. Compound interest
- c. Retained interest
- d. Net interest margin securities

62. _____ is a fee, paid on borrowed capital. Assets lent include money, shares, consumer goods through hire purchase, major assets such as aircraft, and even entire factories in finance lease arrangements. The _____ is calculated upon the value of the assets in the same manner as upon money.

- a. A Mathematical Theory of Communication
- b. Interest sensitivity gap
- c. Interest expense
- d. Interest

63. In mathematics, a _____ is a natural number which has exactly two distinct natural number divisors: 1 and itself. An infinitude of _____s exists, as demonstrated by Euclid around 300 BC. The first twenty-five _____s are:

Chapter 10. NONLINEAR FUNCTIONS

2, 3, 5, 7, 11, 13, 17, 19, 23, 29, 31, 37, 41, 43, 47, 53, 59, 61, 67, 71, 73, 79, 83, 89, 97.

a. Pronic number
c. Perrin number

b. Highly composite number
d. Prime number

64. In abstract algebra, a module S over a ring R is called _____ or irreducible if it is not the zero module 0 and if its only submodules are 0 and S. Understanding the _____ modules over a ring is usually helpful because these modules form the 'building blocks' of all other modules in a certain sense.

Abelian groups are the same as Z-modules.

a. Harmonic series
c. Basis

b. Derivation
d. Simple

65. In calculus, the _____ is a formula for the derivative of the composite of two functions.

In intuitive terms, if a variable, y, depends on a second variable, u, which in turn depends on a third variable, x, then the rate of change of y with respect to x can be computed as the rate of change of y with respect to u multiplied by the rate of change of u with respect to x. Schematically,

$$\frac{dy}{dx} = \frac{dy}{du} \cdot \frac{du}{dx}.$$

For an explanation of notation used in this section, see Function composition.

The _____ states that, under appropriate conditions,

$$(f \circ g)'(x) = f'(g(x))g'(x),$$

which in short form is written as

$$(f \circ g)' = f' \circ g \cdot g'.$$

Alternatively, in the Leibniz notation, the _____ is

$$\frac{dy}{dx} = \frac{dy}{du} \cdot \frac{du}{dx}.$$

In integration, the counterpart to the _____ is the substitution rule.

a. 1-center problem
b. 120-cell
c. Product rule
d. Chain rule

66. In the mathematical area of order theory, every partially ordered set P gives rise to a _____ partially ordered set which is often denoted by P^op or P^d. This _____ order P^op is defined to be the set with the inverse order. It is easy to see that this construction, which can be depicted by flipping the Hasse diagram for P upside down, will indeed yield a partially ordered set.

a. Contraction mapping
b. Christofides heuristics
c. Context-sensitive language
d. Dual

67. _____ is an economics theory, that refers to individuals or societies gaining the maximum amount out of the resources they have available to them. The theory proposed by most economists is that _____ refers to the _____ of profit.

As some economists have begun to find out, this theory does not hold true for all people and cultures.

a. Homogeneity
b. Boundary
c. Composite
d. Maximization

68. _____ occurs when the growth rate of a mathematical function is proportional to the function's current value. In the case of a discrete domain of definition with equal intervals it is also called geometric growth or geometric decay.

With _____ of a positive value its rate of increase steadily increases, or in the case of exponential decay, its rate of decrease steadily decreases.

a. A chemical equation
b. A posteriori
c. Exponential growth
d. A Mathematical Theory of Communication

69. _____ typically deals with the probability of several successive decisions, each of which has two possible outcomes.

The probability of an event can be expressed as a _____ if its outcomes can be broken down into two probabilities p and q, where p and q are complementary For example, tossing a coin can be either heads or tails, each which have a probability of 0.5. Rolling a four on a six-sided die can be expressed as the probability of getting a 4 or the probability of rolling something else.

a. Marginal distribution
b. Quantile
c. Markov chain
d. Binomial probability

70. _____ is the likelihood or chance that something is the case or will happen. Theoretical _____ is used extensively in areas such as statistics, mathematics, science and philosophy to draw conclusions about the likelihood of potential events and the underlying mechanics of complex systems.

The word _____ does not have a consistent direct definition.

Chapter 10. NONLINEAR FUNCTIONS

a. Statistical significance
c. Discrete random variable
b. Probability
d. Standardized moment

71. In mathematics, the _____ of a number to a given base is the power or exponent to which the base must be raised in order to produce the number.

For example, the _____ of 1000 to the base 10 is 3, because 3 is how many 10s one must multiply to get 1000: thus 10 × 10 × 10 = 1000; the base-2 _____ of 32 is 5 because 5 is how many 2s one must multiply to get 32: thus 2 × 2 × 2 × 2 × 2 = 32. In the language of exponents: 10^3 = 1000, so $\log_{10} 1000$ = 3, and 2^5 = 32, so $\log_2 32$ = 5.

a. 120-cell
c. 2-3 heap
b. Logarithm
d. 1-center problem

72. The function $\log_b(x)$ depends on both b and x, but the term _____ (or logarithmic function) in standard usage refers to a function of the form $\log_b(x)$ in which the base b is fixed and so the only argument is x. Thus there is one _____ for each value of the base b (which must be positive and must differ from 1.) Viewed in this way, the base-b _____ is the inverse function of the exponential function b^x.

a. 2-3 heap
c. 1-center problem
b. Logarithm function
d. 120-cell

73. In mathematics, a _____ is a statement that can be proved on the basis of explicitly stated or previously agreed assumptions.

a. Disjunction introduction
c. Boolean function
b. Logical value
d. Theorem

74. In mathematics, the _____ of a number n is the number that, when added to n, yields zero. The _____ of n is denoted −n. For example, 7 is −7, because 7 + (−7) = 0, and the _____ of −0.3 is 0.3, because −0.3 + 0.3 = 0.

a. Associativity
c. Algebraic structure
b. Arity
d. Additive inverse

75. In mathematics, _____ is a technique for optimization of a linear objective function, subject to linear equality and linear inequality constraints. Informally, _____ determines the way to achieve the best outcome in a given mathematical model given some list of requirements represented as linear equations.

More formally, given a polytope, and a real-valued affine function

$$f(x_1, x_2, \ldots, x_n) = c_1 x_1 + c_2 x_2 + \cdots + c_n x_n + d$$

defined on this polytope, a _____ method will find a point in the polytope where this function has the smallest value.

a. Lin-Kernighan
c. Descent direction
b. Linear programming
d. Linear programming relaxation

Chapter 10. NONLINEAR FUNCTIONS

76. The _____ is the period of time required for a quantity to double in size or value.
   a. Doubling time
   b. Zenzizenzizenzic
   c. Power law
   d. Stretched exponential function

77. In computational complexity theory, an algorithm is said to take _____ if the asymptotic upper bound for the time it requires is proportional to the size of the input, which is usually denoted n.

Informally spoken, the running time increases linearly with the size of the input. For example, a procedure that adds up all elements of a list requires time proportional to the length of the list.

   a. Truth table reduction
   b. Constructible function
   c. Linear time
   d. Time-constructible function

78. The _____ program is a directory search utility on Unix-like platforms. It searches through one or more directory trees of a filesystem, locating files based on some user-specified criteria. By default, _____ returns all files below the current working directory.
   a. 2-3 heap
   b. Find
   c. 1-center problem
   d. 120-cell

79. In mathematics, the concept of a '_____' is used to describe the behavior of a function as its argument or input either 'gets close' to some point, or as the argument becomes arbitrarily large; or the behavior of a sequence's elements as their index increases indefinitely. _____s are used in calculus and other branches of mathematical analysis to define derivatives and continuity.

In formulas, _____ is usually abbreviated as lim.

   a. Duality
   b. Contact
   c. Copula
   d. Limit

80. In mathematics, a _____ of a set S in a topological space X is a point x in X that can be 'approximated' by points of S other than x itself. This concept profitably generalizes the notion of a limit and is the underpinning of concepts such as closed set and topological closure. Indeed, a set is closed if and only if it contains all of its _____s, and the topological closure operation can be thought of as an operation that enriches a set by adding its _____s.
   a. Limit point
   b. 1-center problem
   c. 2-3 heap
   d. 120-cell

81. In mathematics, an algebraic group G contains a unique maximal normal solvable subgroup; and this subgroup is closed. Its identity component is called the _____ of G.
   a. Barycentric coordinates
   b. Radical
   c. Block size
   d. Composite

82.

A _____ is a scale of measurement that uses the logarithm of a physical quantity instead of the quantity itself.

Chapter 10. NONLINEAR FUNCTIONS

Presentation of data on a _____ can be helpful when the data covers a large range of values - the logarithm reduces this to a more manageable range. Some of our senses operate in a logarithmic fashion, which makes _____s for these input quantities especially appropriate.

a. 120-cell
c. Mel scale

b. 1-center problem
d. Logarithmic scale

83. The _____ of a quantity whose value decreases with time is the interval required for the quantity to decay to half of its initial value. The concept originated in describing how long it takes atoms to undergo radioactive decay, but also applies in a wide variety of other situations.

The term '_____' dates to 1907.

a. Half-life
c. 120-cell

b. Radioactive decay
d. 1-center problem

84. _____ is the process in which an unstable atomic nucleus loses energy by emitting ionizing particles and radiation. This decay, or loss of energy, results in an atom of one type, called the parent nuclide transforming to an atom of a different type, called the daughter nuclide. For example: a carbon-14 atom emits radiation and transforms to a nitrogen-14 atom.

a. 1-center problem
c. 120-cell

b. Half-life
d. Radioactive decay

85. _____ is the change in population over time, and can be quantified as the change in the number of individuals in a population using 'per unit time' for measurement. The term _____ can technically refer to any species, but almost always refers to humans, and it is often used informally for the more specific demographic term _____ rate, and is often used to refer specifically to the growth of the population of the world.

Simple models of _____ include the Malthusian Growth Model and the logistic model.

a. 1-center problem
c. Population growth

b. 120-cell
d. Population dynamics

86. _____ in technical analysis is typical price multiplied by volume, a kind of approximation to the dollar value of a day's trading.

_____ index is an oscillator calculated over an N-day period, ranging from 0 to 100, showing _____ on up days as a percentage of the total of up and down days.

a. Money flow
c. 120-cell

b. Technical analysis
d. 1-center problem

Chapter 11. THE DERIVATIVE

1. In mathematics, the concept of a '_____' is used to describe the behavior of a function as its argument or input either 'gets close' to some point, or as the argument becomes arbitrarily large; or the behavior of a sequence's elements as their index increases indefinitely. _____s are used in calculus and other branches of mathematical analysis to define derivatives and continuity.

In formulas, _____ is usually abbreviated as lim.

   a. Contact
   b. Limit
   c. Duality
   d. Copula

2. In mathematics, a _____ of a set S in a topological space X is a point x in X that can be 'approximated' by points of S other than x itself. This concept profitably generalizes the notion of a limit and is the underpinning of concepts such as closed set and topological closure. Indeed, a set is closed if and only if it contains all of its _____s, and the topological closure operation can be thought of as an operation that enriches a set by adding its _____s.

   a. 120-cell
   b. 2-3 heap
   c. 1-center problem
   d. Limit point

3. In mathematics, a _____ is a system which is not linear. Less technically, a _____ is any problem where the variabl to be solved for cannot be written as a linear sum of independent components. A nonhomogenous system, which is linear apart from the presence of a function of the independent variables, is nonlinear according to a strict definition, but such systems are usually studied alongside linear systems, because they can be transformed to a linear system as long as a particular solution is known.

   a. Nonlinear system
   b. Metric system
   c. 1-center problem
   d. George Dantzig

4. In calculus, a _____ is either of the two limits of a function f

$$\lim_{x \to a^+} f(x) \text{ or } \lim_{x \downarrow a} f(x)$$

for the limit as x approaches a from above, and similarly

$$\lim_{x \to a^-} f(x) \text{ or } \lim_{x \uparrow a} f(x)$$

for the limit as x approaches a from below.

The two _____s exist and are equal if and only if the limit of f

   a. Archimedes' use of infinitesimals
   b. Infinite series
   c. One-sided limit
   d. Uniform convergence

5. In mathematics, an _____, or central tendency of a data set refers to a measure of the 'middle' or 'expected' value of the data set. There are many different descriptive statistics that can be chosen as a measurement of the central tendency of the data items.

An _____ is a single value that is meant to typify a list of values.

Chapter 11. THE DERIVATIVE

a. A posteriori
b. A Mathematical Theory of Communication
c. A chemical equation
d. Average

6. The mathematical concept of a _____ expresses the intuitive idea of deterministic dependence between two quantities, one of which is viewed as primary and the other as secondary. A _____ then is a way to associate a unique output for each input of a specified type, for example, a real number or an element of a given set.
a. Grill
b. Function
c. Going up
d. Coherent

7. In linear algebra, _____ is a version of Gaussian elimination that puts zeros both above and below each pivot element as it goes from the top row of the given matrix to the bottom. In other words, _____ brings a matrix to reduced row echelon form, whereas Gaussian elimination takes it only as far as row echelon form. Every matrix has a reduced row echelon form, and this algorithm is guaranteed to produce it.
a. Spheroidal wave functions
b. Lax equivalence theorem
c. Conservation form
d. Gauss-Jordan elimination

8. The _____ program is a directory search utility on Unix-like platforms. It searches through one or more directory trees of a filesystem, locating files based on some user-specified criteria. By default, _____ returns all files below the current working directory.
a. Find
b. 120-cell
c. 1-center problem
d. 2-3 heap

9. _____ is the state of being greater than any finite number, however large.
a. Implicit differentiation
b. Interval notation
c. A Mathematical Theory of Communication
d. Infinity

10. An _____ of a real-valued function y = f(x) is a curve which describes the behavior of f as either x or y tends to infinity.

In other words, as one moves along the graph of f(x) in some direction, the distance between it and the _____ eventually becomes smaller than any distance that one may specify.

If a curve A has the curve B as an _____, one says that A is asymptotic to B. Similarly B is asymptotic to A, so A and B are called asymptotic.

a. Infinite product
b. Asymptote
c. Isoperimetric dimension
d. Improper integral

11. Suppose f is a function. Then the line y = a is a _____ for f if

$$\lim_{x \to \infty} f(x) = a \text{ or } \lim_{x \to -\infty} f(x) = a.$$

Intuitively, this means that f(x) can be made as close as desired to a by making x big enough. How big is big enough depends on how close one wishes to make f(x) to a.

Chapter 11. THE DERIVATIVE

a. 1-center problem
c. 120-cell
b. Horizontal asymptote
d. 2-3 heap

12. A _____ is an annuity that has no definite end, or a stream of cash payments that continues forever. There are few actual perpetuities in existence. A number of types of investments are effectively perpetuities, such as real estate and common stock, and techniques for valuing a _____ can be applied to establish price.
  a. Perpetuity
  b. LIBOR market model
  c. Fisher equation
  d. Stochastic volatility

13. In probability theory, a probability distribution is called _____ if its cumulative distribution function is _____. That is equivalent to saying that for random variables X with the distribution in question, Pr[X = a] = 0 for all real numbers a. If the distribution of X is _____ then X is called a _____ random variable.
  a. Conull set
  b. Concatenated codes
  c. Continuous phase modulation
  d. Continuous

14. In mathematics, a _____ is a function for which, intuitively, small changes in the input result in small changes in the output. Otherwise, a function is said to be discontinuous. A _____ with a continuous inverse function is called bicontinuous.
  a. Continuous function
  b. Contraction mapping
  c. Charles's Law
  d. Beth numbers

15. Then, the point $x_0 = 1$ is a _____. The function in example 2, a jump discontinuity

2. Consider the function

$$f(x) = \begin{cases} x^2 & \text{for } x < 1 \\ 0 & \text{for } x = 1 \\ 2 - (x-1)^2 & \text{for } x > 1 \end{cases}$$

Then, the point $x_0 = 1$ is a jump discontinuity.

a. 120-cell
c. 1-center problem
b. 2-3 heap
d. Removable discontinuity

16. Continuous functions are of utmost importance in mathematics and applications. However, not all functions are continuous. If a function is not continuous at a point in its domain, one says that it has a _____ there. The set of all points of _____ of a function may be a discrete set, a dense set, or even the entire domain of the function.
  a. Core
  b. Derivation
  c. Cusp
  d. Discontinuity

17. In mathematics, a _____ is a set of real numbers with the property that any number that lies between two numbers in the set is also included in the set. For example, the set of all numbers x satisfying $0 \leq x \leq 1$ is an _____ which contains 0 and 1, as well as all numbers between them. Other examples of _____s are the set of all real numbers $\mathbb{R}$, the set of all positive real numbers, and the empty set.

Chapter 11. THE DERIVATIVE

a. Order
b. Annihilator
c. Interval
d. Ideal

18. The _____ is a function in mathematics. The application of this function to a value x is written as ex. Equivalently, this can be written in the form e^x, where e is a mathematical constant, the base of the natural logarithm, which equals approximately 2.718281828, and is also known as Euler's number.
   a. A chemical equation
   b. Area hyperbolic functions
   c. A Mathematical Theory of Communication
   d. Exponential function

19. The function $\log_b(x)$ depends on both b and x, but the term _____ (or logarithmic function) in standard usage refers to a function of the form $\log_b(x)$ in which the base b is fixed and so the only argument is x. Thus there is one _____ for each value of the base b (which must be positive and must differ from 1.) Viewed in this way, the base-b _____ is the inverse function of the exponential function b^x.
   a. 120-cell
   b. 1-center problem
   c. Logarithm function
   d. 2-3 heap

20. In mathematics, a _____ is an expression constructed from variables and constants, using the operations of addition, subtraction, multiplication, and constant non-negative whole number exponents. For example, $x^2 - 4x + 7$ is a _____, but $x^2 - 4/x + 7x^{3/2}$ is not, because its second term involves division by the variable x and also because its third term contains an exponent that is not a whole number.

   _____s are one of the most important concepts in algebra and throughout mathematics and science.

   a. Group extension
   b. Semifield
   c. Coimage
   d. Polynomial

21. In mathematics, a _____ is any function which can be written as the ratio of two polynomial functions. _____ of degree 2 :
$$y = \frac{x^2 - 3x - 2}{x^2 - 4}$$

In the case of one variable, x, a _____ is a function of the form

$$f(x) = \frac{P(x)}{Q(x)}$$

where P and Q are polynomial function in x and Q is not the zero polynomial. The domain of f is the set of all points x for which the denominator Q

a. 1-center problem
b. Legendre rational functions
c. Rational function
d. 120-cell

Chapter 11. THE DERIVATIVE

22. In vascular plants, the _____ is the organ of a plant body that typically lies below the surface of the soil. This is not always the case, however, since a _____ can also be aerial (that is, growing above the ground) or aerating (that is, growing up above the ground or especially above water.) Furthermore, a stem normally occurring below ground is not exceptional either
    a. 2-3 heap
    b. Root
    c. 1-center problem
    d. 120-cell

23. A _____ is a software program that facilitates symbolic mathematics. The core functionality of a CAS is manipulation of mathematical expressions in symbolic form.

The symbolic manipulations supported typically include

- simplification to the smallest possible expression or some standard form, including automatic simplification with assumptions and simplification with constraints
- substitution of symbolic, functors or numeric values for expressions
- change of form of expressions: expanding products and powers, partial and full factorization, rewriting as partial fractions, constraint satisfaction, rewriting trigonometric functions as exponentials, etc.
- partial and total differentiation
- symbolic constrained and unconstrained global optimization
- solution of linear and some non-linear equations over various domains
- solution of some differential and difference equations
- taking some limits
- some indefinite and definite integration, including multidimensional integrals
- integral transforms
- arbitrary-precision numeric operations
- Series operations such as expansion, summation and products
- matrix operations including products, inverses, etc.
- display of mathematical expressions in two-dimensional mathematical form, often using typesetting systems similar to TeX
- add-ons for use in applied mathematics such as physics packages for physical computation
- plotting graphs and parametric plots of functions in two and three dimensions, and animating them
- APIs for linking it on an external program such as a database, or using in a programming language to use the _____
- drawing charts and diagrams
- string manipulation such as matching and searching
- statistical computation
- Theorem proving and verification
- graphic production and editing such as CGI and signal processing as image processing
- sound synthesis

Many also include a programming language, allowing users to implement their own algorithms.

Some _____s focus on a specific area of application; these are typically developed in academia and are free.

Chapter 11. THE DERIVATIVE

a. 120-cell
c. 2-3 heap
b. 1-center problem
d. Computer algebra system

24. The word _____ means curving in or hollowed inward.
    a. Clipping
    c. Harmonic series
    b. Key server
    d. Concavity

25. Exponentiation is a mathematical operation, written a^n, involving two numbers, the base a and the _____ n. When n is a positive integer, exponentiation corresponds to repeated multiplication:

$$a^n = \underbrace{a \times \cdots \times a}_{n},$$

just as multiplication by a positive integer corresponds to repeated addition:

$$a \times n = \underbrace{a + \cdots + a}_{n}.$$

The _____ is usually shown as a superscript to the right of the base. The exponentiation a^n can be read as: a raised to the n-th power, a raised to the power [of] n or possibly a raised to the _____ [of] n, or more briefly: a to the n-th power or a to the power [of] n, or even more briefly: a to the n.

a. Exponent
c. Exponentiating by squaring
b. Exponential sum
d. Exponential tree

26. In economics, business, retail, and accounting, a _____ is the value of money that has been used up to produce something, and hence is not available for use anymore. In business, the _____ may be one of acquisition, in which case the amount of money expended to acquire it is counted as _____. In this case, money is the input that is gone in order to acquire the thing.
    a. 2-3 heap
    c. 1-center problem
    b. 120-cell
    d. Cost

27. In mathematical analysis, the _____ states that for each value between the least upper bound and greatest lower bound of the image of a continuous function there is a corresponding value in its domain mapping to the original. _____

- Version I. The _____ states the following: If the function y = f∈ [a, b] such that f

- Version II. Suppose that I is an interval [a, b] in the real numbers R and that f : I → R is a continuous function. Then the image set f

    f⊇ [f or f(I) ⊇ [f(b), f(a)].

It is frequently stated in the following equivalent form: Suppose that f : [a, b] → R is continuous and that u is a real number satisfying f(a) < u < f(b) or f(a) > u > f(b.) Then for some c ∈ [a, b], f(c) = u.

Chapter 11. THE DERIVATIVE

This captures an intuitive property of continuous functions: given f continuous on [1, 2], if f(1) = 3 and f(2) = 5 then f must take the value 4 somewhere between 1 and 2.

   a. Intermediate value theorem
   b. Equicontinuous
   c. Uniformly continuous
   d. A Mathematical Theory of Communication

28. In mathematics, a _____ is a statement that can be proved on the basis of explicitly stated or previously agreed assumptions.
   a. Logical value
   b. Boolean function
   c. Disjunction introduction
   d. Theorem

29. In mathematics, the _____ is an approach to finding a particular solution to certain inhomogeneous ordinary differential equations and recurrence relations. It is closely related to the annihilator method, but instead of using a particular kind of differential operator in order to find the best possible form of the particular solution, a 'guess' is made as to the appropriate form, which is then tested by differentiating the resulting equation. In this sense, the _____ is less formal but more intuitive than the annihilator method.
   a. Phase line
   b. Differential algebraic equations
   c. Method of undetermined coefficients
   d. Linear differential equation

30. In mathematics, a _____ is the end result of a division problem. It can also be expressed as the number of times the divisor divides into the dividend.
   a. Limiting
   b. Marginal cost
   c. Notation
   d. Quotient

31. _____ is used to describe the steepness, incline, gradient, or grade of a straight line. A higher _____ value indicates a steeper incline. The _____ is defined as the ratio of the 'rise' divided by the 'run' between two points on a line, or in other words, the ratio of the altitude change to the horizontal distance between any two points on the line.
   a. Number line
   b. Point plotting
   c. Cognitively Guided Instruction
   d. Slope

32. _____ of an object is its speed in a particular direction.
   a. Discontinuity
   b. Maxima
   c. Rolle's Theorem
   d. Velocity

33. In mathematics and in the sciences, a _____ (plural: _____e, formulæ or _____s) is a concise way of expressing information symbolically (as in a mathematical or chemical _____), or a general relationship between quantities. One of many famous _____e is Albert Einstein's E = mc^2 (see special relativity

In mathematics, a _____ is a key to solve an equation with variables. For example, the problem of determining the volume of a sphere is one that requires a significant amount of integral calculus to solve.

   a. 2-3 heap
   b. 120-cell
   c. 1-center problem
   d. Formula

Chapter 11. THE DERIVATIVE

34. _____ is a term in mathematics. It can refer to:

- a _____ line, in geometry
- the trigonometric function called _____
- the _____ method, a root-finding algorithm in numerical analysis

a. Secant
b. Large set
c. Solvable
d. Separable

35. In trigonometry, the _____ is a function defined as tan x = $^{\sin x}/_{\cos x}$. The function is so-named because it can be defined as the length of a certain segment of a _____ (in the geometric sense) to the unit circle. In plane geometry, a line is _____ to a curve, at some point, if both line and curve pass through the point with the same direction.

a. Hopf conjectures
b. Conformal geometry
c. Projective connection
d. Tangent

36. In geometry, the _____ to a curve at a given point is the straight line that 'just touches' the curve at that point. As it passes through the point of tangency, the _____ is 'going in the same direction' as the curve, and in this sense it is the best straight-line approximation to the curve at that point. The same definition applies to space curves and curves in n-dimensional Euclidean space.

a. Darboux frame
b. Four-vertex theorem
c. Chern-Weil theory
d. Tangent line

37. In mathematics, the concept of a _____ tries to capture the intuitive idea of a geometrical one-dimensional and continuous object. A simple example is the circle. In everyday use of the term '_____', a straight line is not curved, but in mathematical parlance _____s include straight lines and line segments.

a. Kappa curve
b. Curve
c. Quadrifolium
d. Negative pedal curve

38. The _____ expresses the fact that the difference in the y coordinate between two points on a line that is, y − y1 is proportional to the difference in the x coordinate that is, x − x1. The proportionality constant is m (the slope of the line.

a. Point-slope form
b. Cobb-Douglas
c. Square function
d. Rubin Causal Model

39. _____ is a fundamental construction of differential calculus and admits many possible generalizations within the fields of mathematical analysis, combinatorics, algebra, and geometry.

In real, complex, and functional analysis, _____s are generalized to functions of several real or complex variables and functions between topological vector spaces. An important case is the variational _____ in the calculus of variations.

a. Lin-Tsien equation
b. Metric derivative
c. Functional derivative
d. Derivative

40. of the difference quotient as h approaches zero, if this limit exists. If the limit exists, then f is _____ at a. Here f' (a) is one of several common notations for the derivative

a. 120-cell
b. 1-center problem
c. 2-3 heap
d. Differentiable

41. _____, a field in mathematics, is the study of how functions change when their inputs change. The primary object of study in _____ is the derivative. A closely related notion is the differential.
   a. Semi-continuity
   b. Differential calculus
   c. Harmonic analysis
   d. Geometric function theory

42. A _____ typically refers to a class of handheld calculators that are capable of plotting graphs, solving simultaneous equations, and performing numerous other tasks with variables. Most popular _____s are also programmable, allowing the user to create customized programs, typically for scientific/engineering and education applications. Due to their large displays intended for graphing, they can also accommodate several lines of text and calculations at a time.
   a. Genus
   b. Support vector machines
   c. Bump mapping
   d. Graphing calculator

43. _____ or amortisation is the process of decreasing an amount over a period of time. The word comes from Middle English amortisen to kill, alienate in mortmain, from Anglo-French amorteser, alteration of amortir, from Vulgar Latin admortire to kill, from Latin ad- + mort-, mors death. Particular instances of the term include:

   - _____, the allocation of a lump sum amount to different time periods, particularly for loans and other forms of finance, including related interest or other finance charges.
     - _____ schedule, a table detailing each periodic payment on a loan, as generated by an _____ calculator.
     - Negative _____, an _____ schedule where the loan amount actually increases through not paying the full interest
   - Amortized analysis, analyzing the execution cost of algorithms over a sequence of operations.
   - _____ of capital expenditures of certain assets under accounting rules, particularly intangible assets, in a manner analogous to depreciation.
   - _____

_____ is also used in the context of zoning regulations and describes the time in which a property owner has to relocate when the property's use constitutes a preexisting nonconforming use under zoning regulations.

   - Depreciation

   a. Origin
   b. Identity
   c. ISAAC
   d. Amortization

44. An _____ is a table detailing each periodic payment on a amortizing loan, as generated by an amortization calculator.

While a portion of every payment is applied towards both the interest and the principal balance of the loan, the exact amount applied to principal each time varies. An _____ reveals the specific monetary amount put towards interest, as well as the specific put towards the Principal balance, with each payment.

Chapter 11. THE DERIVATIVE

a. A Mathematical Theory of Communication
b. A chemical equation
c. Amortization schedule
d. Accounts receivable

45. A calculation is a deliberate process for transforming one or more inputs into one or more results, with variable change.

The term is used in a variety of senses, from the very definite arithmetical using an algorithm to the vague heuristics of _____ a strategy in a competition or _____ the chance of a successful relationship between two people.

Multiplying 7 by 8 is a simple algorithmic calculation.

a. Calculating
b. Calculation
c. Mathematics Subject Classification
d. Mathematical maturity

46. A _____ is a device for performing mathematical calculations, distinguished from a computer by having a limited problem solving ability and an interface optimized for interactive calculation rather than programming. _____ s can be hardware or software, and mechanical or electronic, and are often built into devices such as PDAs or mobile phones.

Modern electronic _____ s are generally small, digital, and usually inexpensive.

a. 1-center problem
b. 2-3 heap
c. 120-cell
d. Calculator

47. In mathematics, the _____ of a real number is its numerical value without regard to its sign. So, for example, 3 is the _____ of both 3 and −3.

The _____ of a number a is denoted by | a | .

Generalizations of the _____ for real numbers occur in a wide variety of mathematical settings.

a. A Mathematical Theory of Communication
b. A chemical equation
c. Area hyperbolic functions
d. Absolute value

Chapter 12. CALCULATING THE DERIVATIVE

1. _____ is used in mathematics to refer to the elements of matrices or the components of a vector. The formalism of how indices are used varies according to the discipline. In particular, there are different methods for referring to the elements of a list, a vector, or a matrix, depending on whether one is writing a formal mathematical paper for publication, or when one is writing a computer program.

   a. Index notation
   b. Einstein notation
   c. Indexed family
   d. Index set

2. In cryptography, _____ is a pseudorandom number generator and a stream cipher designed by Robert Jenkins to be cryptographically secure. The name is an acronym for Indirection, Shift, Accumulate, Add, and Count.

   The _____ algorithm has similarities with RC4.

   a. Introduction
   b. Order
   c. Imputation
   d. Isaac

3. _____ named in honor of the 17th century German philosopher and mathematician Gottfried Wilhelm Leibniz, was originally the use of expressions such as dx and dy and to represent "infinitely small" or infinitesimal increments of quantities x and y, just as Äx and Äy represent finite increments of x and y respectively.

   a. 120-cell
   b. Leibniz notation
   c. 2-3 heap
   d. 1-center problem

4. _____ was a German polymath who wrote primarily in Latin and French.

   He occupies an equally grand place in both the history of philosophy and the history of mathematics. He invented infinitesimal calculus independently of Newton, and his notation is the one in general use since then.

   a. Harry Hinsley
   b. Raymond Merrill Smullyan
   c. Michel Rolle
   d. Gottfried Wilhelm Leibniz

5. The _____ (symbol: N) is the SI derived unit of force, named after Isaac _____ in recognition of his work on classical mechanics.

   The _____ is the unit of force derived in the SI system; it is equal to the amount of force required to accelerate a mass of one kilogram at a rate of one meter per second per second. Algebraically:

Chapter 12. CALCULATING THE DERIVATIVE

$$1 \text{ N} = 1 \ \frac{\text{kg} \cdot \text{m}}{\text{s}^2}.$$

- 1 N is the force of Earth's gravity on an object with a mass of about 102 g ($\frac{1}{9.8}$ kg) (such as a small apple.)
- On Earth's surface, a mass of 1 kg exerts a force of approximately 9.80665 N [down] (or 1 kgf.) The approximation of 1 kg corresponding to 10 N is sometimes used as a rule of thumb in everyday life and in engineering.
- The force of Earth's gravity on a human being with a mass of 70 kg is approximately 687 N.
- The dot product of force and distance is mechanical work. Thus, in SI units, a force of 1 N exerted over a distance of 1 m is 1 NÂ·m of work. The Work-Energy Theorem states that the work done on a body is equal to the change in energy of the body. 1 NÂ·m = 1 J (joule), the SI unit of energy.
- It is common to see forces expressed in kilonewtons or kN, where 1 kN = 1 000 N.

a. Newton
c. 1-center problem
b. 120-cell
d. 2-3 heap

6. In mathematics, a _____ is a function whose values do not vary and thus are constant. For example, if we have the function f→ B is a _____ iff f
   a. Linear operator
   c. Constant function
   b. Point reflection
   d. Squeeze mapping

7. In mathematics, a _____ is a system which is not linear. Less technically, a _____ is any problem where the variabl to be solved for cannot be written as a linear sum of independent components. A nonhomogenous system, which is linear apart from the presence of a function of the independent variables, is nonlinear according to a strict definition, but such systems are usually studied alongside linear systems, because they can be transformed to a linear system as long as a particular solution is known.
   a. Metric system
   c. 1-center problem
   b. George Dantzig
   d. Nonlinear system

8. In mathematics, an _____, or central tendency of a data set refers to a measure of the 'middle' or 'expected' value of the data set. There are many different descriptive statistics that can be chosen as a measurement of the central tendency of the data items.

An _____ is a single value that is meant to typify a list of values.

   a. A Mathematical Theory of Communication
   c. A posteriori
   b. Average
   d. A chemical equation

9. _____ is a fundamental construction of differential calculus and admits many possible generalizations within the fields of mathematical analysis, combinatorics, algebra, and geometry.

Chapter 12. CALCULATING THE DERIVATIVE

In real, complex, and functional analysis, _____s are generalized to functions of several real or complex variables and functions between topological vector spaces. An important case is the variational _____ in the calculus of variations.

a. Derivative
b. Lin-Tsien equation
c. Functional derivative
d. Metric derivative

10. The mathematical concept of a _____ expresses the intuitive idea of deterministic dependence between two quantities, one of which is viewed as primary and the other as secondary. A _____ then is a way to associate a unique output for each input of a specified type, for example, a real number or an element of a given set.

a. Function
b. Going up
c. Coherent
d. Grill

11. In elementary algebra, a _____ is a polynomial with two terms: the sum of two monomials. It is the simplest kind of polynomial except for a monomial.

The _____ $a^2 - b^2$ can be factored as the product of two other _____s:

$a^2 - b^2$.

The product of a pair of linear _____s a x + b and c x + d is:

2 +x + bd.

A _____ raised to the nth power, represented as

n

can be expanded by means of the _____ theorem or, equivalently, using Pascal's triangle.

a. Rational root theorem
b. Cylindrical algebraic decomposition
c. Binomial
d. Real structure

12. In mathematics, the _____ is an important formula giving the expansion of powers of sums. Its simplest version states that

$$(x+y)^n = \sum_{k=0}^{n} \binom{n}{k} x^{n-k} y^k \qquad (1)$$

for any real or complex numbers x and y, and any nonnegative integer n. The binomial coefficient appearing in may be defined in terms of the factorial function n!:

$$\binom{n}{k} = \frac{n!}{k!\,(n-k)!}.$$

For example, here are the cases where 2 ≤ n ≤ 5:

$$(x+y)^2 = x^2 + 2xy + y^2$$
$$(x+y)^3 = x^3 + 3x^2y + 3xy^2 + y^3$$
$$(x+y)^4 = x^4 + 4x^3y + 6x^2y^2 + 4xy^3 + y^4$$
$$(x+y)^5 = x^5 + 5x^4y + 10x^3y^2 + 10x^2y^3 + 5xy^4 + y^5.$$

Formula is valid more generally for any elements x and y of a semiring as long as xy = yx..

a. Hypergeometric identities
b. Binomial theorem
c. Lah numbers
d. Stirling transform

13. This article will state and prove the _____ for differentiation, and then use it to prove these two formulas.

The _____ for differentiation states that for every natural number n, the derivative of $f(x) = x^n$ is $f'(x) = nx^{n-1}$, that is,

$$(x^n)' = nx^{n-1}.$$

The _____ for integration

$$\int x^n\,dx = \frac{x^{n+1}}{n+1} + C$$

for natural n is then an easy consequence. One just needs to take the derivative of this equality and use the _____ and linearity of differentiation on the right-hand side.

a. Periodic function
b. Functional integration
c. Standard part function
d. Power rule

14. In mathematics, a _____ is a statement that can be proved on the basis of explicitly stated or previously agreed assumptions.

a. Boolean function
b. Logical value
c. Disjunction introduction
d. Theorem

15. A _____ is a software program that facilitates symbolic mathematics. The core functionality of a CAS is manipulation of mathematical expressions in symbolic form.

The symbolic manipulations supported typically include

- simplification to the smallest possible expression or some standard form, including automatic simplification with assumptions and simplification with constraints
- substitution of symbolic, functors or numeric values for expressions
- change of form of expressions: expanding products and powers, partial and full factorization, rewriting as partial fractions, constraint satisfaction, rewriting trigonometric functions as exponentials, etc.
- partial and total differentiation
- symbolic constrained and unconstrained global optimization
- solution of linear and some non-linear equations over various domains
- solution of some differential and difference equations
- taking some limits
- some indefinite and definite integration, including multidimensional integrals
- integral transforms
- arbitrary-precision numeric operations
- Series operations such as expansion, summation and products
- matrix operations including products, inverses, etc.
- display of mathematical expressions in two-dimensional mathematical form, often using typesetting systems similar to TeX
- add-ons for use in applied mathematics such as physics packages for physical computation
- plotting graphs and parametric plots of functions in two and three dimensions, and animating them
- APIs for linking it on an external program such as a database, or using in a programming language to use the _____
- drawing charts and diagrams
- string manipulation such as matching and searching
- statistical computation
- Theorem proving and verification
- graphic production and editing such as CGI and signal processing as image processing
- sound synthesis

Many also include a programming language, allowing users to implement their own algorithms.

Some _____ s focus on a specific area of application; these are typically developed in academia and are free.

a. 1-center problem
b. 120-cell
c. 2-3 heap
d. Computer algebra system

Chapter 12. CALCULATING THE DERIVATIVE 113

16. In computational complexity theory, an algorithm is said to take _____ if the asymptotic upper bound for the time it requires is proportional to the size of the input, which is usually denoted n.

Informally spoken, the running time increases linearly with the size of the input. For example, a procedure that adds up all elements of a list requires time proportional to the length of the list.

a. Time-constructible function
c. Truth table reduction
b. Constructible function
d. Linear time

17. _____, a field in mathematics, is the study of how functions change when their inputs change. The primary object of study in _____ is the derivative. A closely related notion is the differential.

a. Geometric function theory
c. Harmonic analysis
b. Semi-continuity
d. Differential calculus

18. A _____ typically refers to a class of handheld calculators that are capable of plotting graphs, solving simultaneous equations, and performing numerous other tasks with variables. Most popular _____s are also programmable, allowing the user to create customized programs, typically for scientific/engineering and education applications. Due to their large displays intended for graphing, they can also accommodate several lines of text and calculations at a time.

a. Graphing calculator
c. Bump mapping
b. Genus
d. Support vector machines

19. _____ or amortisation is the process of decreasing an amount over a period of time. The word comes from Middle English amortisen to kill, alienate in mortmain, from Anglo-French amorteser, alteration of amortir, from Vulgar Latin admortire to kill, from Latin ad- + mort-, mors death. Particular instances of the term include:

- _____, the allocation of a lump sum amount to different time periods, particularly for loans and other forms of finance, including related interest or other finance charges.
    - _____ schedule, a table detailing each periodic payment on a loan, as generated by an _____ calculator.
    - Negative _____, an _____ schedule where the loan amount actually increases through not paying the full interest
- Amortized analysis, analyzing the execution cost of algorithms over a sequence of operations.
- _____ of capital expenditures of certain assets under accounting rules, particularly intangible assets, in a manner analogous to depreciation.
- _____

_____ is also used in the context of zoning regulations and describes the time in which a property owner has to relocate when the property's use constitutes a preexisting nonconforming use under zoning regulations.

- Depreciation

a. Identity
c. ISAAC
b. Amortization
d. Origin

Chapter 12. CALCULATING THE DERIVATIVE

20. An _____ is a table detailing each periodic payment on a amortizing loan, as generated by an amortization calculator.

While a portion of every payment is applied towards both the interest and the principal balance of the loan, the exact amount applied to principal each time varies. An _____ reveals the specific monetary amount put towards interest, as well as the specific put towards the Principal balance, with each payment.

a. Accounts receivable
b. Amortization schedule
c. A chemical equation
d. A Mathematical Theory of Communication

21. A _____ is a device for performing mathematical calculations, distinguished from a computer by having a limited problem solving ability and an interface optimized for interactive calculation rather than programming. _____s can be hardware or software, and mechanical or electronic, and are often built into devices such as PDAs or mobile phones.

Modern electronic _____s are generally small, digital, and usually inexpensive.

a. 120-cell
b. 1-center problem
c. 2-3 heap
d. Calculator

22. _____ is the change in total cost that arises when the quantity produced changes by one unit.

a. Marginal cost
b. Limiting
c. Differential Algebra
d. Notation

23. In economics, business, retail, and accounting, a _____ is the value of money that has been used up to produce something, and hence is not available for use anymore. In business, the _____ may be one of acquisition, in which case the amount of money expended to acquire it is counted as _____. In this case, money is the input that is gone in order to acquire the thing.

a. Cost
b. 120-cell
c. 2-3 heap
d. 1-center problem

24. In microeconomics, _____ is the term used to refer to total when marginal cost is subtracted from marginal revenue. Under the marginal approach to profit maximization, to maximize profits, a firm should continue to produce a good until _____ is zero. Profit Maximization - The Marginal Approach

{{Economics-stub}}

a. 2-3 heap
b. 1-center problem
c. 120-cell
d. Marginal profit

25. The _____ governs the differentiation of products of differentiable functions.

a. 120-cell
b. Product rule
c. 1-center problem
d. Reciprocal Rule

26. In mathematics, a _____ is the end result of a division problem. It can also be expressed as the number of times the divisor divides into the dividend.

a. Limiting
b. Marginal cost
c. Notation
d. Quotient

27. In economics, _____ is equal to total cost divided by the number of goods produced Quantity-Q. It is also equal to the sum of average variable costs total variable costs divided by Q plus average fixed costs total fixed costs divided by Q. _____s may be dependent on the time period considered increasing production may be expensive or impossible in the short term, for example. _____s affect the supply curve and are a fundamental component of supply and demand.

a. Uncertainty quantification
b. Extreme value theorem
c. Equity
d. Average cost

28. In mathematics, a _____ is a polynomial equation of the second degree. The general form is

$$ax^2 + bx + c = 0,$$

where a ≠ 0.

The letters a, b, and c are called coefficients: the quadratic coefficient a is the coefficient of x^2, the linear coefficient b is the coefficient of x, and c is the constant coefficient, also called the free term or constant term.

a. Quadratic equation
b. Quartic equation
c. Linear equation
d. Difference of two squares

29. A quadratic equation with real solutions, called roots, which may be real or complex, is given by the _____: $x = \frac{-b \pm \sqrt{b^2 - 4ac}}{2a}$.

a. Parametric continuity
b. Quotient
c. Quadratic formula
d. Differential Algebra

30. In mathematics and in the sciences, a _____ (plural: _____e, formulæ or _____s) is a concise way of expressing information symbolically (as in a mathematical or chemical _____), or a general relationship between quantities. One of many famous _____e is Albert Einstein's E = mc^2 (see special relativity

In mathematics, a _____ is a key to solve an equation with variables. For example, the problem of determining the volume of a sphere is one that requires a significant amount of integral calculus to solve.

a. 120-cell
b. 2-3 heap
c. 1-center problem
d. Formula

31. A _____ number is a positive integer which has a positive divisor other than one or itself. By definition, every integer greater than one is either a prime number or a _____ number.zero and one are considered to be neither prime nor _____. For example, the integer 14 is a _____ number because it can be factored as 2 × 7.

a. Composite
b. Discontinuity
c. Key server
d. Basis

32. In calculus, the _____ is a formula for the derivative of the composite of two functions.

Chapter 12. CALCULATING THE DERIVATIVE

In intuitive terms, if a variable, y, depends on a second variable, u, which in turn depends on a third variable, x, then the rate of change of y with respect to x can be computed as the rate of change of y with respect to u multiplied by the rate of change of u with respect to x. Schematically,

$$\frac{dy}{dx} = \frac{dy}{du} \cdot \frac{du}{dx}.$$

For an explanation of notation used in this section, see Function composition.

The _____ states that, under appropriate conditions,

$$(f \circ g)'(x) = f'(g(x))g'(x),$$

which in short form is written as

$$(f \circ g)' = f' \circ g \cdot g'.$$

Alternatively, in the Leibniz notation, the _____ is

$$\frac{dy}{dx} = \frac{dy}{du} \cdot \frac{du}{dx}.$$

In integration, the counterpart to the _____ is the substitution rule.

a. 120-cell
c. 1-center problem
b. Product rule
d. Chain rule

33. In mathematics, hyperbolic n-space, denoted H^n, is the maximally symmetric, simply connected, n-dimensional Riemannian manifold with constant sectional curvature −1. _____ is the principal example of a space exhibiting hyperbolic geometry. It can be thought of as the negative-curvature analogue of the n-sphere.
  a. Horocycle
  c. Hyperbolic geometry
  b. Margulis lemma
  d. Hyperbolic space

34. _____ is the concept of adding accumulated interest back to the principal, so that interest is earned on interest from that moment on. The act of declaring interest to be principal is called compounding. A loan, for example, may have its interest compounded every month: in this case, a loan with $100 principal and 1% interest per month would have a balance of $101 at the end of the first month.
  a. Compound interest
  c. Net interest margin securities
  b. Net interest margin
  d. Retained interest

35. In probability theory, a probability distribution is called _____ if its cumulative distribution function is _____. That is equivalent to saying that for random variables X with the distribution in question, Pr[X = a] = 0 for all real numbers a. If the distribution of X is _____ then X is called a _____ random variable.

Chapter 12. CALCULATING THE DERIVATIVE

a. Continuous
b. Conull set
c. Concatenated codes
d. Continuous phase modulation

36. _____ is a fee, paid on borrowed capital. Assets lent include money, shares, consumer goods through hire purchase, major assets such as aircraft, and even entire factories in finance lease arrangements. The _____ is calculated upon the value of the assets in the same manner as upon money.
   a. A Mathematical Theory of Communication
   b. Interest sensitivity gap
   c. Interest expense
   d. Interest

37. _____ of an object is its speed in a particular direction.
   a. Rolle's Theorem
   b. Maxima
   c. Discontinuity
   d. Velocity

38. The _____ is a function in mathematics. The application of this function to a value x is written as ex. Equivalently, this can be written in the form e^x, where e is a mathematical constant, the base of the natural logarithm, which equals approximately 2.718281828, and is also known as Euler's number.
   a. A chemical equation
   b. Area hyperbolic functions
   c. A Mathematical Theory of Communication
   d. Exponential function

39. A _____ or logistic curve is the most common sigmoid curve. It models the S-curve of growth of some set P, where P might be thought of as population. The initial stage of growth is approximately exponential; then, as saturation begins, the growth slows, and at maturity, growth stops.
   a. Spin-weighted spherical harmonics
   b. Jack function
   c. Legendre forms
   d. Logistic function

40. The function $\log_b(x)$ depends on both b and x, but the term _____ (or logarithmic function) in standard usage refers to a function of the form $\log_b(x)$ in which the base b is fixed and so the only argument is x. Thus there is one _____ for each value of the base b (which must be positive and must differ from 1.) Viewed in this way, the base-b _____ is the inverse function of the exponential function b^x.
   a. Logarithm function
   b. 120-cell
   c. 1-center problem
   d. 2-3 heap

41. In mathematics, the _____ of a number to a given base is the power or exponent to which the base must be raised in order to produce the number.

For example, the _____ of 1000 to the base 10 is 3, because 3 is how many 10s one must multiply to get 1000: thus 10 × 10 × 10 = 1000; the base-2 _____ of 32 is 5 because 5 is how many 2s one must multiply to get 32: thus 2 × 2 × 2 × 2 × 2 = 32. In the language of exponents: 10^3 = 1000, so $\log_{10} 1000$ = 3, and 2^5 = 32, so $\log_2 32$ = 5.

   a. 1-center problem
   b. 120-cell
   c. Logarithm
   d. 2-3 heap

118

Chapter 13. GRAPHS AND THE DERIVATIVE

1. _____ is a fundamental construction of differential calculus and admits many possible generalizations within the fields of mathematical analysis, combinatorics, algebra, and geometry.

In real, complex, and functional analysis, _____s are generalized to functions of several real or complex variables and functions between topological vector spaces. An important case is the variational _____ in the calculus of variations.

a. Metric derivative
b. Derivative
c. Functional derivative
d. Lin-Tsien equation

2. A _____ is a software program that facilitates symbolic mathematics. The core functionality of a CAS is manipulation of mathematical expressions in symbolic form.

The symbolic manipulations supported typically include

- simplification to the smallest possible expression or some standard form, including automatic simplification with assumptions and simplification with constraints
- substitution of symbolic, functors or numeric values for expressions
- change of form of expressions: expanding products and powers, partial and full factorization, rewriting as partial fractions, constraint satisfaction, rewriting trigonometric functions as exponentials, etc.
- partial and total differentiation
- symbolic constrained and unconstrained global optimization
- solution of linear and some non-linear equations over various domains
- solution of some differential and difference equations
- taking some limits
- some indefinite and definite integration, including multidimensional integrals
- integral transforms
- arbitrary-precision numeric operations
- Series operations such as expansion, summation and products
- matrix operations including products, inverses, etc.
- display of mathematical expressions in two-dimensional mathematical form, often using typesetting systems similar to TeX
- add-ons for use in applied mathematics such as physics packages for physical computation
- plotting graphs and parametric plots of functions in two and three dimensions, and animating them
- APIs for linking it on an external program such as a database, or using in a programming language to use the _____
- drawing charts and diagrams
- string manipulation such as matching and searching
- statistical computation
- Theorem proving and verification
- graphic production and editing such as CGI and signal processing as image processing
- sound synthesis

Many also include a programming language, allowing users to implement their own algorithms.

Chapter 13. GRAPHS AND THE DERIVATIVE

Some _____s focus on a specific area of application; these are typically developed in academia and are free.

a. 2-3 heap
b. 120-cell
c. 1-center problem
d. Computer algebra system

3. The word _____ means curving in or hollowed inward.
   a. Clipping
   b. Key server
   c. Harmonic series
   d. Concavity

4. In calculus, a function f defined on a subset of the real numbers with real values is called monotonic (also monotonically increasing or non-_____), if for all x and y such that x ≤ y one has f(x) ≤ f(y), so f preserves the order. In layman's terms, the sign of the slope is always positive (the curve tending upwards) or zero (i.e., non-_____, or asymptotic, or depicted as a horizontal, flat line) Likewise, a function is called monotonically _____ (non-increasing) if, whenever x ≤ y, then f(x) ≥ f(y), so it reverses the order.
   a. Dual pair
   b. Tensor product of Hilbert spaces
   c. Circular convolution
   d. Decreasing

5. The mathematical concept of a _____ expresses the intuitive idea of deterministic dependence between two quantities, one of which is viewed as primary and the other as secondary. A _____ then is a way to associate a unique output for each input of a specified type, for example, a real number or an element of a given set.
   a. Coherent
   b. Grill
   c. Going up
   d. Function

6. In trigonometry, the _____ is a function defined as $\tan x = \sin x / \cos x$. The function is so-named because it can be defined as the length of a certain segment of a _____ (in the geometric sense) to the unit circle. In plane geometry, a line is _____ to a curve, at some point, if both line and curve pass through the point with the same direction.
   a. Hopf conjectures
   b. Conformal geometry
   c. Projective connection
   d. Tangent

7. In geometry, the _____ to a curve at a given point is the straight line that 'just touches' the curve at that point. As it passes through the point of tangency, the _____ is 'going in the same direction' as the curve, and in this sense it is the best straight-line approximation to the curve at that point. The same definition applies to space curves and curves in n-dimensional Euclidean space.
   a. Tangent line
   b. Chern-Weil theory
   c. Four-vertex theorem
   d. Darboux frame

8. In combinatorial mathematics, a _____ is an un-ordered collection of distinct elements, usually of a prescribed size and taken from a given set. Given such a set S, a _____ of elements of S is just a subset of S, where as always forsets the order of the elements is not taken into account. Also, as always forsets, no elements can be repeated more than once in a _____; this is often referred to as a 'collection without repetition'.
   a. Heawood number
   b. Sparsity
   c. Fill-in
   d. Combination

Chapter 13. GRAPHS AND THE DERIVATIVE

9. _____ is used to describe the steepness, incline, gradient, or grade of a straight line. A higher _____ value indicates a steeper incline. The _____ is defined as the ratio of the 'rise' divided by the 'run' between two points on a line, or in other words, the ratio of the altitude change to the horizontal distance between any two points on the line.
    a. Cognitively Guided Instruction
    b. Slope
    c. Point plotting
    d. Number line

10. In mathematics, a _____ is a system which is not linear. Less technically, a _____ is any problem where the variabl to be solved for cannot be written as a linear sum of independent components. A nonhomogenous system, which is linear apart from the presence of a function of the independent variables, is nonlinear according to a strict definition, but such systems are usually studied alongside linear systems, because they can be transformed to a linear system as long as a particular solution is known.
    a. George Dantzig
    b. Metric system
    c. 1-center problem
    d. Nonlinear system

11. In mathematics, an _____, or central tendency of a data set refers to a measure of the 'middle' or 'expected' value of the data set. There are many different descriptive statistics that can be chosen as a measurement of the central tendency of the data items.

    An _____ is a single value that is meant to typify a list of values.

    a. A chemical equation
    b. A Mathematical Theory of Communication
    c. A posteriori
    d. Average

12. In mathematics, a critical point (or _____) is a point on the domain of a function where:

    - one dimension: the derivative (or slope of the line when visualized) is equal to zero or a point where the function ceases to be differentiable.
    - in general: there are two distinct concepts: either the derivative (Jacobian) vanishes, or it is not of full rank (or, in either case, the function is not differentiable); these agree in one dimension.

    Note that in one dimension, a critical value or _____ x of function f is the domain element at which the derivative is zero or undefined, whereas the associated ordered pair (x, y) is the critical point. In higher dimensions a critical value is in the range whereas a critical point is in the domain.

    There are two situations in which a point becomes a critical point of a function of one variable. The first of which is that the value of the first derivative is equal to zero.

    a. Hessian matrix
    b. Critical number
    c. Jacobian
    d. Multivariable calculus

13. In mathematics, a _____ is a point on the domain of a function where:

    - one dimension: the derivative is equal to zero or a point where the function ceases to be differentiable.
    - in general: there are two distinct concepts: either the derivative vanishes, or it is not of full rank; these agree in one dimension.

Chapter 13. GRAPHS AND THE DERIVATIVE

Note that in one dimension, a critical value or critical number x of function f is the domain element at which the derivative is zero or undefined, whereas the associated ordered pair is the _____. In higher dimensions a critical value is in the range whereas a _____ is in the domain.

There are two situations in which a point becomes a _____ of a function of one variable. The first of which is that the value of the derivative is equal to zero.

a. Critical point
b. Decimal system
c. Derivative algebra
d. Going up

14. In mathematics, a _____ is an expression constructed from variables and constants, using the operations of addition, subtraction, multiplication, and constant non-negative whole number exponents. For example, $x^2 - 4x + 7$ is a _____, but $x^2 - 4/x + 7x^{3/2}$ is not, because its second term involves division by the variable x and also because its third term contains an exponent that is not a whole number.

_____s are one of the most important concepts in algebra and throughout mathematics and science.

a. Polynomial
b. Group extension
c. Semifield
d. Coimage

15. In probability theory, a probability distribution is called _____ if its cumulative distribution function is _____. That is equivalent to saying that for random variables X with the distribution in question, Pr[X = a] = 0 for all real numbers a. If the distribution of X is _____ then X is called a _____ random variable.

a. Concatenated codes
b. Conull set
c. Continuous phase modulation
d. Continuous

16. In mathematics, an _____ is a statement about the relative size or order of two objects, or about whether they are the same or not

- The notation a < b means that a is less than b.
- The notation a > b means that a is greater than b.
- The notation a ≠ b means that a is not equal to b, but does not say that one is bigger than the other or even that they can be compared in size.

In all these cases, a is not equal to b, hence, '_____'.

These relations are known as strict _____

- The notation a ≤ b means that a is less than or equal to b;
- The notation a ≥ b means that a is greater than or equal to b;

Chapter 13. GRAPHS AND THE DERIVATIVE

An additional use of the notation is to show that one quantity is much greater than another, normally by several orders of magnitude.

- The notation a << b means that a is much less than b.
- The notation a >> b means that a is much greater than b.

If the sense of the _____ is the same for all values of the variables for which its members are defined, then the _____ is called an 'absolute' or 'unconditional' _____. If the sense of an _____ holds only for certain values of the variables involved, but is reversed or destroyed for other values of the variables, it is called a conditional _____.

An _____ may appear unsolvable because it only states whether a number is larger or smaller than another number; but it is possible to apply the same operations for equalities to inequalities. For example, to find x for the _____ 10x > 23 one would divide 23 by 10.

a. A chemical equation   b. A Mathematical Theory of Communication
c. A posteriori   d. Inequality

17. A _____ typically refers to a class of handheld calculators that are capable of plotting graphs, solving simultaneous equations, and performing numerous other tasks with variables. Most popular _____s are also programmable, allowing the user to create customized programs, typically for scientific/engineering and education applications. Due to their large displays intended for graphing, they can also accommodate several lines of text and calculations at a time.

a. Graphing calculator   b. Genus
c. Support vector machines d. Bump mapping

18. _____ or amortisation is the process of decreasing an amount over a period of time. The word comes from Middle English amortisen to kill, alienate in mortmain, from Anglo-French amorteser, alteration of amortir, from Vulgar Latin admortire to kill, from Latin ad- + mort-, mors death. Particular instances of the term include:

- _____, the allocation of a lump sum amount to different time periods, particularly for loans and other forms of finance, including related interest or other finance charges.
  - _____ schedule, a table detailing each periodic payment on a loan, as generated by an _____ calculator.
  - Negative _____, an _____ schedule where the loan amount actually increases through not paying the full interest
- Amortized analysis, analyzing the execution cost of algorithms over a sequence of operations.
- _____ of capital expenditures of certain assets under accounting rules, particularly intangible assets, in a manner analogous to depreciation.
- _____

Chapter 13. GRAPHS AND THE DERIVATIVE

_____ is also used in the context of zoning regulations and describes the time in which a property owner has to relocate when the property's use constitutes a preexisting nonconforming use under zoning regulations.

- Depreciation

    a. Origin
    c. Amortization
    b. Identity
    d. ISAAC

19. An _____ is a table detailing each periodic payment on a amortizing loan, as generated by an amortization calculator.

While a portion of every payment is applied towards both the interest and the principal balance of the loan, the exact amount applied to principal each time varies. An _____ reveals the specific monetary amount put towards interest, as well as the specific put towards the Principal balance, with each payment.

    a. Amortization schedule
    c. Accounts receivable
    b. A Mathematical Theory of Communication
    d. A chemical equation

20. A _____ is a device for performing mathematical calculations, distinguished from a computer by having a limited problem solving ability and an interface optimized for interactive calculation rather than programming. _____s can be hardware or software, and mechanical or electronic, and are often built into devices such as PDAs or mobile phones.

Modern electronic _____s are generally small, digital, and usually inexpensive.

    a. 1-center problem
    c. 120-cell
    b. 2-3 heap
    d. Calculator

21. In linear algebra, _____ is a version of Gaussian elimination that puts zeros both above and below each pivot element as it goes from the top row of the given matrix to the bottom. In other words, _____ brings a matrix to reduced row echelon form, whereas Gaussian elimination takes it only as far as row echelon form. Every matrix has a reduced row echelon form, and this algorithm is guaranteed to produce it.

    a. Gauss-Jordan elimination
    c. Lax equivalence theorem
    b. Spheroidal wave functions
    d. Conservation form

22. In mathematics, specifically in combinatorial commutative algebra, a convex lattice polytope P is called _____ if it has the following property: given any positive integer n, every lattice point of the dilation nP, obtained from P by scaling its vertices by the factor n and taking the convex hull of the resulting points, can be written as the sum of exactly n lattice points in P. This property plays an important role in the theory of toric varieties, where it corresponds to projective normality of the toric variety determined by P.

The simplex in R^k with the vertices at the origin and along the unit coordinate vectors is _____.

a. Demihypercubes
b. Polytetrahedron
c. Normal
d. Hypercube

23. _____ is a quantity expressing the two-dimensional size of a defined part of a surface, typically a region bounded by a closed curve. The term surface _____ refers to the total _____ of the exposed surface of a 3-dimensional solid, such as the sum of the _____s of the exposed sides of a polyhedron. _____ is an important invariant in the differential geometry of surfaces.
   a. A Mathematical Theory of Communication
   b. A chemical equation
   c. Area
   d. A posteriori

24. In mathematics, the concept of a _____ tries to capture the intuitive idea of a geometrical one-dimensional and continuous object. A simple example is the circle. In everyday use of the term '_____', a straight line is not curved, but in mathematical parlance _____s include straight lines and line segments.
   a. Negative pedal curve
   b. Quadrifolium
   c. Curve
   d. Kappa curve

25. _____ is the likelihood or chance that something is the case or will happen. Theoretical _____ is used extensively in areas such as statistics, mathematics, science and philosophy to draw conclusions about the likelihood of potential events and the underlying mechanics of complex systems.

    The word _____ does not have a consistent direct definition.

   a. Statistical significance
   b. Discrete random variable
   c. Standardized moment
   d. Probability

26. A _____, in mathematics, is a polynomial function of the form $f(x) = ax^2 + bx + c$, where $a \neq 0$. The graph of a _____ is a parabola whose major axis is parallel to the y-axis.

    The expression ax² + bx + c in the definition of a _____ is a polynomial of degree 2 or a 2nd degree polynomial, because the highest exponent of x is 2.

   a. Multivariate division algorithm
   b. Laguerre polynomials
   c. Discriminant
   d. Quadratic function

27. Let f be a differentiable function, and let f'(x) be its derivative. The derivative of f'(x) (if it has one) is written f''(x) and is called the _____ of f. Similarly, the derivative of a _____, if it exists, is written f'''(x) and is called the third derivative of f.
   a. 2-3 heap
   b. Second derivative
   c. 1-center problem
   d. 120-cell

28. Let f be a differentiable function, and let f'(x) be its derivative. The derivative of f'(x) (if it has one) is written f''(x) and is called the second derivative of f. Similarly, the derivative of a second derivative, if it exists, is written f'''(x) and is called the _____ of f.

| a. Third derivative | b. 1-center problem |
| c. 2-3 heap | d. 120-cell |

29. _____ of an object is its speed in a particular direction.
| a. Discontinuity | b. Maxima |
| c. Rolle's Theorem | d. Velocity |

30. In mathematics and in the sciences, a _____ (plural: _____ e, formulæ or _____ s) is a concise way of expressing information symbolically (as in a mathematical or chemical _____), or a general relationship between quantities. One of many famous _____ e is Albert Einstein's E = mc² (see special relativity

In mathematics, a _____ is a key to solve an equation with variables. For example, the problem of determining the volume of a sphere is one that requires a significant amount of integral calculus to solve.

| a. 2-3 heap | b. 120-cell |
| c. 1-center problem | d. Formula |

31. In differential calculus, an inflection point, or _____ (or inflexion) is a point on a curve at which the curvature changes sign. The curve changes from being concave upwards (positive curvature) to concave downwards (negative curvature), or vice versa. If one imagines driving a vehicle along the curve, it is a point at which the steering-wheel is momentarily 'straight', being turned from left to right or vice versa.
| a. Metric derivative | b. Gradient |
| c. Directional derivative | d. Point of inflection |

32. In calculus, a branch of mathematics, the _____ is a criterion often useful for determining whether a given stationary point of a function is a local maximum or a local minimum.

The test states: If the function f is twice differentiable in a neighborhood of a stationary point x, meaning that $f'(x) = 0$, then:

- If $f''(x) < 0$ then f has a local maximum at x.
- If 0" src="http://upload.wikimedia.org/math/e/0/0/e000178f7f6b9c3307e0f9e4e9e077e9.png"> then f has a local minimum at x.
- If $f''(x) = 0$, the _____ says nothing about the point x.

In the last case, the function may have a local maximum or minimum there, but the function is sufficiently 'flat' that this is undetected by the second derivative. In this case one has to examine the third derivative. Such an example is f4.

| a. Differentiation under the integral sign | b. Second derivative test |
| c. Functional derivative | d. Normal derivative |

Chapter 13. GRAPHS AND THE DERIVATIVE

33. In mathematics, a _____ is any function which can be written as the ratio of two polynomial functions. _____ of degree 2 :

$$y = \frac{x^2 - 3x - 2}{x^2 - 4}$$

In the case of one variable, x, a _____ is a function of the form

$$f(x) = \frac{P(x)}{Q(x)}$$

where P and Q are polynomial function in x and Q is not the zero polynomial. The domain of f is the set of all points x for which the denominator Q

a. Rational function
b. 1-center problem
c. Legendre rational functions
d. 120-cell

34. Exponentiation is a mathematical operation, written a^n, involving two numbers, the base a and the _____ n. When n is a positive integer, exponentiation corresponds to repeated multiplication:

$$a^n = \underbrace{a \times \cdots \times a}_{n},$$

just as multiplication by a positive integer corresponds to repeated addition:

$$a \times n = \underbrace{a + \cdots + a}_{n}.$$

The _____ is usually shown as a superscript to the right of the base. The exponentiation a^n can be read as: a raised to the n-th power, a raised to the power [of] n or possibly a raised to the _____ [of] n, or more briefly: a to the n-th power or a to the power [of] n, or even more briefly: a to the n.

a. Exponent
b. Exponentiating by squaring
c. Exponential sum
d. Exponential tree

35. An _____ of a real-valued function y = f(x) is a curve which describes the behavior of f as either x or y tends to infinity.

In other words, as one moves along the graph of f(x) in some direction, the distance between it and the _____ eventually becomes smaller than any distance that one may specify.

If a curve A has the curve B as an _____, one says that A is asymptotic to B. Similarly B is asymptotic to A, so A and B are called asymptotic.

Chapter 13. GRAPHS AND THE DERIVATIVE

    a. Infinite product   b. Asymptote
    c. Isoperimetric dimension   d. Improper integral

36. The function $\log_b(x)$ depends on both b and x, but the term _____ (or logarithmic function) in standard usage refers to a function of the form $\log_b(x)$ in which the base b is fixed and so the only argument is x. Thus there is one _____ for each value of the base b (which must be positive and must differ from 1.) Viewed in this way, the base-b _____ is the inverse function of the exponential function b^x.

    a. Logarithm function   b. 120-cell
    c. 2-3 heap   d. 1-center problem

Chapter 14. APPLICATIONS OF THE DERIVATIVE

1. _____ is a fundamental construction of differential calculus and admits many possible generalizations within the fields of mathematical analysis, combinatorics, algebra, and geometry.

In real, complex, and functional analysis, _____s are generalized to functions of several real or complex variables and functions between topological vector spaces. An important case is the variational _____ in the calculus of variations.

- a. Lin-Tsien equation
- b. Derivative
- c. Functional derivative
- d. Metric derivative

2. A _____ is a software program that facilitates symbolic mathematics. The core functionality of a CAS is manipulation of mathematical expressions in symbolic form.

The symbolic manipulations supported typically include

- simplification to the smallest possible expression or some standard form, including automatic simplification with assumptions and simplification with constraints
- substitution of symbolic, functors or numeric values for expressions
- change of form of expressions: expanding products and powers, partial and full factorization, rewriting as partial fractions, constraint satisfaction, rewriting trigonometric functions as exponentials, etc.
- partial and total differentiation
- symbolic constrained and unconstrained global optimization
- solution of linear and some non-linear equations over various domains
- solution of some differential and difference equations
- taking some limits
- some indefinite and definite integration, including multidimensional integrals
- integral transforms
- arbitrary-precision numeric operations
- Series operations such as expansion, summation and products
- matrix operations including products, inverses, etc.
- display of mathematical expressions in two-dimensional mathematical form, often using typesetting systems similar to TeX
- add-ons for use in applied mathematics such as physics packages for physical computation
- plotting graphs and parametric plots of functions in two and three dimensions, and animating them
- APIs for linking it on an external program such as a database, or using in a programming language to use the _____
- drawing charts and diagrams
- string manipulation such as matching and searching
- statistical computation
- Theorem proving and verification
- graphic production and editing such as CGI and signal processing as image processing
- sound synthesis

Many also include a programming language, allowing users to implement their own algorithms.

Chapter 14. APPLICATIONS OF THE DERIVATIVE

Some _____s focus on a specific area of application; these are typically developed in academia and are free.

a. 1-center problem
b. 120-cell
c. 2-3 heap
d. Computer algebra system

3. In calculus, the _____ states that if a real-valued function f is continuous in the closed interval, then f must attain its maximum and minimum value, each at least once.

a. Average cost
b. Uncertainty quantification
c. Extreme value theorem
d. Equity

4. In mathematics, a _____ is a statement that can be proved on the basis of explicitly stated or previously agreed assumptions.

a. Theorem
b. Boolean function
c. Disjunction introduction
d. Logical value

5. In linear algebra, _____ is a version of Gaussian elimination that puts zeros both above and below each pivot element as it goes from the top row of the given matrix to the bottom. In other words, _____ brings a matrix to reduced row echelon form, whereas Gaussian elimination takes it only as far as row echelon form. Every matrix has a reduced row echelon form, and this algorithm is guaranteed to produce it.

a. Spheroidal wave functions
b. Lax equivalence theorem
c. Conservation form
d. Gauss-Jordan elimination

6. _____ methods are common techniques to compute the equilibrium configuration of molecules. The basic idea is that a stable state of a molecular system should correspond to a local minimum of their potential energy. This kind of calculation generally starts from an arbitrary state of molecules, then the mathematical procedure of optimization allows us to move atoms in a way to reduce the net forces to nearly zero.

a. A Mathematical Theory of Communication
b. Energy minimization
c. A posteriori
d. A chemical equation

7. The mathematical concept of a _____ expresses the intuitive idea of deterministic dependence between two quantities, one of which is viewed as primary and the other as secondary. A _____ then is a way to associate a unique output for each input of a specified type, for example, a real number or an element of a given set.

a. Coherent
b. Going up
c. Grill
d. Function

8. _____s is the social science that studies the production, distribution, and consumption of goods and services.

The term _____s comes from the Ancient Greek oá¼°κονομῖα (oikonomia, 'management of a household, administration') from oá¼¶κος (oikos, 'house') + vĺŒμος (nomos, 'custom' or 'law'), hence 'rules of the house(hold)'.

Current _____ models developed out of the broader field of political economy in the late 19th century, owing to a desire to use an empirical approach more akin to the physical sciences.

a. A Mathematical Theory of Communication
b. Economic
c. Experimental economics
d. A chemical equation

9. In mathematics, an _____ in the sense of ring theory is a subring $\mathcal{O}$ of a ring R that satisfies the conditions

   1. R is a ring which is a finite-dimensional algebra over the rational number field $\mathbb{Q}$
   2. $\mathcal{O}$ spans R over $\mathbb{Q}$, so that $\mathbb{Q}\mathcal{O} = R$, and
   3. $\mathcal{O}$ is a lattice in R.

The third condition can be stated more accurately, in terms of the extension of scalars of R to the real numbers, embedding R in a real vector space. In less formal terms, additively $\mathcal{O}$ should be a free abelian group generated by a basis for R over $\mathbb{Q}$.

The leading example is the case where R is a number field K and $\mathcal{O}$ is its ring of integers. In algebraic number theory there are examples for any K other than the rational field of proper subrings of the ring of integers that are also _____s.

a. Efficiency
b. Order
c. Algebraic
d. Annihilator

10. Price _____ is defined as the measure of responsivenesses in the quantity demanded for a commodity as a result of change in price of the same commodity. In other words, it is percentage change in quantity demanded as per the percentage change in price of the same commodity. In economics and business studies, the price _____ is a measure of the sensitivity of quantity demanded to changes in price. It is measured as elasticity, that is it measures the relationship as the ratio of percentage changes between quantity demanded of a good and changes in its price.

a. A Mathematical Theory of Communication
b. Elasticity of demand
c. A posteriori
d. A chemical equation

11. _____, a field in mathematics, is the study of how functions change when their inputs change. The primary object of study in _____ is the derivative. A closely related notion is the differential.

a. Geometric function theory
b. Harmonic analysis
c. Semi-continuity
d. Differential calculus

12. _____ is to give an equation R(x,y) = S(x,y) that at least in part has the same graph as y = f(x).

a. Ordinary differential equation
b. Inflection point
c. Implicit function
d. Implicit differentiation

13. _____ and independent variables refer to values that change in relationship to each other. The _____ are those that are observed to change in response to the independent variables. The independent variables are those that are deliberately manipulated to invoke a change in the _____.

a. Yates analysis
b. Round robin test
c. Dependent variables
d. Steiner system

Chapter 14. APPLICATIONS OF THE DERIVATIVE

14. Dependent variables and _____ refer to values that change in relationship to each other. The dependent variables are those that are observed to change in response to the _____. The _____ are those that are deliberately manipulated to invoke a change in the dependent variables.
    a. Operational confound
    b. Experimental design diagram
    c. One-factor-at-a-time method
    d. Independent variables

15. In Geometry, the _____ is an algebraic curve defined by the equation

$$x^3 + y^3 - 3axy = 0$$

It forms a loop in the first quadrant with a double point at the origin and asymptote

$$x + y + a = 0$$

It is symmetrical about y = x.

    a. Quadratrix
    b. Sextic plane curve
    c. Trisectrix
    d. Folium of Descartes

16. In trigonometry, the _____ is a function defined as tan x = $\sin x / \cos x$. The function is so-named because it can be defined as the length of a certain segment of a _____ (in the geometric sense) to the unit circle. In plane geometry, a line is _____ to a curve, at some point, if both line and curve pass through the point with the same direction.
    a. Hopf conjectures
    b. Conformal geometry
    c. Projective connection
    d. Tangent

17. In geometry, the _____ to a curve at a given point is the straight line that 'just touches' the curve at that point. As it passes through the point of tangency, the _____ is 'going in the same direction' as the curve, and in this sense it is the best straight-line approximation to the curve at that point. The same definition applies to space curves and curves in n-dimensional Euclidean space.
    a. Darboux frame
    b. Chern-Weil theory
    c. Four-vertex theorem
    d. Tangent line

18. In mathematics, the _____ is an approach to finding a particular solution to certain inhomogeneous ordinary differential equations and recurrence relations. It is closely related to the annihilator method, but instead of using a particular kind of differential operator in order to find the best possible form of the particular solution, a 'guess' is made as to the appropriate form, which is then tested by differentiating the resulting equation. In this sense, the _____ is less formal but more intuitive than the annihilator method.
    a. Method of undetermined coefficients
    b. Linear differential equation
    c. Differential algebraic equations
    d. Phase line

19. The _____ expresses the fact that the difference in the y coordinate between two points on a line that is, y − y1 is proportional to the difference in the x coordinate that is, x − x1. The proportionality constant is m (the slope of the line.
    a. Square function
    b. Cobb-Douglas
    c. Point-slope form
    d. Rubin Causal Model

20. In mathematics, an _____ is a particular type of curve: a hypocycloid with four cusps. _____s are also superellipses: all _____s are scaled versions of the curve specified by the equation

$$x^{2/3} + y^{2/3} = 1.$$

Its modern name comes from the Greek word for 'star'.

a. Ogive
b. Algebraic curve
c. Inverse curve
d. Astroid

21. In geometry, the _____ or Gutschoven's curve is a two-dimensional algebraic curve resembling the Greek letter κ.

Using the Cartesian coordinate system it can be expressed as:

x²2y²

or, using parametric equations:

$$x = a \cos t \cot t$$
$$y = a \cos t$$

In polar coordinates its equation is even simpler:

r = atanθ

It has two vertical asymptotes at $x = \pm a$, , shown as dashed blue lines in the figure at right.

The _____'s curvature:

$$\kappa(\theta) = \frac{8\left(3 - \sin^2\theta\right)\sin^4\theta}{a\left[\sin^2(2\theta) + 4\right]^{\frac{3}{2}}}$$

Tangential angle:

$$\phi(\theta) = -\arctan\left[\frac{1}{2}\sin(2\theta)\right]$$

The _____ was first studied by Gérard van Gutschoven around 1662.

a. Centered trochoid
b. Swastika curve
c. Kappa curve
d. Parallel

22. In mathematics, the _____ is an algebraic curve described by a Cartesian equation of the form:

$$(x^2 + y^2)^2 = 2a^2(x^2 - y^2).$$

The curve has a shape similar to the numeral 8 and to the ∞ symbol.

The lemniscate was first described in 1694 by Jakob Bernoulli as a modification of an ellipse, which is the locus of points for which the sum of the distances to each of two fixed focal points is a constant. A Cassini oval, by contrast, is the locus of points for which the product of these distances is constant.

a. Lemniscate of Bernoulli
b. Hypocycloid
c. Trisectrix of Maclaurin
d. Truncus

23. In mathematics, the concept of a _____ tries to capture the intuitive idea of a geometrical one-dimensional and continuous object. A simple example is the circle. In everyday use of the term '_____', a straight line is not curved, but in mathematical parlance _____s include straight lines and line segments.

a. Kappa curve
b. Negative pedal curve
c. Quadrifolium
d. Curve

24. In computational complexity theory, an algorithm is said to take _____ if the asymptotic upper bound for the time it requires is proportional to the size of the input, which is usually denoted n.

Informally spoken, the running time increases linearly with the size of the input. For example, a procedure that adds up all elements of a list requires time proportional to the length of the list.

a. Time-constructible function
b. Truth table reduction
c. Constructible function
d. Linear time

25. Exponentiation is a mathematical operation, written a^n, involving two numbers, the base a and the _____ n. When n is a positive integer, exponentiation corresponds to repeated multiplication:

$$a^n = \underbrace{a \times \cdots \times a}_{n},$$

just as multiplication by a positive integer corresponds to repeated addition:

$$a \times n = \underbrace{a + \cdots + a}_{n}.$$

The _____ is usually shown as a superscript to the right of the base. The exponentiation a^n can be read as: a raised to the n-th power, a raised to the power [of] n or possibly a raised to the _____ [of] n, or more briefly: a to the n-th power or a to the power [of] n, or even more briefly: a to the n.

   a. Exponent
   b. Exponential tree
   c. Exponential sum
   d. Exponentiating by squaring

26. The _____ program is a directory search utility on Unix-like platforms. It searches through one or more directory trees of a filesystem, locating files based on some user-specified criteria. By default, _____ returns all files below the current working directory.
   a. Find
   b. 120-cell
   c. 2-3 heap
   d. 1-center problem

27. In mathematics and in the sciences, a _____ (plural: _____e, formulæ or _____s) is a concise way of expressing information symbolically (as in a mathematical or chemical _____), or a general relationship between quantities. One of many famous _____e is Albert Einstein's $E = mc^2$ (see special relativity

In mathematics, a _____ is a key to solve an equation with variables. For example, the problem of determining the volume of a sphere is one that requires a significant amount of integral calculus to solve.

   a. Formula
   b. 120-cell
   c. 2-3 heap
   d. 1-center problem

28. In mathematics, an _____ is a statement about the relative size or order of two objects, or about whether they are the same or not

   - The notation a < b means that a is less than b.
   - The notation a > b means that a is greater than b.
   - The notation a ≠ b means that a is not equal to b, but does not say that one is bigger than the other or even that they can be compared in size.

In all these cases, a is not equal to b, hence, '_____'.

These relations are known as strict _____

   - The notation a ≤ b means that a is less than or equal to b;
   - The notation a ≥ b means that a is greater than or equal to b;

An additional use of the notation is to show that one quantity is much greater than another, normally by several orders of magnitude.

   - The notation a << b means that a is much less than b.
   - The notation a >> b means that a is much greater than b.

Chapter 14. APPLICATIONS OF THE DERIVATIVE

If the sense of the _____ is the same for all values of the variables for which its members are defined, then the _____ is called an 'absolute' or 'unconditional' _____. If the sense of an _____ holds only for certain values of the variables involved, but is reversed or destroyed for other values of the variables, it is called a conditional _____.

An _____ may appear unsolvable because it only states whether a number is larger or smaller than another number; but it is possible to apply the same operations for equalities to inequalities. For example, to find x for the _____ 10x > 23 one would divide 23 by 10.

a. Inequality
c. A Mathematical Theory of Communication
b. A chemical equation
d. A posteriori

29. In mathematics, the concept of a '_____' is used to describe the behavior of a function as its argument or input either 'gets close' to some point, or as the argument becomes arbitrarily large; or the behavior of a sequence's elements as their index increases indefinitely. _____s are used in calculus and other branches of mathematical analysis to define derivatives and continuity.

In formulas, _____ is usually abbreviated as lim.

a. Contact
c. Duality
b. Copula
d. Limit

30. In mathematics, a _____ of a set S in a topological space X is a point x in X that can be 'approximated' by points of S other than x itself. This concept profitably generalizes the notion of a limit and is the underpinning of concepts such as closed set and topological closure. Indeed, a set is closed if and only if it contains all of its _____s, and the topological closure operation can be thought of as an operation that enriches a set by adding its _____s.

a. 1-center problem
c. 120-cell
b. 2-3 heap
d. Limit point

31. In mathematics, a _____ is an expression constructed from variables and constants, using the operations of addition, subtraction, multiplication, and constant non-negative whole number exponents. For example, $x^2 - 4x + 7$ is a _____, but $x^2 - 4/x + 7x^{3/2}$ is not, because its second term involves division by the variable x and also because its third term contains an exponent that is not a whole number.

_____s are one of the most important concepts in algebra and throughout mathematics and science.

a. Semifield
c. Group extension
b. Coimage
d. Polynomial

32. In mathematics, an algebraic group G contains a unique maximal normal solvable subgroup; and this subgroup is closed. Its identity component is called the _____ of G.

a. Barycentric coordinates
c. Composite
b. Radical
d. Block size

Chapter 14. APPLICATIONS OF THE DERIVATIVE

33. Suppose that φ : M → N is a smooth map between smooth manifolds; then the _____ of φ at a point x is, in some sense, the best linear approximation of φ near x. It can be viewed as generalization of the total derivative of ordinary calculus. Explicitly, it is a linear map from the tangent space of M at x to the tangent space of N at φ
   a. Boundary
   b. Concurrent
   c. Grill
   d. Differential

34. _____s is concerned with the tasks of developing and applying quantitative or statistical methods to the study and elucidation of economic principles. _____s combines economic theory with statistics to analyze and test economic relationships. Theoretical _____s considers questions about the statistical properties of estimators and tests, while applied _____s is concerned with the application of _____ methods to assess economic theories.
   a. Economic
   b. A Mathematical Theory of Communication
   c. A chemical equation
   d. Econometric

35. _____ is a quantity expressing the two-dimensional size of a defined part of a surface, typically a region bounded by a closed curve. The term surface _____ refers to the total _____ of the exposed surface of a 3-dimensional solid, such as the sum of the _____s of the exposed sides of a polyhedron. _____ is an important invariant in the differential geometry of surfaces.
   a. A chemical equation
   b. A posteriori
   c. A Mathematical Theory of Communication
   d. Area

36. In economics, business, retail, and accounting, a _____ is the value of money that has been used up to produce something, and hence is not available for use anymore. In business, the _____ may be one of acquisition, in which case the amount of money expended to acquire it is counted as _____. In this case, money is the input that is gone in order to acquire the thing.
   a. Cost
   b. 1-center problem
   c. 2-3 heap
   d. 120-cell

37. In economics, the cross elasticity of demand and _____ measures the responsiveness of the quantity demanded of a good to a change in the price of another good.

It is measured as the percentage change in quantity demanded for the first good that occurs in response to a percentage change in price of the second good. For example, if, in response to a 10% increase in the price of fuel, the quantity of new cars that are fuel inefficient demanded decreased by 20%, the cross elasticity of demand would be -20%/10% = -2.

   a. Supply and demand
   b. Marginal rate of substitution
   c. 1-center problem
   d. Cross price elasticity of demand

38. _____ is the change in total cost that arises when the quantity produced changes by one unit.
   a. Notation
   b. Limiting
   c. Marginal cost
   d. Differential Algebra

39. _____ is the study of algorithms for the problems of continuous mathematics.

Chapter 14. APPLICATIONS OF THE DERIVATIVE 137

One of the earliest mathematical writings is the Babylonian tablet YBC 7289, which gives a sexagesimal numerical approximation of $\sqrt{2}$, the length of the diagonal in a unit square. Being able to compute the sides of a triangle is extremely important, for instance, in carpentry and construction.

    a. Constructions of low-discrepancy sequences   b. Truncation error
    c. Numerical analysis   d. Richardson extrapolation

40. In mathematics, an _____, or central tendency of a data set refers to a measure of the 'middle' or 'expected' value of the data set. There are many different descriptive statistics that can be chosen as a measurement of the central tendency of the data items.

An _____ is a single value that is meant to typify a list of values.

    a. Average   b. A posteriori
    c. A Mathematical Theory of Communication   d. A chemical equation

41. A _____ is a symmetrical geometrical object. In non-mathematical usage, the term is used to refer either to a round ball or to its two-dimensional surface. In mathematics, a _____ is the set of all points in three-dimensional space which are at distance r from a fixed point of that space, where r is a positive real number called the radius of the _____.

    a. Lie derivative   b. Differentiable manifold
    c. Differential geometry of curves   d. Sphere

42. _____ is the calculated approximation of a result which is usable even if input data may be incomplete or uncertain.

In statistics, see _____ theory, estimator.

In mathematics, approximation or _____ typically means finding upper or lower bounds of a quantity that cannot readily be computed precisely and is also an educated guess .

    a. Estimation   b. U-statistic
    c. Estimation theory   d. Estimator

Chapter 15. INTEGRATION

1. In complex analysis, a branch of mathematics, the _____ of a complex-valued function g is a function whose complex derivative is g. More precisely, given an open set U in the complex plane and a function $g: U \to \mathbb{C}$, the _____ of g is a function $f: U \to \mathbb{C}$ that satisfies $\frac{df}{dz} = g$.

As such, this concept is the complex-variable version of the _____ of a real-valued function.

  a. Integral
  b. Integration by parts
  c. Indefinite integral
  d. Antiderivative

2. _____ is a branch of mathematics that includes the study of limits, derivatives, integrals, and infinite series, and constitutes a major part of modern university education. Historically, it has been referred to as 'the _____ of infinitesimals', or 'infinitesimal _____'. Most basically, _____ is the study of change, in the same way that geometry is the study of space.
  a. Hyperbolic angle
  b. Test for Divergence
  c. Calculus
  d. Partial sum

3. Suppose that φ : M → N is a smooth map between smooth manifolds; then the _____ of φ at a point x is, in some sense, the best linear approximation of φ near x. It can be viewed as generalization of the total derivative of ordinary calculus. Explicitly, it is a linear map from the tangent space of M at x to the tangent space of N at φ
  a. Boundary
  b. Grill
  c. Concurrent
  d. Differential

4. _____, a field in mathematics, is the study of how functions change when their inputs change. The primary object of study in _____ is the derivative. A closely related notion is the differential.
  a. Geometric function theory
  b. Harmonic analysis
  c. Semi-continuity
  d. Differential calculus

5. In commutative algebra, the notions of an element _____ over a ring, and of an _____ extension of rings, are a generalization of the notions in field theory of an element being algebraic over a field, and of an algebraic extension of fields.

The special case of greatest interest in number theory is that of complex numbers _____ over the ring of integers Z.

The term ring will be understood to mean commutative ring with a unit.

  a. Antidifferentiation
  b. Integral test for convergence
  c. Arc length
  d. Integral

6. _____ is a core concept of basic mathematics, specifically in the fields of infinitesimal calculus and mathematical analysis. Given a function f

$$\int_a^b f(x)\, dx,$$

is equal to the area of a region in the xy-plane bounded by the graph of f, the x-axis, and the vertical lines x = a and x = b, with areas below the x-axis being subtracted.

The term 'integral' may also refer to the notion of antiderivative, a function F whose derivative is the given function f.

   a. OMAC
   b. Epigraph
   c. Apex
   d. Integration

7. In mathematics, a _____ is a system which is not linear. Less technically, a _____ is any problem where the variabl to be solved for cannot be written as a linear sum of independent components. A nonhomogenous system, which is linear apart from the presence of a function of the independent variables, is nonlinear according to a strict definition, but such systems are usually studied alongside linear systems, because they can be transformed to a linear system as long as a particular solution is known.

   a. Nonlinear system
   b. Metric system
   c. 1-center problem
   d. George Dantzig

8. In mathematics, a _____ is a statement that can be proved on the basis of explicitly stated or previously agreed assumptions.

   a. Boolean function
   b. Disjunction introduction
   c. Theorem
   d. Logical value

9. A _____ is a software program that facilitates symbolic mathematics. The core functionality of a CAS is manipulation of mathematical expressions in symbolic form.

Chapter 15. INTEGRATION

The symbolic manipulations supported typically include

- simplification to the smallest possible expression or some standard form, including automatic simplification with assumptions and simplification with constraints
- substitution of symbolic, functors or numeric values for expressions
- change of form of expressions: expanding products and powers, partial and full factorization, rewriting as partial fractions, constraint satisfaction, rewriting trigonometric functions as exponentials, etc.
- partial and total differentiation
- symbolic constrained and unconstrained global optimization
- solution of linear and some non-linear equations over various domains
- solution of some differential and difference equations
- taking some limits
- some indefinite and definite integration, including multidimensional integrals
- integral transforms
- arbitrary-precision numeric operations
- Series operations such as expansion, summation and products
- matrix operations including products, inverses, etc.
- display of mathematical expressions in two-dimensional mathematical form, often using typesetting systems similar to TeX
- add-ons for use in applied mathematics such as physics packages for physical computation
- plotting graphs and parametric plots of functions in two and three dimensions, and animating them
- APIs for linking it on an external program such as a database, or using in a programming language to use the _____
- drawing charts and diagrams
- string manipulation such as matching and searching
- statistical computation
- Theorem proving and verification
- graphic production and editing such as CGI and signal processing as image processing
- sound synthesis

Many also include a programming language, allowing users to implement their own algorithms.

Some _____s focus on a specific area of application; these are typically developed in academia and are free.

a. 2-3 heap
c. Computer algebra system
b. 1-center problem
d. 120-cell

10. In mathematics, an _____, or central tendency of a data set refers to a measure of the 'middle' or 'expected' value of the data set. There are many different descriptive statistics that can be chosen as a measurement of the central tendency of the data items.

An _____ is a single value that is meant to typify a list of values.

Chapter 15. INTEGRATION

a. A posteriori
b. A Mathematical Theory of Communication
c. Average
d. A chemical equation

11. In grammatical theory, definiteness is a feature of noun phrases, distinguishing between entities which are specific and identifiable in a given context (_____ noun phrases) and entities which are not (indefinite noun phrases Examples are:

- Free form: English the boy.
- Phrasal clitic: as in Basque: Cf. emakume ('woman'), emakume-a (woman-ART: 'the woman'), emakume ederr-a (woman beautiful-ART: 'the beautiful woman')
- Noun affix: as in Romanian: om ('man'), om-ul (man-ART: 'the man'); om-ul bun (man-ART good: 'the good man')
- Prefix on both noun and adjective: Arabic ا̈لÙƒØªØ§Ø¨ اÙ„ÙƒØ¨ÙŠØ± (al-kitÄ b al-kabÄ«r) with two instances of al- (DEF-book-DEF-big, literally, 'the book the big')

Germanic, Romance, Celtic, Semitic, and auxiliary languages generally have a _____ article, sometimes used as a postposition. Many other languages do not.

a. 1-center problem
b. Definite
c. Sentence diagram
d. Syntax

12. The mathematical concept of a _____ expresses the intuitive idea of deterministic dependence between two quantities, one of which is viewed as primary and the other as secondary. A _____ then is a way to associate a unique output for each input of a specified type, for example, a real number or an element of a given set.

a. Coherent
b. Function
c. Going up
d. Grill

13. The _____ specifies the relationship between the two central operations of calculus, differentiation and integration.

The first part of the theorem, sometimes called the first _____, shows that an indefinite integration can be reversed by a differentiation.

The second part, sometimes called the second _____, allows one to compute the definite integral of a function by using any one of its infinitely many antiderivatives.

a. Maxima and minima
b. Hyperbolic angle
c. Fundamental Theorem of Calculus
d. Standard part function

14. In mathematics, a _____ is an expression constructed from variables and constants, using the operations of addition, subtraction, multiplication, and constant non-negative whole number exponents. For example, $x^2 - 4x + 7$ is a _____, but $x^2 - 4/x + 7x^{3/2}$ is not, because its second term involves division by the variable x and also because its third term contains an exponent that is not a whole number.

_____s are one of the most important concepts in algebra and throughout mathematics and science.

a. Semifield
b. Group extension
c. Coimage
d. Polynomial

15. _____ is the change in population over time, and can be quantified as the change in the number of individuals in a population using 'per unit time' for measurement. The term _____ can technically refer to any species, but almost always refers to humans, and it is often used informally for the more specific demographic term _____ rate, and is often used to refer specifically to the growth of the population of the world.

Simple models of _____ include the Malthusian Growth Model and the logistic model.

a. Population dynamics
b. 1-center problem
c. 120-cell
d. Population growth

16. In combinatorial mathematics, a _____ is an un-ordered collection of distinct elements, usually of a prescribed size and taken from a given set. Given such a set S, a _____ of elements of S is just a subset of S, where as always forsets the order of the elements is not taken into account. Also, as always forsets, no elements can be repeated more than once in a _____; this is often referred to as a 'collection without repetition'.

a. Fill-in
b. Heawood number
c. Combination
d. Sparsity

17. In the absence of a more specific context, convergence denotes the approach toward a definite value, as time goes on; or to a definite point, a common view or opinion, or toward a fixed or equilibrium state. _____ is the adjectival form, and also a noun meaning an iterative approximation.

In mathematics, convergence describes limiting behaviour, particularly of an infinite sequence or series, toward some limit.

a. Word problem
b. Convergent
c. Prime ideal theorem
d. Separable

18. In calculus, an antiderivative, primitive or _____ of a function f is a function F whose derivative is equal to f. The process of solving for antiderivatives is antidifferentiation. Antiderivatives are related to definite integrals through the fundamental theorem of calculus, and provide a convenient means for calculating the definite integrals of many functions.

a. Indefinite Integral
b. Integral
c. Integral test for convergence
d. Integration by parts operator

19. In mathematics, an _____ is a statement about the relative size or order of two objects, or about whether they are the same or not

- The notation a < b means that a is less than b.
- The notation a > b means that a is greater than b.
- The notation a ≠ b means that a is not equal to b, but does not say that one is bigger than the other or even that they can be compared in size.

In all these cases, a is not equal to b, hence, '_____'.

Chapter 15. INTEGRATION

These relations are known as strict _____

- The notation a ≤ b means that a is less than or equal to b;
- The notation a ≥ b means that a is greater than or equal to b;

An additional use of the notation is to show that one quantity is much greater than another, normally by several orders of magnitude.

- The notation a << b means that a is much less than b.
- The notation a >> b means that a is much greater than b.

If the sense of the _____ is the same for all values of the variables for which its members are defined, then the _____ is called an 'absolute' or 'unconditional' _____. If the sense of an _____ holds only for certain values of the variables involved, but is reversed or destroyed for other values of the variables, it is called a conditional _____.

An _____ may appear unsolvable because it only states whether a number is larger or smaller than another number; but it is possible to apply the same operations for equalities to inequalities. For example, to find x for the _____ 10x > 23 one would divide 23 by 10.

a. A Mathematical Theory of Communication
c. Inequality

b. A posteriori
d. A chemical equation

20. _____ is the mathematical operation of scaling one number by another. It is one of the four basic operations in elementary arithmetic.

_____ is defined for whole numbers in terms of repeated addition; for example, 4 multiplied by 3 can be calculated by adding 3 copies of 4 together:

$$4 + 4 + 4 = 12.$$

_____ of rational numbers and real numbers is defined by systematic generalization of this basic idea.

a. The number 0 is even.
c. Highest common factor

b. Least common multiple
d. Multiplication

21. In mathematics, a _____ is a natural number which has exactly two distinct natural number divisors: 1 and itself. An infinitude of _____s exists, as demonstrated by Euclid around 300 BC. The first twenty-five _____s are:

2, 3, 5, 7, 11, 13, 17, 19, 23, 29, 31, 37, 41, 43, 47, 53, 59, 61, 67, 71, 73, 79, 83, 89, 97.

a. Pronic number
c. Perrin number

b. Highly composite number
d. Prime number

22. _____ was a German polymath who wrote primarily in Latin and French.

He occupies an equally grand place in both the history of philosophy and the history of mathematics. He invented infinitesimal calculus independently of Newton, and his notation is the one in general use since then.

   a. Harry Hinsley
   b. Michel Rolle
   c. Raymond Merrill Smullyan
   d. Gottfried Wilhelm Leibniz

23. This article will state and prove the _____ for differentiation, and then use it to prove these two formulas.

The _____ for differentiation states that for every natural number n, the derivative of $f(x) = x^n$ is $f'(x) = nx^{n-1}$, that is,

$$(x^n)' = nx^{n-1}.$$

The _____ for integration

$$\int x^n \, dx = \frac{x^{n+1}}{n+1} + C$$

for natural n is then an easy consequence. One just needs to take the derivative of this equality and use the _____ and linearity of differentiation on the right-hand side.

   a. Power rule
   b. Periodic function
   c. Standard part function
   d. Functional integration

24. In mathematics, the _____ of a Euclidean space is a special point, usually denoted by the letter O, used as a fixed point of reference for the geometry of the surrounding space. In a Cartesian coordinate system, the _____ is the point where the axes of the system intersect. In Euclidean geometry, the _____ may be chosen freely as any convenient point of reference.

   a. Autonomous system
   b. Interval
   c. Origin
   d. OMAC

25. The _____ is a function in mathematics. The application of this function to a value x is written as ex. Equivalently, this can be written in the form e^x, where e is a mathematical constant, the base of the natural logarithm, which equals approximately 2.718281828, and is also known as Euler's number.

   a. A chemical equation
   b. A Mathematical Theory of Communication
   c. Area hyperbolic functions
   d. Exponential function

26. In mathematics, the _____ of a real number is its numerical value without regard to its sign. So, for example, 3 is the _____ of both 3 and −3.

The _____ of a number a is denoted by $|a|$.

Chapter 15. INTEGRATION

Generalizations of the _____ for real numbers occur in a wide variety of mathematical settings.

a. Area hyperbolic functions
c. A chemical equation
b. A Mathematical Theory of Communication
d. Absolute value

27. In mathematics, hyperbolic n-space, denoted H^n, is the maximally symmetric, simply connected, n-dimensional Riemannian manifold with constant sectional curvature −1. _____ is the principal example of a space exhibiting hyperbolic geometry. It can be thought of as the negative-curvature analogue of the n-sphere.

a. Margulis lemma
c. Hyperbolic space
b. Horocycle
d. Hyperbolic geometry

28. _____ of an object is its speed in a particular direction.

a. Maxima
c. Velocity
b. Rolle's Theorem
d. Discontinuity

29. In mathematics and in the sciences, a _____ (plural: _____e, formulæ or _____s) is a concise way of expressing information symbolically (as in a mathematical or chemical _____), or a general relationship between quantities. One of many famous _____e is Albert Einstein's E = mc² (see special relativity

In mathematics, a _____ is a key to solve an equation with variables. For example, the problem of determining the volume of a sphere is one that requires a significant amount of integral calculus to solve.

a. Formula
c. 120-cell
b. 2-3 heap
d. 1-center problem

30. In calculus, the _____ is a formula for the derivative of the composite of two functions.

In intuitive terms, if a variable, y, depends on a second variable, u, which in turn depends on a third variable, x, then the rate of change of y with respect to x can be computed as the rate of change of y with respect to u multiplied by the rate of change of u with respect to x. Schematically,

$$\frac{dy}{dx} = \frac{dy}{du} \cdot \frac{du}{dx}.$$

For an explanation of notation used in this section, see Function composition.

The _____ states that, under appropriate conditions,

$$(f \circ g)'(x) = f'(g(x))g'(x),$$

which in short form is written as

$$(f \circ g)' = f' \circ g \cdot g'.$$

Alternatively, in the Leibniz notation, the _____ is

$$\frac{dy}{dx} = \frac{dy}{du} \cdot \frac{du}{dx}.$$

In integration, the counterpart to the _____ is the substitution rule.

a. 1-center problem
b. 120-cell
c. Product rule
d. Chain rule

31. _____ is a fundamental construction of differential calculus and admits many possible generalizations within the fields of mathematical analysis, combinatorics, algebra, and geometry.

In real, complex, and functional analysis, _____s are generalized to functions of several real or complex variables and functions between topological vector spaces. An important case is the variational _____ in the calculus of variations.

a. Derivative
b. Lin-Tsien equation
c. Functional derivative
d. Metric derivative

32. _____s is concerned with the tasks of developing and applying quantitative or statistical methods to the study and elucidation of economic principles. _____s combines economic theory with statistics to analyze and test economic relationships. Theoretical _____s considers questions about the statistical properties of estimators and tests, while applied _____s is concerned with the application of _____ methods to assess economic theories.

a. Economic
b. A chemical equation
c. A Mathematical Theory of Communication
d. Econometric

33. In linear algebra, _____ is a version of Gaussian elimination that puts zeros both above and below each pivot element as it goes from the top row of the given matrix to the bottom. In other words, _____ brings a matrix to reduced row echelon form, whereas Gaussian elimination takes it only as far as row echelon form. Every matrix has a reduced row echelon form, and this algorithm is guaranteed to produce it.

a. Spheroidal wave functions
b. Lax equivalence theorem
c. Conservation form
d. Gauss-Jordan elimination

34. In mathematics, the _____ is a conic section, the intersection of a right circular conical surface and a plane parallel to a generating straight line of that surface. Given a point and a line that lie in a plane, the locus of points in that plane that are equidistant to them is a _____.

A particular case arises when the plane is tangent to the conical surface of a circle.

Chapter 15. INTEGRATION

a. Parabola
b. Matrix representation of conic sections
c. Directrix
d. Dandelin sphere

35. _____ is a quantity expressing the two-dimensional size of a defined part of a surface, typically a region bounded by a closed curve. The term surface _____ refers to the total _____ of the exposed surface of a 3-dimensional solid, such as the sum of the _____ s of the exposed sides of a polyhedron. _____ is an important invariant in the differential geometry of surfaces.
a. Area
b. A chemical equation
c. A posteriori
d. A Mathematical Theory of Communication

36. A set S of real numbers is called _____ from above if there is a real number k such that k ≥ s for all s in S. The number k is called an upper bound of S. The terms _____ from below and lower bound are similarly defined.
a. Derivative algebra
b. Harmonic series
c. Descent
d. Bounded

37. In mathematics, the concept of a _____ tries to capture the intuitive idea of a geometrical one-dimensional and continuous object. A simple example is the circle. In everyday use of the term '_____', a straight line is not curved, but in mathematical parlance _____ s include straight lines and line segments.
a. Curve
b. Kappa curve
c. Quadrifolium
d. Negative pedal curve

38. A trapezoid or a _____ is a quadrilateral that has at least one pair of parallel lines for sides.

Some authors define it as a quadrilateral having exactly one pair of parallel sides, so as to exclude parallelograms, which otherwise would be regarded as a special type of trapezoid, but most mathematicians use the inclusive definition.

In North America, the term _____ is used to refer to a quadrilateral with no parallel sides.

a. Rhomboid
b. Tangential quadrilateral
c. Lozenge
d. Trapezium

39. A _____ or a trapezium is a quadrilateral that has at least one pair of parallel lines for sides.

Some authors define it as a quadrilateral having exactly one pair of parallel sides, so as to exclude parallelograms, which otherwise would be regarded as a special type of _____, but most mathematicians use the inclusive definition.

In North America, the term trapezium is used to refer to a quadrilateral with no parallel sides.

a. Trapezium
b. Trapezoid
c. Rhomboid
d. Lozenge

40. In mathematics, the trapezium rule or _____ is a way to approximately calculate the definite integral

Chapter 15. INTEGRATION

$$\int_a^b f(x)\,dx.$$

The trapezium rule works by approximating the region under the graph of the function f by a trapezium and calculating its area. It follows that

$$\int_a^b f(x)\,dx \approx (b-a)\frac{f(a)+f(b)}{2}.$$

To calculate this integral more accurately, one first splits the interval of integration [a,b] into n smaller subintervals, and then applies the trapezium rule on each of them. One obtains the composite trapezium rule:

$$\int_a^b f(x)\,dx \approx \frac{b-a}{n}\left[\frac{f(a)+f(b)}{2} + \sum_{k=1}^{n-1} f\left(a+k\frac{b-a}{n}\right)\right].$$

This can alternatively be written as:

$$\int_a^b f(x)\,dx \approx \frac{b-a}{2n}\left(f(x_0) + 2f(x_1) + 2f(x_2) + \cdots + 2f(x_{n-1}) + f(x_n)\right)$$

where

$$x_k = a + k\frac{b-a}{n}, \text{ for } k = 0, 1, \ldots, n.$$

- a. 120-cell
- b. 2-3 heap
- c. 1-center problem
- d. Trapezoidal rule

41. In mathematics, the concept of a '_____' is used to describe the behavior of a function as its argument or input either 'gets close' to some point, or as the argument becomes arbitrarily large; or the behavior of a sequence's elements as their index increases indefinitely. _____s are used in calculus and other branches of mathematical analysis to define derivatives and continuity.

In formulas, _____ is usually abbreviated as lim.

- a. Copula
- b. Contact
- c. Duality
- d. Limit

42. In mathematics, a _____ of a set S in a topological space X is a point x in X that can be 'approximated' by points of S other than x itself. This concept profitably generalizes the notion of a limit and is the underpinning of concepts such as closed set and topological closure. Indeed, a set is closed if and only if it contains all of its _____s, and the topological closure operation can be thought of as an operation that enriches a set by adding its _____s.

Chapter 15. INTEGRATION

a. 1-center problem
b. 120-cell
c. 2-3 heap
d. Limit point

43. _____ is the addition of a set of numbers; the result is their sum or total. An interim or present total of a _____ process is termed the running total. The 'numbers' to be summed may be natural numbers, complex numbers, matrices, or still more complicated objects.
a. 2-3 heap
b. 120-cell
c. 1-center problem
d. Summation

44. _____ is a branch of mathematics which focuses on the study of matrices. Initially a sub-branch of linear algebra, it has grown to cover subjects related to graph theory, algebra, combinatorics, and statistics as well.

The term matrix was first coined in 1848 by J.J. Sylvester as a name of an array of numbers.

a. Pairing
b. Segre classification
c. Semi-simple operators
d. Matrix theory

45. A _____ typically refers to a class of handheld calculators that are capable of plotting graphs, solving simultaneous equations, and performing numerous other tasks with variables. Most popular _____s are also programmable, allowing the user to create customized programs, typically for scientific/engineering and education applications. Due to their large displays intended for graphing, they can also accommodate several lines of text and calculations at a time.
a. Bump mapping
b. Support vector machines
c. Genus
d. Graphing calculator

46. Georg Friedrich Bernhard _____ was a German mathematician who made important contributions to analysis and differential geometry, some of them paving the way for the later development of general relativity.

_____ was born in Breselenz, a village near Dannenberg in the Kingdom of Hanover in what is today Germany. His father, Friedrich Bernhard _____, was a poor Lutheran pastor in Breselenz who fought in the Napoleonic Wars.

a. Brook Taylor
b. Gustave Bertrand
c. Paul C. van Oorschot
d. Riemann

47. In the branch of mathematics known as real analysis, the _____, created by Bernhard Riemann, was the first rigorous definition of the integral of a function on an interval. While the _____ is unsuitable for many theoretical purposes, it is one of the easiest integrals to define. Some of these technical deficiencies can be remedied by the Riemann-Stieltjes integral, and most of them disappear in the Lebesgue integral.
a. Darboux integral
b. Skorokhod integral
c. Russo-Vallois integral
d. Riemann integral

48. In mathematics, a _____ is a method for approximating the total area underneath a curve on a graph, otherwise known as an integral. It may also be used to define the integration operation. The sums are named after the German mathematician Bernhard Riemann.

a. Multiple integral
c. Singular measure
b. Riemann sum
d. Solid of revolution

49. _____ or amortisation is the process of decreasing an amount over a period of time. The word comes from Middle English amortisen to kill, alienate in mortmain, from Anglo-French amorteser, alteration of amortir, from Vulgar Latin admortire to kill, from Latin ad- + mort-, mors death. Particular instances of the term include:

- _____, the allocation of a lump sum amount to different time periods, particularly for loans and other forms of finance, including related interest or other finance charges.
  - _____ schedule, a table detailing each periodic payment on a loan, as generated by an _____ calculator.
  - Negative _____, an _____ schedule where the loan amount actually increases through not paying the full interest
- Amortized analysis, analyzing the execution cost of algorithms over a sequence of operations.
- _____ of capital expenditures of certain assets under accounting rules, particularly intangible assets, in a manner analogous to depreciation.
- _____

_____ is also used in the context of zoning regulations and describes the time in which a property owner has to relocate when the property's use constitutes a preexisting nonconforming use under zoning regulations.

- Depreciation

a. ISAAC
c. Identity
b. Origin
d. Amortization

50. An _____ is a table detailing each periodic payment on a amortizing loan, as generated by an amortization calculator.

While a portion of every payment is applied towards both the interest and the principal balance of the loan, the exact amount applied to principal each time varies. An _____ reveals the specific monetary amount put towards interest, as well as the specific put towards the Principal balance, with each payment.

a. Accounts receivable
c. Amortization schedule
b. A chemical equation
d. A Mathematical Theory of Communication

51. A _____ is a device for performing mathematical calculations, distinguished from a computer by having a limited problem solving ability and an interface optimized for interactive calculation rather than programming. _____s can be hardware or software, and mechanical or electronic, and are often built into devices such as PDAs or mobile phones.

Modern electronic _____s are generally small, digital, and usually inexpensive.

a. 120-cell
c. 1-center problem
b. 2-3 heap
d. Calculator

Chapter 15. INTEGRATION

52. _____ (20 August 1710 - 14 May 1761) was a British mathematician, inventor and eponym of Simpson's rule to approximate definite integrals. However, this rule was also found 200 years earlier from Johannes Kepler, in the so-called Keplersche Fassregel.

Simpson was born in Market Bosworth, Leicestershire.

- a. Kunihiko Kodaira
- b. Felix Hausdorff
- c. Raj Chandra Bose
- d. Thomas Simpson

53. _____ is the study of algorithms for the problems of continuous mathematics.

One of the earliest mathematical writings is the Babylonian tablet YBC 7289, which gives a sexagesimal numerical approximation of $\sqrt{2}$, the length of the diagonal in a unit square. Being able to compute the sides of a triangle is extremely important, for instance, in carpentry and construction.

- a. Numerical analysis
- b. Constructions of low-discrepancy sequences
- c. Truncation error
- d. Richardson extrapolation

54. _____ is the study of kind and quantity of error that occurs, particularly in the fields of applied mathematics, applied linguistics and statistics.

In numerical simulation or modelling of real systems, _____ is concerned with the changes in the output of the model as the parameters to the model vary about a mean.

For instance, in a system modelled as a function of two variables z = f.

- a. Error analysis
- b. Infix notation
- c. Inverse relationship
- d. Inventory control problem

55. The _____ of a material is defined as its mass per unit volume:

$$\rho = \frac{m}{V}$$

Different materials usually have different densities, so _____ is an important concept regarding buoyancy, metal purity and packaging.

In some cases _____ is expressed as the dimensionless quantities specific gravity or relative _____, in which case it is expressed in multiples of the _____ of some other standard material, usually water or air.

In a well-known story, Archimedes was given the task of determining whether King Hiero's goldsmith was embezzling gold during the manufacture of a wreath dedicated to the gods and replacing it with another, cheaper alloy.

a. 2-3 heap
c. 1-center problem
b. 120-cell
d. Density

56. In differential geometry, a discipline within mathematics, a _____ is a subset of the tangent bundle of a manifold satisfying certain properties. _____s are used to build up notions of integrability, and specifically of a foliation of a manifold
   a. Coherence
   c. Constraint
   b. Distribution
   d. Discontinuity

57. The _____ or Dirac's delta is a mathematical construct introduced by the British theoretical physicist Paul Dirac. Informally, it is a function representing an infinitely sharp peak bounding unit area: a function that has the value zero everywhere except at x = 0 where its value is infinitely large in such a way that its total integral is 1. It is a continuous analogue of the discrete Kronecker delta.
   a. Weak derivative
   c. Hyperfunction
   b. Schwartz kernel theorem
   d. Dirac delta

58. In elementary algebra, a _____ is a polynomial with two terms: the sum of two monomials. It is the simplest kind of polynomial except for a monomial.

The _____ $a^2 - b^2$ can be factored as the product of two other _____s:

$a^2 - b^2$.

The product of a pair of linear _____s a x + b and c x + d is:

2 +x + bd.

A _____ raised to the nth power, represented as

n

can be expanded by means of the _____ theorem or, equivalently, using Pascal's triangle.

   a. Real structure
   c. Cylindrical algebraic decomposition
   b. Rational root theorem
   d. Binomial

59. In mathematics, specifically in combinatorial commutative algebra, a convex lattice polytope P is called _____ if it has the following property: given any positive integer n, every lattice point of the dilation nP, obtained from P by scaling its vertices by the factor n and taking the convex hull of the resulting points, can be written as the sum of exactly n lattice points in P. This property plays an important role in the theory of toric varieties, where it corresponds to projective normality of the toric variety determined by P.

The simplex in R^k with the vertices at the origin and along the unit coordinate vectors is _____.

a. Polytetrahedron
b. Hypercube
c. Demihypercubes
d. Normal

60. The _____ is an important family of continuous probability distributions, applicable in many fields. Each member of the family may be defined by two parameters, location and scale: the mean and variance respectively. The standard _____ is the _____ with a mean of zero and a variance of one.
   a. Coefficient of variation
   b. Null hypothesis
   c. Percentile rank
   d. Normal Distribution

61. In calculus, an antiderivative, primitive or indefinite integral of a function f is a function F whose derivative is equal to f. The process of solving for antiderivatives is _____. Antiderivatives are related to definite integrals through the fundamental theorem of calculus, and provide a convenient means for calculating the definite integrals of many functions.
   a. Integration by parts operator
   b. Indefinite integral
   c. Arc length
   d. Antidifferentiation

Chapter 16. FURTHER TECHNIQUES AND APPLICATIONS OF INTEGRATION

1. _____ is a branch of mathematics that includes the study of limits, derivatives, integrals, and infinite series, and constitutes a major part of modern university education. Historically, it has been referred to as 'the _____ of infinitesimals', or 'infinitesimal _____'. Most basically, _____ is the study of change, in the same way that geometry is the study of space.
   - a. Hyperbolic angle
   - b. Partial sum
   - c. Test for Divergence
   - d. Calculus

2. The _____ specifies the relationship between the two central operations of calculus, differentiation and integration.

   The first part of the theorem, sometimes called the first _____, shows that an indefinite integration can be reversed by a differentiation.

   The second part, sometimes called the second _____, allows one to compute the definite integral of a function by using any one of its infinitely many antiderivatives.

   - a. Maxima and minima
   - b. Hyperbolic angle
   - c. Fundamental Theorem of Calculus
   - d. Standard part function

3. In mathematics, a _____ is a statement that can be proved on the basis of explicitly stated or previously agreed assumptions.
   - a. Disjunction introduction
   - b. Theorem
   - c. Boolean function
   - d. Logical value

4. _____ is a core concept of basic mathematics, specifically in the fields of infinitesimal calculus and mathematical analysis. Given a function f

$$\int_a^b f(x)\, dx,$$

is equal to the area of a region in the xy-plane bounded by the graph of f, the x-axis, and the vertical lines x = a and x = b, with areas below the x-axis being subtracted.

The term 'integral' may also refer to the notion of antiderivative, a function F whose derivative is the given function f.

   - a. Apex
   - b. OMAC
   - c. Epigraph
   - d. Integration

5. In complex analysis, a branch of mathematics, the _____ of a complex-valued function g is a function whose complex derivative is g. More precisely, given an open set U in the complex plane and a function $g : U \to \mathbb{C}$, the _____ of g is a function $f : U \to \mathbb{C}$ that satisfies $\frac{df}{dz} = g$.

As such, this concept is the complex-variable version of the _____ of a real-valued function.

Chapter 16. FURTHER TECHNIQUES AND APPLICATIONS OF INTEGRATION

a. Integral
c. Indefinite integral
b. Integration by parts
d. Antiderivative

6. In grammatical theory, definiteness is a feature of noun phrases, distinguishing between entities which are specific and identifiable in a given context (_____ noun phrases) and entities which are not (indefinite noun phrases Examples are:

- Free form: English the boy.
- Phrasal clitic: as in Basque: Cf. emakume ('woman'), emakume-a (woman-ART: 'the woman'), emakume ederr-a (woman beautiful-ART: 'the beautiful woman')
- Noun affix: as in Romanian: om ('man'), om-ul (man-ART: 'the man'); om-ul bun (man-ART good: 'the good man')
- Prefix on both noun and adjective: Arabic ا‎لﻜﺘﺎب الﻜﺒير (al-kitÄ b al-kabÄ«r) with two instances of al- (DEF-book-DEF-big, literally, 'the book the big')

Germanic, Romance, Celtic, Semitic, and auxiliary languages generally have a _____ article, sometimes used as a postposition. Many other languages do not.

a. Sentence diagram
c. 1-center problem
b. Syntax
d. Definite

7. In commutative algebra, the notions of an element _____ over a ring, and of an _____ extension of rings, are a generalization of the notions in field theory of an element being algebraic over a field, and of an algebraic extension of fields.

The special case of greatest interest in number theory is that of complex numbers _____ over the ring of integers Z.

The term ring will be understood to mean commutative ring with a unit.

a. Arc length
c. Integral test for convergence
b. Antidifferentiation
d. Integral

8. A _____ is a software program that facilitates symbolic mathematics. The core functionality of a CAS is manipulation of mathematical expressions in symbolic form.

Chapter 16. FURTHER TECHNIQUES AND APPLICATIONS OF INTEGRATION

The symbolic manipulations supported typically include

- simplification to the smallest possible expression or some standard form, including automatic simplification with assumptions and simplification with constraints
- substitution of symbolic, functors or numeric values for expressions
- change of form of expressions: expanding products and powers, partial and full factorization, rewriting as partial fractions, constraint satisfaction, rewriting trigonometric functions as exponentials, etc.
- partial and total differentiation
- symbolic constrained and unconstrained global optimization
- solution of linear and some non-linear equations over various domains
- solution of some differential and difference equations
- taking some limits
- some indefinite and definite integration, including multidimensional integrals
- integral transforms
- arbitrary-precision numeric operations
- Series operations such as expansion, summation and products
- matrix operations including products, inverses, etc.
- display of mathematical expressions in two-dimensional mathematical form, often using typesetting systems similar to TeX
- add-ons for use in applied mathematics such as physics packages for physical computation
- plotting graphs and parametric plots of functions in two and three dimensions, and animating them
- APIs for linking it on an external program such as a database, or using in a programming language to use the _____
- drawing charts and diagrams
- string manipulation such as matching and searching
- statistical computation
- Theorem proving and verification
- graphic production and editing such as CGI and signal processing as image processing
- sound synthesis

Many also include a programming language, allowing users to implement their own algorithms.

Some _____s focus on a specific area of application; these are typically developed in academia and are free.

a. 2-3 heap
c. 1-center problem
b. Computer algebra system
d. 120-cell

9. In the absence of a more specific context, convergence denotes the approach toward a definite value, as time goes on; or to a definite point, a common view or opinion, or toward a fixed or equilibrium state. _____ is the adjective form, and also a noun meaning an iterative approximation.

In mathematics, convergence describes limiting behaviour, particularly of an infinite sequence or series, toward some limit.

Chapter 16. FURTHER TECHNIQUES AND APPLICATIONS OF INTEGRATION

a. Separable
b. Word problem
c. Prime ideal theorem
d. Convergent

10. In linear algebra, _____ is a version of Gaussian elimination that puts zeros both above and below each pivot element as it goes from the top row of the given matrix to the bottom. In other words, _____ brings a matrix to reduced row echelon form, whereas Gaussian elimination takes it only as far as row echelon form. Every matrix has a reduced row echelon form, and this algorithm is guaranteed to produce it.

a. Conservation form
b. Lax equivalence theorem
c. Spheroidal wave functions
d. Gauss-Jordan elimination

11. In mathematics, engineering, and manufacturing, a _____ is a solid figure obtained by rotating a plane curve around some straight line (the axis) that lies on the same plane.

Assuming that the curve does not cross the axis, the solid's volume is equal to the length of the circle described by the figure's centroid, times the figure's area (Pappus's second centroid Theorem.)

Rotating a curve

A representative disk is a three-dimensional volume element of a _____.

a. Risch algorithm
b. Signed measure
c. Solid of revolution
d. Riemann sum

12. The _____ of any solid, plasma, vacuum or theoretical object is how much three-dimensional space it occupies, often quantified numerically. One-dimensional figures and two-dimensional shapes are assigned zero _____ in the three-dimensional space. _____ is presented as ml or cm^3.

_____s of straight-edged and circular shapes are calculated using arithmetic formulae.

a. Volume
b. Stress-energy tensor
c. Thermodynamic limit
d. Cauchy momentum equation

13. In mathematics, an _____, or central tendency of a data set refers to a measure of the 'middle' or 'expected' value of the data set. There are many different descriptive statistics that can be chosen as a measurement of the central tendency of the data items.

An _____ is a single value that is meant to typify a list of values.

a. A posteriori
b. Average
c. A chemical equation
d. A Mathematical Theory of Communication

14. _____ is a three-dimensional geometric shape formed by straight lines through a fixed point vertex to the points of a fixed curve directrix.

a. 2-3 heap
b. 1-center problem
c. 120-cell
d. Right circular cone

Chapter 16. FURTHER TECHNIQUES AND APPLICATIONS OF INTEGRATION

15. In mathematics, the _____ s are analogs of the ordinary trigonometric functions. The basic _____ s are the hyperbolic sine 'sinh', and the hyperbolic cosine 'cosh', from which are derived the hyperbolic tangent 'tanh', etc., in analogy to the derived trigonometric functions. The inverse _____ are the area hyperbolic sine 'arsinh' (also called 'asinh', or sometimes by the misnomer of 'arcsinh') and so on.
   a. Square root
   b. Heaviside step function
   c. Rectangular function
   d. Hyperbolic function

16. A _____ is a three-dimensional geometric shape that tapers smoothly from a flat, round base to a point called the apex or vertex. More precisely, it is the solid figure bounded by a plane base and the surface formed by the locus of all straight line segments joining the apex to the perimeter of the base. The term '_____' sometimes refers just to the surface of this solid figure, or just to the lateral surface.
   a. Blocking
   b. Characteristic
   c. Gravity waves
   d. Cone

17. In mathematics, a _____ is a system which is not linear. Less technically, a _____ is any problem where the variabl to be solved for cannot be written as a linear sum of independent components. A nonhomogenous system, which is linear apart from the presence of a function of the independent variables, is nonlinear according to a strict definition, but such systems are usually studied alongside linear systems, because they can be transformed to a linear system as long as a particular solution is known.
   a. Metric system
   b. 1-center problem
   c. George Dantzig
   d. Nonlinear system

18. The mathematical concept of a _____ expresses the intuitive idea of deterministic dependence between two quantities, one of which is viewed as primary and the other as secondary. A _____ then is a way to associate a unique output for each input of a specified type, for example, a real number or an element of a given set.
   a. Function
   b. Coherent
   c. Going up
   d. Grill

19. In probability theory, a probability distribution is called _____ if its cumulative distribution function is _____. That is equivalent to saying that for random variables X with the distribution in question, Pr[X = a] = 0 for all real numbers a. If the distribution of X is _____ then X is called a _____ random variable.
   a. Conull set
   b. Concatenated codes
   c. Continuous
   d. Continuous phase modulation

20. _____ in technical analysis is typical price multiplied by volume, a kind of approximation to the dollar value of a day's trading.

_____ index is an oscillator calculated over an N-day period, ranging from 0 to 100, showing _____ on up days as a percentage of the total of up and down days.

   a. 120-cell
   b. Technical analysis
   c. Money flow
   d. 1-center problem

Chapter 16. FURTHER TECHNIQUES AND APPLICATIONS OF INTEGRATION

21. _____ is a quantity expressing the two-dimensional size of a defined part of a surface, typically a region bounded by a closed curve. The term surface _____ refers to the total _____ of the exposed surface of a 3-dimensional solid, such as the sum of the _____s of the exposed sides of a polyhedron. _____ is an important invariant in the differential geometry of surfaces.
    a. A chemical equation
    b. A posteriori
    c. A Mathematical Theory of Communication
    d. Area

22. In mathematics and in the sciences, a _____ (plural: _____e, formulæ or _____s) is a concise way of expressing information symbolically (as in a mathematical or chemical _____), or a general relationship between quantities. One of many famous _____e is Albert Einstein's E = mc² (see special relativity

In mathematics, a _____ is a key to solve an equation with variables. For example, the problem of determining the volume of a sphere is one that requires a significant amount of integral calculus to solve.

    a. 1-center problem
    b. 120-cell
    c. 2-3 heap
    d. Formula

23. In mathematics, the _____ of a number to a given base is the power or exponent to which the base must be raised in order to produce the number.

For example, the _____ of 1000 to the base 10 is 3, because 3 is how many 10s one must multiply to get 1000: thus 10 × 10 × 10 = 1000; the base-2 _____ of 32 is 5 because 5 is how many 2s one must multiply to get 32: thus 2 × 2 × 2 × 2 × 2 = 32. In the language of exponents: 10^3 = 1000, so $\log_{10} 1000$ = 3, and 2^5 = 32, so $\log_2 32$ = 5.

    a. Logarithm
    b. 2-3 heap
    c. 1-center problem
    d. 120-cell

24. In calculus, an _____ is the limit of a definite integral as an endpoint of the interval of integration approaches either a specified real number or ∞ or −∞ or, in some cases, as both endpoints approach limits.

Specifically, an _____ is a limit of the form

$$\lim_{b \to \infty} \int_a^b f(x)\, dx, \qquad \lim_{a \to -\infty} \int_a^b f(x)\, dx,$$

or of the form

$$\lim_{c \to b^-} \int_a^c f(x)\, dx, \qquad \lim_{c \to a^+} \int_c^b f(x)\, dx,$$

in which one takes a limit in one or the other endpoints . _____s may also occur at an interior point of the domain of integration, or at multiple such points.

a. Infinite product
b. Isoperimetric dimension
c. Elliptic boundary value problem
d. Improper integral

25. In mathematics, the concept of a _____ tries to capture the intuitive idea of a geometrical one-dimensional and continuous object. A simple example is the circle. In everyday use of the term '_____', a straight line is not curved, but in mathematical parlance _____s include straight lines and line segments.
  a. Kappa curve
  b. Quadrifolium
  c. Curve
  d. Negative pedal curve

26. _____ is the state of being greater than any finite number, however large.
  a. A Mathematical Theory of Communication
  b. Implicit differentiation
  c. Interval notation
  d. Infinity

27. In mathematics, the concept of a '_____' is used to describe the behavior of a function as its argument or input either 'gets close' to some point, or as the argument becomes arbitrarily large; or the behavior of a sequence's elements as their index increases indefinitely. _____s are used in calculus and other branches of mathematical analysis to define derivatives and continuity.

In formulas, _____ is usually abbreviated as lim.

  a. Copula
  b. Contact
  c. Duality
  d. Limit

28. In mathematics, a _____ of a set S in a topological space X is a point x in X that can be 'approximated' by points of S other than x itself. This concept profitably generalizes the notion of a limit and is the underpinning of concepts such as closed set and topological closure. Indeed, a set is closed if and only if it contains all of its _____s, and the topological closure operation can be thought of as an operation that enriches a set by adding its _____s.
  a. 120-cell
  b. 2-3 heap
  c. Limit point
  d. 1-center problem

29. In mathematics, and in particular in abstract algebra, distributivity is a property of binary operations that generalises the _____ law from elementary algebra.
  a. General linear group
  b. Permutation
  c. Distributive
  d. Closure with a twist

30. Suppose that φ : M → N is a smooth map between smooth manifolds; then the _____ of φ at a point x is, in some sense, the best linear approximation of φ near x. It can be viewed as generalization of the total derivative of ordinary calculus. Explicitly, it is a linear map from the tangent space of M at x to the tangent space of N at φ
  a. Grill
  b. Boundary
  c. Concurrent
  d. Differential

31. _____s arise in many problems in physics, engineering, etc. The following examples show how to solve _____s in a few simple cases when an exact solution exists.

Chapter 16. FURTHER TECHNIQUES AND APPLICATIONS OF INTEGRATION

A separable linear ordinary _____ of the first order has the general form:

$$\frac{dy}{dt} + f(t)y = 0$$

where f is some known function.

   a. Nahm equations   b. Differential equation
   c. Homogeneous differential equation   d. Nullcline

32. In mathematics, hyperbolic n-space, denoted H^n, is the maximally symmetric, simply connected, n-dimensional Riemannian manifold with constant sectional curvature −1. _____ is the principal example of a space exhibiting hyperbolic geometry. It can be thought of as the negative-curvature analogue of the n-sphere.

   a. Hyperbolic space   b. Hyperbolic geometry
   c. Horocycle   d. Margulis lemma

33. Initial objects are also called _____, and terminal objects are also called final.
   a. Direct limit   b. Terminal object
   c. Colimit   d. Coterminal

34. In mathematics, in the field of differential equations, an _____ is an ordinary differential equation together with specified value, called the initial condition, of the unknown function at a given point in the domain of the solution. In physics or other sciences, modeling a system frequently amounts to solving an _____; in this context, the differential equation is an evolution equation specifying how, given initial conditions, the system will evolve with time.

An _____ is a differential equation

$$y'(t) = f(t, y(t)) \quad \text{with} \quad f : \mathbb{R} \times \mathbb{R} \to \mathbb{R}$$

together with a point in the domain of f

$$(t_0, y_0) \in \mathbb{R} \times \mathbb{R},$$

called the initial condition.

   a. Initial value problem   b. A chemical equation
   c. A Mathematical Theory of Communication   d. A posteriori

35. _____ is the concept of adding accumulated interest back to the principal, so that interest is earned on interest from that moment on. The act of declaring interest to be principal is called compounding. A loan, for example, may have its interest compounded every month: in this case, a loan with $100 principal and 1% interest per month would have a balance of $101 at the end of the first month.

Chapter 16. FURTHER TECHNIQUES AND APPLICATIONS OF INTEGRATION

  a. Net interest margin
  c. Compound interest
  b. Net interest margin securities
  d. Retained interest

36. In mathematics, an algebraic field extension L/K is _____ if it can be generated by adjoining to K a set each of whose elements is a root of a _____ polynomial over K. In that case, each β in L has a _____ minimal polynomial over K.

The condition of separability is central in Galois theory.

  a. Separable
  c. Computational mathematics
  b. Small set
  d. Normal form

37. In mathematics, _____ is any of several methods for solving ordinary and partial differential equations, in which algebra allows one to re-write an equation so that each of two variables occurs on a different side of the equation.

Suppose a differential equation can be written in the form

$$\frac{d}{dx}f(x) = g(x)h(f(x)), \qquad (1)$$

which we can write more simply by letting y = f:

$$\frac{dy}{dx} = g(x)h(y).$$

As long as h≠ 0, we can rearrange terms to obtain:

$$\frac{dy}{h(y)} = g(x)dx,$$

so that the two variables x and y have been separated.

Some who dislike Leibniz's notation may prefer to write this as

$$\frac{1}{h(y)}\frac{dy}{dx} = g(x),$$

but that fails to make it quite as obvious why this is called '_____'.

  a. Wronskian
  c. Normal mode
  b. Sturm-Liouville equation
  d. Separation of variables

38. In calculus, the _____ is a formula for the derivative of the composite of two functions.

Chapter 16. FURTHER TECHNIQUES AND APPLICATIONS OF INTEGRATION

In intuitive terms, if a variable, y, depends on a second variable, u, which in turn depends on a third variable, x, then the rate of change of y with respect to x can be computed as the rate of change of y with respect to u multiplied by the rate of change of u with respect to x. Schematically,

$$\frac{dy}{dx} = \frac{dy}{du} \cdot \frac{du}{dx}.$$

For an explanation of notation used in this section, see Function composition.

The _____ states that, under appropriate conditions,

$$(f \circ g)'(x) = f'(g(x))g'(x),$$

which in short form is written as

$$(f \circ g)' = f' \circ g \cdot g'.$$

Alternatively, in the Leibniz notation, the _____ is

$$\frac{dy}{dx} = \frac{dy}{du} \cdot \frac{du}{dx}.$$

In integration, the counterpart to the _____ is the substitution rule.

    a. Chain rule   b. 120-cell
    c. Product rule   d. 1-center problem

39. _____ is a fee, paid on borrowed capital. Assets lent include money, shares, consumer goods through hire purchase, major assets such as aircraft, and even entire factories in finance lease arrangements. The _____ is calculated upon the value of the assets in the same manner as upon money.
    a. A Mathematical Theory of Communication   b. Interest
    c. Interest sensitivity gap   d. Interest expense

40. _____ occurs when the growth rate of a mathematical function is proportional to the function's current value. In the case of a discrete domain of definition with equal intervals it is also called geometric growth or geometric decay.

With _____ of a positive value its rate of increase steadily increases, or in the case of exponential decay, its rate of decrease steadily decreases.

    a. A posteriori   b. A chemical equation
    c. A Mathematical Theory of Communication   d. Exponential growth

41. The supportable population of an organism, given the food, habitat, water and other necessities available within an environment is known as the environment's _____ for that organism. For the human population, more complex variables such as sanitation and medical care are sometimes considered as part of the necessary infrastructure.

As population density increases, birth rate often increases and death rates typically decrease.

a. Carrying capacity
b. 1-center problem
c. 2-3 heap
d. 120-cell

42. A _____ or logistic curve is the most common sigmoid curve. It models the S-curve of growth of some set P, where P might be thought of as population. The initial stage of growth is approximately exponential; then, as saturation begins, the growth slows, and at maturity, growth stops.

a. Spin-weighted spherical harmonics
b. Logistic function
c. Legendre forms
d. Jack function

43. In mathematics, a _____ is an expression constructed from variables and constants, using the operations of addition, subtraction, multiplication, and constant non-negative whole number exponents. For example, $x^2 - 4x + 7$ is a _____, but $x^2 - 4/x + 7x^{3/2}$ is not, because its second term involves division by the variable x and also because its third term contains an exponent that is not a whole number.

_____s are one of the most important concepts in algebra and throughout mathematics and science.

a. Coimage
b. Group extension
c. Semifield
d. Polynomial

44. _____ is the change in population over time, and can be quantified as the change in the number of individuals in a population using 'per unit time' for measurement. The term _____ can technically refer to any species, but almost always refers to humans, and it is often used informally for the more specific demographic term _____ rate, and is often used to refer specifically to the growth of the population of the world.

Simple models of _____ include the Malthusian Growth Model and the logistic model.

a. 1-center problem
b. Population dynamics
c. 120-cell
d. Population growth

45. In mathematics, an _____ is a statement about the relative size or order of two objects, or about whether they are the same or not

- The notation a < b means that a is less than b.
- The notation a > b means that a is greater than b.
- The notation a ≠ b means that a is not equal to b, but does not say that one is bigger than the other or even that they can be compared in size.

In all these cases, a is not equal to b, hence, '_____'.

Chapter 16. FURTHER TECHNIQUES AND APPLICATIONS OF INTEGRATION

These relations are known as strict _____

- The notation a ≤ b means that a is less than or equal to b;
- The notation a ≥ b means that a is greater than or equal to b;

An additional use of the notation is to show that one quantity is much greater than another, normally by several orders of magnitude.

- The notation a << b means that a is much less than b.
- The notation a >> b means that a is much greater than b.

If the sense of the _____ is the same for all values of the variables for which its members are defined, then the _____ is called an 'absolute' or 'unconditional' _____. If the sense of an _____ holds only for certain values of the variables involved, but is reversed or destroyed for other values of the variables, it is called a conditional _____.

An _____ may appear unsolvable because it only states whether a number is larger or smaller than another number; but it is possible to apply the same operations for equalities to inequalities. For example, to find x for the _____ 10x > 23 one would divide 23 by 10.

a. Inequality
c. A posteriori

b. A Mathematical Theory of Communication
d. A chemical equation

46. _____ is the mathematical operation of scaling one number by another. It is one of the four basic operations in elementary arithmetic.

_____ is defined for whole numbers in terms of repeated addition; for example, 4 multiplied by 3 can be calculated by adding 3 copies of 4 together:

$$4 + 4 + 4 = 12.$$

_____ of rational numbers and real numbers is defined by systematic generalization of this basic idea.

a. Multiplication
c. Least common multiple

b. Highest common factor
d. The number 0 is even.

47. In mathematics, a _____ is a natural number which has exactly two distinct natural number divisors: 1 and itself. An infinitude of _____s exists, as demonstrated by Euclid around 300 BC. The first twenty-five _____s are:

2, 3, 5, 7, 11, 13, 17, 19, 23, 29, 31, 37, 41, 43, 47, 53, 59, 61, 67, 71, 73, 79, 83, 89, 97.

a. Highly composite number
c. Prime number

b. Perrin number
d. Pronic number

Chapter 16. FURTHER TECHNIQUES AND APPLICATIONS OF INTEGRATION

48. A logistic function or _____ is the most common sigmoid curve. It models the S-curve of growth of some set P, where P might be thought of as population. The initial stage of growth is approximately exponential; then, as saturation begins, the growth slows, and at maturity, growth stops.
    a. Polylogarithm
    b. Logistic curve
    c. Logarithmic integral function
    d. Lambert W function

49. A _____ of a number is a number a such that $a^3 = x$.
    a. Golden function
    b. Cube root
    c. Hyperbolic functions
    d. Square root

50. In mathematics, a _____ is traditionally a map from a vector space to the field underlying the vector space, which is usually the real numbers. In other words, it is a function that takes a vector as its argument or input and returns a scalar. Its use goes back to the calculus of variations where one searches for a function which minimizes a certain _____.
    a. Derivation
    b. Functional
    c. Kernel
    d. Curl

51. A trapezoid or a _____ is a quadrilateral that has at least one pair of parallel lines for sides.

Some authors define it as a quadrilateral having exactly one pair of parallel sides, so as to exclude parallelograms, which otherwise would be regarded as a special type of trapezoid, but most mathematicians use the inclusive definition.

In North America, the term _____ is used to refer to a quadrilateral with no parallel sides.

   a. Lozenge
   b. Rhomboid
   c. Tangential quadrilateral
   d. Trapezium

52. A _____ or a trapezium is a quadrilateral that has at least one pair of parallel lines for sides.

Some authors define it as a quadrilateral having exactly one pair of parallel sides, so as to exclude parallelograms, which otherwise would be regarded as a special type of _____, but most mathematicians use the inclusive definition.

In North America, the term trapezium is used to refer to a quadrilateral with no parallel sides.

   a. Lozenge
   b. Trapezium
   c. Rhomboid
   d. Trapezoid

53. In mathematics, the trapezium rule or _____ is a way to approximately calculate the definite integral

$$\int_a^b f(x)\,dx.$$

Chapter 16. FURTHER TECHNIQUES AND APPLICATIONS OF INTEGRATION

The trapezium rule works by approximating the region under the graph of the function f by a trapezium and calculating its area. It follows that

$$\int_a^b f(x)\,dx \approx (b-a)\frac{f(a)+f(b)}{2}.$$

To calculate this integral more accurately, one first splits the interval of integration [a,b] into n smaller subintervals, and then applies the trapezium rule on each of them. One obtains the composite trapezium rule:

$$\int_a^b f(x)\,dx \approx \frac{b-a}{n}\left[\frac{f(a)+f(b)}{2}+\sum_{k=1}^{n-1} f\left(a+k\frac{b-a}{n}\right)\right].$$

This can alternatively be written as:

$$\int_a^b f(x)\,dx \approx \frac{b-a}{2n}\left(f(x_0)+2f(x_1)+2f(x_2)+\cdots+2f(x_{n-1})+f(x_n)\right)$$

where

$$x_k = a + k\frac{b-a}{n}, \text{ for } k=0,1,\ldots,n.$$

a. 120-cell
c. 2-3 heap
b. 1-center problem
d. Trapezoidal rule

54. In vascular plants, the _____ is the organ of a plant body that typically lies below the surface of the soil. This is not always the case, however, since a _____ can also be aerial (that is, growing above the ground) or aerating (that is, growing up above the ground or especially above water.) Furthermore, a stem normally occurring below ground is not exceptional either

a. 2-3 heap
c. 1-center problem
b. 120-cell
d. Root

Chapter 17. MULTIVARIABLE CALCULUS

1. In mathematics, a _____ is a statement that can be proved on the basis of explicitly stated or previously agreed assumptions.
   a. Theorem
   b. Logical value
   c. Disjunction introduction
   d. Boolean function

2. _____ calculus is the extension of calculus in one variable to calculus in several variables: the functions which are differentiated and integrated involve several variables rather than one variable.
   a. Convergence of measures
   b. Cook reduction
   c. Convex and concave
   d. Multivariable

3. _____ and independent variables refer to values that change in relationship to each other. The _____ are those that are observed to change in response to the independent variables. The independent variables are those that are deliberately manipulated to invoke a change in the _____.
   a. Yates analysis
   b. Dependent variables
   c. Steiner system
   d. Round robin test

4. In mathematics, especially in the area of abstract algebra known as ring theory, a _____ is a ring with $0 \neq 1$ such that $ab = 0$ implies that either $a = 0$ or $b = 0$. That is, it is a nontrivial ring without left or right zero divisors. A commutative _____ is called an integral _____.
   a. Domain
   b. Left primitive ring
   c. Simple ring
   d. Modular representation theory

5. Dependent variables and _____ refer to values that change in relationship to each other. The dependent variables are those that are observed to change in response to the _____. The _____ are those that are deliberately manipulated to invoke a change in the dependent variables.
   a. One-factor-at-a-time method
   b. Operational confound
   c. Independent variables
   d. Experimental design diagram

6. _____ is the extension of calculus in one variable to calculus in several variables: the functions which are differentiated and integrated involve several variables rather than one variable.

A study of limits and continuity in multiple dimensions yields many counter-intuitive and pathological results not demonstrated by single-variable functions. There exist, for example, scalar functions of two variables having points in their domain which, when approached along any arbitrary line, give a particular limit, yet give a different limit when approached along a parabola.

   a. Multivariable calculus
   b. Surface integral
   c. Shift theorem
   d. Total derivative

7. In mathematics, a _____ is a system which is not linear. Less technically, a _____ is any problem where the variabl to be solved for cannot be written as a linear sum of independent components. A nonhomogenous system, which is linear apart from the presence of a function of the independent variables, is nonlinear according to a strict definition, but such systems are usually studied alongside linear systems, because they can be transformed to a linear system as long as a particular solution is known.
   a. Metric system
   b. George Dantzig
   c. 1-center problem
   d. Nonlinear system

Chapter 17. MULTIVARIABLE CALCULUS

8. In descriptive statistics, the _____ is the length of the smallest interval which contains all the data. It is calculated by subtracting the smallest observations from the greatest and provides an indication of statistical dispersion.

It is measured in the same units as the data.

   a. Bandwidth
   b. Kernel
   c. Class
   d. Range

9. In mathematics, an _____, or central tendency of a data set refers to a measure of the 'middle' or 'expected' value of the data set. There are many different descriptive statistics that can be chosen as a measurement of the central tendency of the data items.

An _____ is a single value that is meant to typify a list of values.

   a. A Mathematical Theory of Communication
   b. Average
   c. A posteriori
   d. A chemical equation

10. _____ is a branch of mathematics that includes the study of limits, derivatives, integrals, and infinite series, and constitutes a major part of modern university education. Historically, it has been referred to as 'the _____ of infinitesimals', or 'infinitesimal _____'. Most basically, _____ is the study of change, in the same way that geometry is the study of space.
   a. Calculus
   b. Partial sum
   c. Hyperbolic angle
   d. Test for Divergence

11. The multiple integral is a type of definite integral extended to functions of more than one real variable, for example, $fz = x^2 + y^2$. The rectangular region at the bottom of the body is the domain of integration, while the surface is the graph of the two-variable function to be integrated.

Introduction

Just as the definite integral of a positive function of one variable represents the area of the region between the graph of the function and the x-axis, the _____ of a positive function of two variables represents the volume of the region between the surface defined by the function and the plane which contains its domain.

   a. Double integral
   b. Risch algorithm
   c. Signed measure
   d. Solid of revolution

12. The mathematical concept of a _____ expresses the intuitive idea of deterministic dependence between two quantities, one of which is viewed as primary and the other as secondary. A _____ then is a way to associate a unique output for each input of a specified type, for example, a real number or an element of a given set.
   a. Going up
   b. Coherent
   c. Grill
   d. Function

13. In commutative algebra, the notions of an element _____ over a ring, and of an _____ extension of rings, are a generalization of the notions in field theory of an element being algebraic over a field, and of an algebraic extension of fields.

Chapter 17. MULTIVARIABLE CALCULUS

The special case of greatest interest in number theory is that of complex numbers _____ over the ring of integers Z.

The term ring will be understood to mean commutative ring with a unit.

- a. Integral
- b. Arc length
- c. Antidifferentiation
- d. Integral test for convergence

14. The word _____ means curving in or hollowed inward.
    - a. Harmonic series
    - b. Concavity
    - c. Key server
    - d. Clipping

15. In quantum field theory and statistical mechanics in the thermodynamic limit, a system with a global symmetry can have more than one phase. For parameters where the symmetry is spontaneously broken, the system is said to be _____. When the global symmetry is unbroken the system is disordered.
    - a. Ordered
    - b. Ursell function
    - c. Einstein relation
    - d. Isoenthalpic-isobaric ensemble

16. In mathematics, a _____ is, informally, an infinitely vast and infinitely thin sheet. _____s may be thought of as objects in some higher dimensional space, or they may be considered without any outside space, as in the setting of Euclidean geometry
    - a. Blocking
    - b. Group
    - c. Bandwidth
    - d. Plane

17. In mathematics, a level set of a real-valued function f of n variables is a set of the form

    $\{ [x_1,...,x_n] \mid f[x_1,...,x_n] = c \}$

    where c is a constant. That is, it is the set where the function takes on a given constant value.

    When the number of variables is two, this is a _____, if it is three this is a level surface, and for higher values of n the level set is a level hypersurface.

    - a. Shift theorem
    - b. Parametric equations
    - c. Multipole moment
    - d. Level curve

18. In mathematics, a _____ is a quadric surface of special kind. There are two kinds of _____s: elliptic and hyperbolic. The elliptic _____ is shaped like an oval cup and can have a maximum or minimum point.
    - a. Paraboloid
    - b. Spheroid
    - c. Dupin cyclide
    - d. Homoeoid

Chapter 17. MULTIVARIABLE CALCULUS

19. In mathematics, specifically in topology, a _____ is a two-dimensional manifold. The most familiar examples are those that arise as the boundaries of solid objects in ordinary three-dimensional Euclidean space, $E³$. On the other hand, there are also more exotic _____s, that are so 'contorted' that they cannot be embedded in three-dimensional space at all.
   a. Standard torus
   b. Cross-cap
   c. Homoeoid
   d. Surface

20. In linear algebra, the _____ of an n-by-n square matrix A is defined to be the sum of the elements on the main diagonal of A. wikimedia.org/math/8/2/b/82be32fa00bd97ebbc066aec3dfe72da.png">

   where a_{ij} represents the entry on the ith row and jth column of A. Equivalently, the _____ of a matrix is the sum of its eigenvalues, making it an invariant with respect to a change of basis.

   a. Constructivism
   b. Lattice
   c. Blinding
   d. Trace

21. In mathematics, the concept of a _____ tries to capture the intuitive idea of a geometrical one-dimensional and continuous object. A simple example is the circle. In everyday use of the term '_____', a straight line is not curved, but in mathematical parlance _____s include straight lines and line segments.
   a. Quadrifolium
   b. Negative pedal curve
   c. Kappa curve
   d. Curve

22. _____ is a geometric model of the physical universe in which we live. The three dimensions are commonly called length, width, and depth (or height), although any three mutually perpendicular directions can serve as the three dimensions.

   In physics, our _____ is viewed as embedded in 4-dimensional space-time, called Minkowski space (see special relativity.)

   a. Surface of constant width
   b. Steinmetz solid
   c. Solid geometry
   d. Three-dimensional space

23. In economics, the _____ functional form of production functions is widely used to represent the relationship of an output to inputs. It was proposed by Knut Wicksell, and tested against statistical evidence by Paul Douglas and Charles Cobb in 1928.
   a. State price vector
   b. Cobb-Douglas
   c. Burden of proof
   d. State price

24. In economics, a _____ is a function that specifies the output of a firm, an industry, or an entire economy for all combinations of inputs. A meta-_____ compares the practice of the existing entities converting inputs X into output y to determine the most efficient practice _____ of the existing entities, whether the most efficient feasible practice production or the most efficient actual practice production. In either case, the maximum output of a technologically-determined production process is a mathematical function of input factors of production.
   a. Long-run
   b. Production function
   c. 1-center problem
   d. Short-run

25. An _____ is a type of quadric surface that is a higher dimensional analogue of an ellipse. The equation of a standard _____ body in an xyz-Cartesian coordinate system is

$$\frac{x^2}{a^2} + \frac{y^2}{b^2} + \frac{z^2}{c^2} = 1$$

where a and b are the equatorial radii and c is the polar radius, all of which are fixed positive real numbers determining the shape of the _____.

If all three radii are equal, the solid body is a sphere; if two radii are equal, the _____ is a spheroid:

- $a = b = c$: Sphere;
- c:,!" src="http://upload.wikimedia.org/math/1/c/1/1c101f69cb5c9fca2549cc52aa371d02.png"> Oblate spheroid;
- $a = b < c$: Prolate spheroid;
- b>c:,!" src="http://upload.wikimedia.org/math/f/f/4/ff41a00b219ea3edb0d41dce4d26cc46.png"> Scalene _____.

The points, and lie on the surface and the line segments from the origin to these points are called the semi-principal axes. These correspond to the semi-major axis and semi-minor axis of the appropriate ellipses.

a. A posteriori
b. A chemical equation
c. A Mathematical Theory of Communication
d. Ellipsoid

26. In mathematics, a _____ is a quadric, a type of surface in three dimensions, described by the equation

$$\frac{x^2}{a^2} + \frac{y^2}{b^2} - \frac{z^2}{c^2} = 1$$

or

$$-\frac{x^2}{a^2} - \frac{y^2}{b^2} + \frac{z^2}{c^2} = 1$$

If, and only if, a = b, it is a _____ of revolution. A _____ of revolution of one sheet can be obtained by revolving a hyperbola around its semi-minor axis.

a. Hyperboloid of two sheets
b. Hyperboloid
c. 120-cell
d. 1-center problem

27. In mathematical optimization, the method of _____s is a method for finding the maximum/minimum of a function subject to constraints.

Chapter 17. MULTIVARIABLE CALCULUS

For example if we want to solve:

$$\text{maximize } f(x, y)$$
$$\text{subject to } g(x, y) = c$$

We introduce a new variable called a _____ to rewrite the problem as:

$$\text{maximize } f(x, y) + \lambda(g(x, y) - c)$$

Solving this new unconstrained problem for x, y, and λ will give us the solution for our original constrained problem.

Introduction

Consider a two-dimensional case.

a. 120-cell
b. 1-center problem
c. Radfar ratio
d. Lagrange multiplier

28. In mathematics, a _____ of a function of several variables is its derivative with respect to one of those variables with the others held constant. _____s are useful in vector calculus and differential geometry.

The _____ of a function f with respect to the variable x is written as f_x, $\partial_x f$, or $\partial f/\partial x$.

a. Laplacian
b. Critical number
c. Laplace invariant
d. Partial derivative

29. _____ is a fundamental construction of differential calculus and admits many possible generalizations within the fields of mathematical analysis, combinatorics, algebra, and geometry.

In real, complex, and functional analysis, _____s are generalized to functions of several real or complex variables and functions between topological vector spaces. An important case is the variational _____ in the calculus of variations.

a. Lin-Tsien equation
b. Functional derivative
c. Derivative
d. Metric derivative

30. In Fourier analysis, a _____ is a kind of linear operator, or transformation of functions. These operators multiply the Fourier coefficients of a function by a specified function, hence the name. Among the multipliers one can count some simple operators, such as translations and differentiation, but also some more complicated ones such as the convolutions, Hilbert transform, and others.

Chapter 17. MULTIVARIABLE CALCULUS

a. Fourier multiplier
c. Poisson summation formula
b. Reality condition
d. Modulated complex lapped transform

31. In calculus, the _____ is a formula for the derivative of the composite of two functions.

In intuitive terms, if a variable, y, depends on a second variable, u, which in turn depends on a third variable, x, then the rate of change of y with respect to x can be computed as the rate of change of y with respect to u multiplied by the rate of change of u with respect to x. Schematically,

$$\frac{dy}{dx} = \frac{dy}{du} \cdot \frac{du}{dx}.$$

For an explanation of notation used in this section, see Function composition.

The _____ states that, under appropriate conditions,

$$(f \circ g)'(x) = f'(g(x))g'(x),$$

which in short form is written as

$$(f \circ g)' = f' \circ g \cdot g'.$$

Alternatively, in the Leibniz notation, the _____ is

$$\frac{dy}{dx} = \frac{dy}{du} \cdot \frac{du}{dx}.$$

In integration, the counterpart to the _____ is the substitution rule.

a. Product rule
c. Chain rule
b. 120-cell
d. 1-center problem

32. _____ is a quantity expressing the two-dimensional size of a defined part of a surface, typically a region bounded by a closed curve. The term surface _____ refers to the total _____ of the exposed surface of a 3-dimensional solid, such as the sum of the _____ s of the exposed sides of a polyhedron. _____ is an important invariant in the differential geometry of surfaces.

a. Area
c. A chemical equation
b. A posteriori
d. A Mathematical Theory of Communication

33. A _____ is a software program that facilitates symbolic mathematics. The core functionality of a CAS is manipulation of mathematical expressions in symbolic form.

Chapter 17. MULTIVARIABLE CALCULUS

The symbolic manipulations supported typically include

- simplification to the smallest possible expression or some standard form, including automatic simplification with assumptions and simplification with constraints
- substitution of symbolic, functors or numeric values for expressions
- change of form of expressions: expanding products and powers, partial and full factorization, rewriting as partial fractions, constraint satisfaction, rewriting trigonometric functions as exponentials, etc.
- partial and total differentiation
- symbolic constrained and unconstrained global optimization
- solution of linear and some non-linear equations over various domains
- solution of some differential and difference equations
- taking some limits
- some indefinite and definite integration, including multidimensional integrals
- integral transforms
- arbitrary-precision numeric operations
- Series operations such as expansion, summation and products
- matrix operations including products, inverses, etc.
- display of mathematical expressions in two-dimensional mathematical form, often using typesetting systems similar to TeX
- add-ons for use in applied mathematics such as physics packages for physical computation
- plotting graphs and parametric plots of functions in two and three dimensions, and animating them
- APIs for linking it on an external program such as a database, or using in a programming language to use the _____
- drawing charts and diagrams
- string manipulation such as matching and searching
- statistical computation
- Theorem proving and verification
- graphic production and editing such as CGI and signal processing as image processing
- sound synthesis

Many also include a programming language, allowing users to implement their own algorithms.

Some _____s focus on a specific area of application; these are typically developed in academia and are free.

a. 1-center problem
c. 120-cell
b. Computer algebra system
d. 2-3 heap

34. _____ is a phenomenon which arises in the region of a continuous phase transition. Originally reported by Thomas Andrews in 1869 for the liquid-gas transition in carbon dioxide, many other examples have been discovered since. The phenomenon is most commonly demonstrated in binary fluid mixtures, such as methanol and cyclohexane.
a. Critical temperature
c. Fermi point
b. Percolation threshold
d. Critical opalescence

Chapter 17. MULTIVARIABLE CALCULUS

35. _____ of an object is its speed in a particular direction.
   a. Discontinuity
   b. Rolle's Theorem
   c. Velocity
   d. Maxima

36. In mathematics and in the sciences, a _____ (plural: _____e, formulæ or _____s) is a concise way of expressing information symbolically (as in a mathematical or chemical _____), or a general relationship between quantities. One of many famous _____e is Albert Einstein's $E = mc^2$ (see special relativity

In mathematics, a _____ is a key to solve an equation with variables. For example, the problem of determining the volume of a sphere is one that requires a significant amount of integral calculus to solve.

   a. 2-3 heap
   b. 120-cell
   c. Formula
   d. 1-center problem

37. In mathematics, _____ and minima, known collectively as extrema, are the largest value or smallest value, that a function takes in a point either within a given neighbourhood or on the function domain in its entirety.

A real-valued function f' defined on the real line is said to have a local maximum point at the point x^*, if there exists some ε > 0, such that f≥ f½x − x*| < ε. The value of the function at this point is called maximum of the function.

   a. Decimal system
   b. Field
   c. Maxima
   d. Descent

38. _____ are points in the domain of a function at which the function takes a largest value or smallest value, either within a given neighborhood or on the function domain in its entirety.
   a. Minima
   b. Test for Divergence
   c. Calculus controversy
   d. Maxima and minima

39. In mathematics, maxima and _____, known collectively as extrema, are the largest value or smallest value, that a function takes in a point either within a given neighbourhood or on the function domain in its entirety.

A real-valued function f' defined on the real line is said to have a local maximum point at the point x^*, if there exists some ε > 0, such that f≥ f½x − x*| < ε. The value of the function at this point is called maximum of the function.

   a. Periodic function
   b. Minima
   c. Dirichlet integral
   d. Calculus

40. In mathematics, a _____ is a point on the domain of a function where:

   - one dimension: the derivative is equal to zero or a point where the function ceases to be differentiable.
   - in general: there are two distinct concepts: either the derivative vanishes, or it is not of full rank; these agree in one dimension.

Chapter 17. MULTIVARIABLE CALCULUS

Note that in one dimension, a critical value or critical number x of function f is the domain element at which the derivative is zero or undefined, whereas the associated ordered pair is the _____. In higher dimensions a critical value is in the range whereas a _____ is in the domain.

There are two situations in which a point becomes a _____ of a function of one variable. The first of which is that the value of the derivative is equal to zero.

a. Going up
b. Decimal system
c. Derivative algebra
d. Critical point

41. In mathematics, a _____ is a point in the domain of a function of two variables which is a stationary point but not a local extremum. At such a point, in general, the surface resembles a saddle that curves up in one direction, and curves down in a different direction. In terms of contour lines, a _____ can be recognized, in general, by a contour that appears to intersect itself.

a. Gauss-Codazzi equations
b. 1-center problem
c. Gauss map
d. Saddle point

42. Let f be a differentiable function, and let f'(x) be its derivative. The derivative of f'(x) (if it has one) is written f''(x) and is called the _____ of f. Similarly, the derivative of a _____, if it exists, is written f'''(x) and is called the third derivative of f.

a. 1-center problem
b. 120-cell
c. 2-3 heap
d. Second derivative

43. In calculus, a branch of mathematics, the _____ is a criterion often useful for determining whether a given stationary point of a function is a local maximum or a local minimum.

The test states: If the function f is twice differentiable in a neighborhood of a stationary point x, meaning that $f'(x) = 0$, then:

- If $f''(x) < 0$ then f has a local maximum at x.
- If 0" src="http://upload.wikimedia.org/math/e/0/0/e000178f7f6b9c3307e0f9e4e9e077e9.png"> then f has a local minimum at x.
- If $f''(x) = 0$, the _____ says nothing about the point x.

In the last case, the function may have a local maximum or minimum there, but the function is sufficiently 'flat' that this is undetected by the second derivative. In this case one has to examine the third derivative. Such an example is f4.

a. Differentiation under the integral sign
b. Normal derivative
c. Functional derivative
d. Second derivative test

44. In linear algebra, _____ is a version of Gaussian elimination that puts zeros both above and below each pivot element as it goes from the top row of the given matrix to the bottom. In other words, _____ brings a matrix to reduced row echelon form, whereas Gaussian elimination takes it only as far as row echelon form. Every matrix has a reduced row echelon form, and this algorithm is guaranteed to produce it.
   a. Spheroidal wave functions
   b. Gauss-Jordan elimination
   c. Lax equivalence theorem
   d. Conservation form

45. In mathematics, a _____ is a condition that a solution to an optimization problem must satisfy. There are two types of _____s: equality _____s and inequality _____s. The set of solutions that satisfy all _____s is called the feasible set.
   a. Foci
   b. Concurrent
   c. Constraint
   d. Decidable

46. The _____ of any solid, plasma, vacuum or theoretical object is how much three-dimensional space it occupies, often quantified numerically. One-dimensional figures and two-dimensional shapes are assigned zero _____ in the three-dimensional space. _____ is presented as ml or cm³.

   _____s of straight-edged and circular shapes are calculated using arithmetic formulae.

   a. Thermodynamic limit
   b. Stress-energy tensor
   c. Cauchy momentum equation
   d. Volume

47. Suppose that φ : M → N is a smooth map between smooth manifolds; then the _____ of φ at a point x is, in some sense, the best linear approximation of φ near x. It can be viewed as generalization of the total derivative of ordinary calculus. Explicitly, it is a linear map from the tangent space of M at x to the tangent space of N at φ
   a. Grill
   b. Differential
   c. Boundary
   d. Concurrent

48. _____s is concerned with the tasks of developing and applying quantitative or statistical methods to the study and elucidation of economic principles. _____s combines economic theory with statistics to analyze and test economic relationships. Theoretical _____s considers questions about the statistical properties of estimators and tests, while applied _____s is concerned with the application of _____ methods to assess economic theories.
   a. Economic
   b. A chemical equation
   c. Econometric
   d. A Mathematical Theory of Communication

49. In mathematics, a _____ is a certain kind of ordinary differential equation which is widely used in physics and engineering.

Given a simply connected and open subset D of R² and two functions I and J which are continuous on D then an implicit first-order ordinary differential equation of the form

$$I(x,y)\,dx + J(x,y)\,dy = 0,$$

is called exact differential equation if there exists a continuously differentiable function F, called the potential function, so that

$$\frac{\partial F}{\partial x}(x,y) = I$$

and

$$\frac{\partial F}{\partial y}(x,y) = J.$$

The nomenclature of 'exact differential equation' refers to the exact derivative (or total derivative) of a function. For a function F $(x_0, x_1, ..., x_{n-1}, x_n)$, the exact or total derivative with respect to x_0 is given by

$$\frac{dF}{dx_0} = \frac{\partial F}{\partial x_0} + \sum_{i=1}^{n} \frac{\partial F}{\partial x_i} \frac{dx_i}{dx_0}.$$

The function

$$F(x,y) := \frac{1}{2}(x^2 + y^2)$$

is a potential function for the differential equation

$$xx' + yy' = 0.$$

In physical applications the functions I and J are usually not only continuous but even continuously differentiable.

a. Sturm-Liouville equation
c. Total differential equation
b. Riccati equation
d. Wronskian

50. In the absence of a more specific context, convergence denotes the approach toward a definite value, as time goes on; or to a definite point, a common view or opinion, or toward a fixed or equilibrium state. _____ is the adjectival form, and also a noun meaning an iterative approximation.

In mathematics, convergence describes limiting behaviour, particularly of an infinite sequence or series, toward some limit.

a. Convergent
c. Prime ideal theorem
b. Separable
d. Word problem

Chapter 17. MULTIVARIABLE CALCULUS

51. In grammatical theory, definiteness is a feature of noun phrases, distinguishing between entities which are specific and identifiable in a given context (_____ noun phrases) and entities which are not (indefinite noun phrases Examples are:

- Free form: English the boy.
- Phrasal clitic: as in Basque: Cf. emakume ('woman'), emakume-a (woman-ART: 'the woman'), emakume ederr-a (woman beautiful-ART: 'the beautiful woman')
- Noun affix: as in Romanian: om ('man'), om-ul (man-ART: 'the man'); om-ul bun (man-ART good: 'the good man')
- Prefix on both noun and adjective: Arabic ا„ƒªØ§Ø¨ ا„ƒØ¨ÙŠØ± (al-kitÄ b al-kabÄ«r) with two instances of al- (DEF-book-DEF-big, literally, 'the book the big')

Germanic, Romance, Celtic, Semitic, and auxiliary languages generally have a _____ article, sometimes used as a postposition. Many other languages do not.

    a. Sentence diagram   b. 1-center problem
    c. Definite   d. Syntax

52. In combinatorial mathematics, a _____ is an un-ordered collection of distinct elements, usually of a prescribed size and taken from a given set. Given such a set S, a _____ of elements of S is just a subset of S, where as always forsets the order of the elements is not taken into account. Also, as always forsets, no elements can be repeated more than once in a _____; this is often referred to as a 'collection without repetition'.

    a. Heawood number   b. Sparsity
    c. Combination   d. Fill-in

53. In calculus, an antiderivative, primitive or _____ of a function f is a function F whose derivative is equal to f. The process of solving for antiderivatives is antidifferentiation. Antiderivatives are related to definite integrals through the fundamental theorem of calculus, and provide a convenient means for calculating the definite integrals of many functions.

    a. Integral   b. Integral test for convergence
    c. Indefinite Integral   d. Integration by parts operator

54. The _____ specifies the relationship between the two central operations of calculus, differentiation and integration.

The first part of the theorem, sometimes called the first _____, shows that an indefinite integration can be reversed by a differentiation.

The second part, sometimes called the second _____, allows one to compute the definite integral of a function by using any one of its infinitely many antiderivatives.

    a. Standard part function   b. Fundamental Theorem of Calculus
    c. Maxima and minima   d. Hyperbolic angle

55. _____ is a core concept of basic mathematics, specifically in the fields of infinitesimal calculus and mathematical analysis. Given a function f

$$\int_a^b f(x)\,dx,$$

is equal to the area of a region in the xy-plane bounded by the graph of f, the x-axis, and the vertical lines x = a and x = b, with areas below the x-axis being subtracted.

The term 'integral' may also refer to the notion of antiderivative, a function F whose derivative is the given function f.

a. Epigraph
b. Integration
c. OMAC
d. Apex

56. The _____ program is a directory search utility on Unix-like platforms. It searches through one or more directory trees of a filesystem, locating files based on some user-specified criteria. By default, _____ returns all files below the current working directory.

a. Find
b. 2-3 heap
c. 1-center problem
d. 120-cell

57. In mathematics, specifically in combinatorial commutative algebra, a convex lattice polytope P is called _____ if it has the following property: given any positive integer n, every lattice point of the dilation nP, obtained from P by scaling its vertices by the factor n and taking the convex hull of the resulting points, can be written as the sum of exactly n lattice points in P. This property plays an important role in the theory of toric varieties, where it corresponds to projective normality of the toric variety determined by P.

The simplex in R^k with the vertices at the origin and along the unit coordinate vectors is _____.

a. Polytetrahedron
b. Normal
c. Demihypercubes
d. Hypercube

58. In mathematics, the concept of a '_____' is used to describe the behavior of a function as its argument or input either 'gets close' to some point, or as the argument becomes arbitrarily large; or the behavior of a sequence's elements as their index increases indefinitely. _____s are used in calculus and other branches of mathematical analysis to define derivatives and continuity.

In formulas, _____ is usually abbreviated as lim.

a. Contact
b. Copula
c. Duality
d. Limit

59. In mathematics, a _____ of a set S in a topological space X is a point x in X that can be 'approximated' by points of S other than x itself. This concept profitably generalizes the notion of a limit and is the underpinning of concepts such as closed set and topological closure. Indeed, a set is closed if and only if it contains all of its _____s, and the topological closure operation can be thought of as an operation that enriches a set by adding its _____s.

a. 1-center problem
c. 2-3 heap
b. 120-cell
d. Limit point

Chapter 18. PROBABILITY AND CALCULUS

1. In probability theory, a probability distribution is called _____ if its cumulative distribution function is _____. That is equivalent to saying that for random variables X with the distribution in question, Pr[X = a] = 0 for all real numbers a. If the distribution of X is _____ then X is called a _____ random variable.
   a. Concatenated codes
   b. Continuous
   c. Continuous phase modulation
   d. Conull set

2. _____ is the likelihood or chance that something is the case or will happen. Theoretical _____ is used extensively in areas such as statistics, mathematics, science and philosophy to draw conclusions about the likelihood of potential events and the underlying mechanics of complex systems.

   The word _____ does not have a consistent direct definition.

   a. Discrete random variable
   b. Statistical significance
   c. Standardized moment
   d. Probability

3. In mathematics, _____ are used in the study of chance and probability. They were developed to assist in the analysis of games of chance, stochastic events, and the results of scientific experiments by capturing only the mathematical properties necessary to answer probabilistic questions. Further formalizations have firmly grounded the entity in the theoretical domains of mathematics by making use of measure theory.
   a. Statistics
   b. Statistical dispersion
   c. Median polish
   d. Random variables

4. The mathematical concept of a _____ expresses the intuitive idea of deterministic dependence between two quantities, one of which is viewed as primary and the other as secondary. A _____ then is a way to associate a unique output for each input of a specified type, for example, a real number or an element of a given set.
   a. Coherent
   b. Going up
   c. Grill
   d. Function

5. In ecology, predation describes a biological interaction where a _____ (an organism that is hunting) feeds on its prey, the organism that is attacked. _____s may or may not kill their prey prior to feeding on them, but the act of predation always results in the death of the prey. The other main category of consumption is detritivory, the consumption of dead organic material (detritus.)
   a. Prey
   b. 120-cell
   c. Predator
   d. 1-center problem

6. In differential geometry, a discipline within mathematics, a _____ is a subset of the tangent bundle of a manifold satisfying certain properties. _____s are used to build up notions of integrability, and specifically of a foliation of a manifold
   a. Discontinuity
   b. Constraint
   c. Coherence
   d. Distribution

7. The _____ or Dirac's delta is a mathematical construct introduced by the British theoretical physicist Paul Dirac. Informally, it is a function representing an infinitely sharp peak bounding unit area: a function that has the value zero everywhere except at x = 0 where its value is infinitely large in such a way that its total integral is 1. It is a continuous analogue of the discrete Kronecker delta.

a. Dirac delta
b. Schwartz kernel theorem
c. Hyperfunction
d. Weak derivative

8. In statistics, a _____ is a graphical display of tabulated frequencies, shown as bars. It shows what proportion of cases fall into each of several categories. A _____ differs from a bar chart in that it is the area of the bar that denotes the value, not the height as in bar charts, a crucial distinction when the categories are not of uniform width.
   a. Histogram
   b. First-hitting-time models
   c. Standardized moment
   d. Probability distribution

9. In elementary algebra, a _____ is a polynomial with two terms: the sum of two monomials. It is the simplest kind of polynomial except for a monomial.

The _____ $a^2 - b^2$ can be factored as the product of two other _____s:

$a^2 - b^2$.

The product of a pair of linear _____s $ax + b$ and $cx + d$ is:

$2 + x + bd$.

A _____ raised to the nth power, represented as

n

can be expanded by means of the _____ theorem or, equivalently, using Pascal's triangle.

   a. Rational root theorem
   b. Cylindrical algebraic decomposition
   c. Real structure
   d. Binomial

10. _____ typically deals with the probability of several successive decisions, each of which has two possible outcomes.

The probability of an event can be expressed as a _____ if its outcomes can be broken down into two probabilities p and q, where p and q are complementary For example, tossing a coin can be either heads or tails, each which have a probability of 0.5. Rolling a four on a six-sided die can be expressed as the probability of getting a 4 or the probability of rolling something else.

   a. Marginal distribution
   b. Quantile
   c. Markov chain
   d. Binomial probability

11. In probability theory and statistics, the _____ of a random variable is the integral of the random variable with respect to its probability measure. For discrete random variables this is equivalent to the probability-weighted sum of the possible values, and for continuous random variables with a density function it is the probability density -weighted integral of the possible values.

Chapter 18. PROBABILITY AND CALCULUS

The _____ may be intuitively understood by the law of large numbers: The _____, when it exists, is almost surely the limit of the sample mean as sample size grows to infinity.

a. Expected value
c. Illustration

b. Infinitely divisible distribution
d. Event

12. In probability theory and statistics, a _____ identifies either the probability of each value of an unidentified random variable, or the probability of the value falling within a particular interval. The probability function describes the range of possible values that a random variable can attain and the probability that the value of the random variable is within any subset of that range.

When the random variable takes values in the set of real numbers, the _____ is completely described by the cumulative distribution function, whose value at each real x is the probability that the random variable is smaller than or equal to x.

a. Z-test
c. Normal distribution

b. Statistical graphics
d. Probability Distribution

13. In probability theory and statistics, the _____ of a random variable, probability distribution averaging the squared distance of its possible values from the expected value. Whereas the mean is a way to describe the location of a distribution, the _____ is a way to capture its scale or degree of being spread out. The unit of _____ is the square of the unit of the original variable.

a. Nonlinear regression
c. Probability distribution

b. Kendall tau rank correlation coefficient
d. Variance

14. In mathematics, a _____ is a function that represents a probability distribution in terms of integrals.

Formally, a probability distribution has density f, if f is a non-negative Lebesgue-integrable function $\mathbb{R} \to \mathbb{R}$ such that the probability of the interval [a, b] is given by

$$\int_a^b f(x)\, dx$$

for any two numbers a and b. This implies that the total integral of f must be 1.

a. Quantile
c. Pseudocount

b. Law of total variance
d. Probability density function

15. The _____ of a material is defined as its mass per unit volume:

$$\rho = \frac{m}{V}$$

Different materials usually have different densities, so _____ is an important concept regarding buoyancy, metal purity and packaging.

In some cases _____ is expressed as the dimensionless quantities specific gravity or relative _____, in which case it is expressed in multiples of the _____ of some other standard material, usually water or air.

In a well-known story, Archimedes was given the task of determining whether King Hiero's goldsmith was embezzling gold during the manufacture of a wreath dedicated to the gods and replacing it with another, cheaper alloy.

a. 2-3 heap
b. 120-cell
c. Density
d. 1-center problem

16. In calculus, an _____ is the limit of a definite integral as an endpoint of the interval of integration approaches either a specified real number or ∞ or −∞ or, in some cases, as both endpoints approach limits.

Specifically, an _____ is a limit of the form

$$\lim_{b \to \infty} \int_a^b f(x)\, dx, \qquad \lim_{a \to -\infty} \int_a^b f(x)\, dx,$$

or of the form

$$\lim_{c \to b^-} \int_a^c f(x)\, dx, \qquad \lim_{c \to a^+} \int_c^b f(x)\, dx,$$

in which one takes a limit in one or the other endpoints . _____s may also occur at an interior point of the domain of integration, or at multiple such points.

a. Infinite product
b. Improper integral
c. Isoperimetric dimension
d. Elliptic boundary value problem

17. In commutative algebra, the notions of an element _____ over a ring, and of an _____ extension of rings, are a generalization of the notions in field theory of an element being algebraic over a field, and of an algebraic extension of fields.

The special case of greatest interest in number theory is that of complex numbers _____ over the ring of integers Z.

The term ring will be understood to mean commutative ring with a unit.

Chapter 18. PROBABILITY AND CALCULUS

a. Antidifferentiation
b. Integral
c. Integral test for convergence
d. Arc length

18. A _____ is a software program that facilitates symbolic mathematics. The core functionality of a CAS is manipulation of mathematical expressions in symbolic form.

The symbolic manipulations supported typically include

- simplification to the smallest possible expression or some standard form, including automatic simplification with assumptions and simplification with constraints
- substitution of symbolic, functors or numeric values for expressions
- change of form of expressions: expanding products and powers, partial and full factorization, rewriting as partial fractions, constraint satisfaction, rewriting trigonometric functions as exponentials, etc.
- partial and total differentiation
- symbolic constrained and unconstrained global optimization
- solution of linear and some non-linear equations over various domains
- solution of some differential and difference equations
- taking some limits
- some indefinite and definite integration, including multidimensional integrals
- integral transforms
- arbitrary-precision numeric operations
- Series operations such as expansion, summation and products
- matrix operations including products, inverses, etc.
- display of mathematical expressions in two-dimensional mathematical form, often using typesetting systems similar to TeX
- add-ons for use in applied mathematics such as physics packages for physical computation
- plotting graphs and parametric plots of functions in two and three dimensions, and animating them
- APIs for linking it on an external program such as a database, or using in a programming language to use the _____
- drawing charts and diagrams
- string manipulation such as matching and searching
- statistical computation
- Theorem proving and verification
- graphic production and editing such as CGI and signal processing as image processing
- sound synthesis

Many also include a programming language, allowing users to implement their own algorithms.

Some _____s focus on a specific area of application; these are typically developed in academia and are free.

a. 1-center problem
b. Computer algebra system
c. 2-3 heap
d. 120-cell

Chapter 18. PROBABILITY AND CALCULUS

19. In the absence of a more specific context, convergence denotes the approach toward a definite value, as time goes on; or to a definite point, a common view or opinion, or toward a fixed or equilibrium state. _____ is the adjectival form, and also a noun meaning an iterative approximation.

In mathematics, convergence describes limiting behaviour, particularly of an infinite sequence or series, toward some limit.

a. Separable
b. Convergent
c. Word problem
d. Prime ideal theorem

20. In linear algebra, _____ is a version of Gaussian elimination that puts zeros both above and below each pivot element as it goes from the top row of the given matrix to the bottom. In other words, _____ brings a matrix to reduced row echelon form, whereas Gaussian elimination takes it only as far as row echelon form. Every matrix has a reduced row echelon form, and this algorithm is guaranteed to produce it.

a. Conservation form
b. Lax equivalence theorem
c. Spheroidal wave functions
d. Gauss-Jordan elimination

21. In probability theory, a probability distribution is called discrete if it is characterized by a probability mass function. Thus, the distribution of a random variable X is discrete, and X is then called a _____, if

$$\sum_u \Pr(X = u) = 1$$

as u runs through the set of all possible values of X.

If a random variable is discrete, then the set of all values that it can assume with non-zero probability is finite or countably infinite, because the sum of uncountably many positive real numbers always diverges to infinity.

a. First-hitting-time models
b. Regression toward the mean
c. Statistics
d. Discrete random variable

22. In statistics, _____ has two related meanings:

- the arithmetic _____.
- the expected value of a random variable, which is also called the population _____.

It is sometimes stated that the '_____' _____s average. This is incorrect if '_____' is taken in the specific sense of 'arithmetic _____' as there are different types of averages: the _____, median, and mode. For instance, average house prices almost always use the median value for the average.

For a real-valued random variable X, the _____ is the expectation of X.

a. Statistical population
b. Proportional hazards model
c. Probability
d. Mean

Chapter 18. PROBABILITY AND CALCULUS

23. In probability theory and statistics, the _____ is the discrete probability distribution of the number of successes in a sequence of n independent yes/no experiments, each of which yields success with probability p. Such a success/failure experiment is also called a Bernoulli experiment or Bernoulli trial. In fact, when n = 1, the _____ is a Bernoulli distribution.
   a. Biostatistics
   b. Median
   c. Binomial distribution
   d. Coefficient of variation

24. In mathematics, a _____ of a number x is a number r such that r^2 = x, or, in other words, a number r whose square is x. Every non-negative real number x has a unique non-negative _____, called the principal _____, which is denoted with a radical symbol as $\sqrt{x}$, or, using exponent notation, as $x^{1/2}$. For example, the principal _____ of 9 is 3, denoted $\sqrt{9}$ = 3, because 3^2 = 3 × 3 = 9.
   a. Double exponential
   b. Multiplicative inverse
   c. Hyperbolic functions
   d. Square root

25. In probability and statistics, the _____ is a measure of the dispersion of a collection of numbers. It can apply to a probability distribution, a random variable, a population or a data set. The _____ is usually denoted with the letter σ.
   a. Statistical population
   b. Null hypothesis
   c. Standard deviation
   d. Failure rate

26. In mathematics and statistics, _____ is a measure of difference for interval and ratio variables between the observed value and the mean. The sign of _____, either positive or negative, indicates whether the observation is larger than or smaller than the mean. The magnitude of the value reports how different an observation is from the mean.
   a. Deviation
   b. Functional
   c. Conchoid
   d. Filter

27. In mathematics and in the sciences, a _____ (plural: _____e, formulæ or _____s) is a concise way of expressing information symbolically (as in a mathematical or chemical _____), or a general relationship between quantities. One of many famous _____e is Albert Einstein's E = mc^2 (see special relativity

In mathematics, a _____ is a key to solve an equation with variables. For example, the problem of determining the volume of a sphere is one that requires a significant amount of integral calculus to solve.

   a. Formula
   b. 120-cell
   c. 1-center problem
   d. 2-3 heap

28. In vascular plants, the _____ is the organ of a plant body that typically lies below the surface of the soil. This is not always the case, however, since a _____ can also be aerial (that is, growing above the ground) or aerating (that is, growing up above the ground or especially above water.) Furthermore, a stem normally occurring below ground is not exceptional either
   a. 120-cell
   b. 2-3 heap
   c. 1-center problem
   d. Root

Chapter 18. PROBABILITY AND CALCULUS

29. A _____ is a set of standard clothing worn by members of an organization while participating in that organization's activity. Modern _____s are worn by armed forces and paramilitary organisations such as police, emergency services, security guards, in some workplaces and schools and by inmates in prisons. In some countries, some other officials also wear _____s in some of their duties; such is the case of the Commissioned Corps of the United States Public Health Service or the French prefects.
- a. Uniform
- b. A Mathematical Theory of Communication
- c. A posteriori
- d. A chemical equation

30. In probability theory and statistics, the _____ is a family of probability distributions such that for each member of the family, all intervals of the same length on the distribution's support are equally probable. The support is defined by the two parameters, a and b, which are its minimum and maximum values. The distribution is often abbreviated U
- a. Convex conjugation
- b. Continuous uniform distribution
- c. Continuity correction
- d. Convergence of measures

31. In probability theory and statistics, the _____s are a class of continuous probability distributions. They describe the times between events in a Poisson process.

The probability density function of an _____ has the form

$$f(x;\lambda) = \begin{cases} \lambda e^{-\lambda x} &, x \geq 0, \\ 0 &, x < 0. \end{cases}$$

where λ > 0 is a parameter of the distribution, often called the rate parameter.

- a. A chemical equation
- b. A posteriori
- c. A Mathematical Theory of Communication
- d. Exponential distribution

32. In mathematics, specifically in combinatorial commutative algebra, a convex lattice polytope P is called _____ if it has the following property: given any positive integer n, every lattice point of the dilation nP, obtained from P by scaling its vertices by the factor n and taking the convex hull of the resulting points, can be written as the sum of exactly n lattice points in P. This property plays an important role in the theory of toric varieties, where it corresponds to projective normality of the toric variety determined by P.

The simplex in R^k with the vertices at the origin and along the unit coordinate vectors is _____.

- a. Hypercube
- b. Demihypercubes
- c. Polytetrahedron
- d. Normal

33. The _____ is an important family of continuous probability distributions, applicable in many fields. Each member of the family may be defined by two parameters, location and scale: the mean and variance respectively. The standard _____ is the _____ with a mean of zero and a variance of one.
- a. Null hypothesis
- b. Normal distribution
- c. Percentile rank
- d. Coefficient of variation

Chapter 18. PROBABILITY AND CALCULUS

34. _____ is a quantity expressing the two-dimensional size of a defined part of a surface, typically a region bounded by a closed curve. The term surface _____ refers to the total _____ of the exposed surface of a 3-dimensional solid, such as the sum of the _____s of the exposed sides of a polyhedron. _____ is an important invariant in the differential geometry of surfaces.

    a. A chemical equation
    b. A Mathematical Theory of Communication
    c. A posteriori
    d. Area

35. In mathematics, the concept of a _____ tries to capture the intuitive idea of a geometrical one-dimensional and continuous object. A simple example is the circle. In everyday use of the term '_____', a straight line is not curved, but in mathematical parlance _____s include straight lines and line segments.

    a. Kappa curve
    b. Quadrifolium
    c. Negative pedal curve
    d. Curve

36. _____ is a branch of mathematics which focuses on the study of matrices. Initially a sub-branch of linear algebra, it has grown to cover subjects related to graph theory, algebra, combinatorics, and statistics as well.

The term matrix was first coined in 1848 by J.J. Sylvester as a name of an array of numbers.

    a. Pairing
    b. Semi-simple operators
    c. Segre classification
    d. Matrix theory

37. _____ is a dimensionless quantity derived by subtracting the population mean from an individual raw score and then dividing the difference by the population standard deviation.

    a. 1-center problem
    b. 2-3 heap
    c. 120-cell
    d. Z-score

38. In statistics, a standard score is a dimensionless quantity derived by subtracting the population mean from an individual raw score and then dividing the difference by the population standard deviation. This conversion process is called standardizing or normalizing.

Standard scores are also called z-values, _____, normal scores, and standardized variables.

    a. CIE 1931 XYZ color space
    b. Z-scores
    c. Converge absolutely
    d. Bernstein inequalities

39. In computational complexity theory, an algorithm is said to take _____ if the asymptotic upper bound for the time it requires is proportional to the size of the input, which is usually denoted n.

Informally spoken, the running time increases linearly with the size of the input. For example, a procedure that adds up all elements of a list requires time proportional to the length of the list.

    a. Truth table reduction
    b. Time-constructible function
    c. Linear time
    d. Constructible function

40. The word _____ has many distinct meanings in different fields of knowledge, depending on their methodologies and the context of discussion. Broadly speaking we can say that a _____ is some kind of belief or claim that (supposedly) explains, asserts, or consolidates some class of claims. Additionally, in contrast with a theorem the statement of the _____ is generally accepted only in some tentative fashion as opposed to regarding it as having been conclusively established.
   a. Transport of structure
   b. Theory
   c. Per mil
   d. Defined

ANSWER KEY

Chapter 1
1. a	2. d	3. d	4. c	5. b	6. d	7. d	8. d	9. d	10. d
11. a	12. b	13. b	14. d	15. d	16. d	17. a	18. d	19. d	20. a
21. b	22. b	23. d	24. b	25. b	26. d	27. c	28. a	29. d	30. d
31. b	32. d	33. b	34. c	35. d	36. b	37. d	38. d	39. d	40. d
41. d	42. c	43. d	44. d	45. c	46. d	47. d	48. c	49. a	50. d
51. d	52. d	53. a	54. a	55. d	56. b	57. c	58. a	59. b	

Chapter 2
1. a	2. d	3. d	4. b	5. d	6. d	7. d	8. c	9. a	10. d
11. c	12. b	13. b	14. c	15. d	16. d	17. c	18. d	19. d	20. d
21. d	22. b	23. c	24. d	25. b	26. d				

Chapter 3
1. b	2. b	3. d	4. a	5. d	6. a	7. c	8. d	9. c	10. b
11. b	12. d	13. d	14. b	15. a	16. b				

Chapter 4
1. a	2. d	3. b	4. c	5. b	6. d	7. c	8. d	9. d	10. d
11. d	12. d	13. d	14. b	15. d	16. d	17. c	18. b	19. d	20. a
21. b	22. d	23. d	24. d	25. a					

Chapter 5
1. b	2. a	3. a	4. d	5. c	6. d	7. d	8. a	9. c	10. d
11. d	12. a	13. b	14. d	15. b	16. c	17. d	18. d	19. d	20. d
21. d	22. d	23. d							

Chapter 6
1. b	2. b	3. a	4. a	5. b	6. a	7. b	8. b	9. d	10. a
11. c	12. a	13. c	14. d	15. b	16. d	17. c	18. c	19. b	20. c
21. b									

Chapter 7
1. d	2. a	3. d	4. d	5. a	6. d	7. d	8. b	9. b	10. a
11. d	12. d	13. d	14. d	15. d	16. b	17. b	18. c	19. d	20. a
21. c	22. d	23. d	24. d	25. d	26. a	27. d	28. b	29. d	30. d
31. d	32. b	33. d	34. d	35. a	36. d				

Chapter 8
1. a	2. d	3. d	4. a	5. c	6. d	7. d	8. d	9. d	10. d
11. d	12. b	13. a	14. b	15. a	16. d	17. b	18. d	19. d	20. c
21. d	22. d	23. a	24. d	25. d	26. c	27. d	28. d	29. a	30. a
31. b	32. d	33. d	34. b	35. d	36. d	37. d	38. d	39. d	40. b
41. d	42. d								

Chapter 9

1. a	2. a	3. d	4. a	5. b	6. b	7. a	8. c	9. c	10. d
11. c	12. a	13. a	14. d	15. d	16. c	17. d	18. b	19. a	20. a
21. d	22. d	23. d	24. d	25. d	26. a	27. d	28. d	29. a	30. b
31. a	32. d	33. d	34. c	35. a	36. c	37. a	38. b	39. d	40. b
41. d	42. d	43. d	44. d	45. c	46. c	47. c	48. c	49. c	50. d
51. d	52. d	53. b	54. d						

Chapter 10

1. d	2. d	3. d	4. b	5. d	6. b	7. d	8. d	9. d	10. b
11. a	12. b	13. d	14. d	15. d	16. d	17. d	18. d	19. c	20. d
21. d	22. a	23. c	24. d	25. a	26. c	27. a	28. a	29. d	30. a
31. d	32. d	33. d	34. b	35. c	36. d	37. d	38. b	39. d	40. d
41. a	42. d	43. c	44. a	45. d	46. d	47. d	48. d	49. d	50. b
51. d	52. b	53. d	54. b	55. b	56. a	57. d	58. a	59. b	60. c
61. b	62. d	63. d	64. d	65. d	66. d	67. d	68. c	69. d	70. b
71. b	72. b	73. d	74. d	75. b	76. a	77. c	78. b	79. d	80. a
81. b	82. d	83. a	84. d	85. c	86. a				

Chapter 11

1. b	2. d	3. a	4. c	5. d	6. b	7. d	8. a	9. d	10. b
11. b	12. a	13. d	14. a	15. d	16. d	17. c	18. d	19. c	20. d
21. c	22. b	23. d	24. d	25. a	26. d	27. a	28. d	29. c	30. d
31. d	32. d	33. d	34. a	35. d	36. d	37. b	38. a	39. d	40. d
41. b	42. d	43. d	44. c	45. a	46. d	47. d			

Chapter 12

1. a	2. d	3. b	4. d	5. a	6. c	7. d	8. b	9. a	10. a
11. c	12. b	13. d	14. d	15. d	16. d	17. d	18. a	19. b	20. b
21. d	22. a	23. a	24. d	25. b	26. d	27. d	28. a	29. c	30. d
31. a	32. d	33. d	34. a	35. a	36. d	37. d	38. d	39. d	40. a
41. c									

Chapter 13

1. b	2. d	3. d	4. d	5. d	6. d	7. a	8. d	9. b	10. d
11. d	12. b	13. a	14. a	15. d	16. d	17. a	18. c	19. a	20. d
21. a	22. c	23. c	24. c	25. d	26. d	27. b	28. a	29. d	30. d
31. d	32. b	33. a	34. a	35. b	36. a				

ANSWER KEY

Chapter 14

1. b	2. d	3. c	4. a	5. d	6. b	7. d	8. b	9. b	10. b
11. d	12. d	13. c	14. d	15. d	16. d	17. d	18. a	19. c	20. d
21. c	22. a	23. d	24. d	25. a	26. a	27. a	28. a	29. d	30. d
31. d	32. b	33. d	34. d	35. d	36. a	37. d	38. c	39. c	40. a
41. d	42. a								

Chapter 15

1. d	2. c	3. d	4. d	5. d	6. d	7. a	8. c	9. c	10. c
11. b	12. b	13. c	14. d	15. d	16. c	17. b	18. a	19. c	20. d
21. d	22. d	23. a	24. c	25. d	26. d	27. c	28. c	29. a	30. d
31. a	32. d	33. d	34. a	35. a	36. d	37. a	38. d	39. b	40. d
41. d	42. d	43. d	44. d	45. d	46. d	47. d	48. b	49. d	50. c
51. d	52. d	53. a	54. a	55. d	56. b	57. d	58. d	59. d	60. d
61. d									

Chapter 16

1. d	2. c	3. b	4. d	5. d	6. d	7. d	8. b	9. d	10. d
11. c	12. a	13. b	14. d	15. d	16. d	17. d	18. a	19. c	20. c
21. d	22. d	23. a	24. d	25. c	26. d	27. d	28. c	29. c	30. d
31. b	32. a	33. d	34. a	35. c	36. a	37. d	38. a	39. b	40. d
41. a	42. b	43. d	44. d	45. a	46. a	47. c	48. b	49. b	50. b
51. d	52. d	53. d	54. d						

Chapter 17

1. a	2. d	3. b	4. a	5. c	6. a	7. d	8. d	9. b	10. a
11. a	12. d	13. a	14. b	15. a	16. d	17. d	18. a	19. d	20. d
21. d	22. d	23. b	24. b	25. d	26. b	27. d	28. d	29. c	30. a
31. c	32. a	33. b	34. d	35. c	36. c	37. c	38. d	39. b	40. d
41. d	42. d	43. d	44. b	45. c	46. d	47. b	48. c	49. c	50. a
51. c	52. c	53. c	54. b	55. b	56. a	57. b	58. d	59. d	

Chapter 18

1. b	2. d	3. d	4. d	5. c	6. d	7. a	8. a	9. d	10. d
11. a	12. d	13. d	14. d	15. c	16. b	17. b	18. b	19. b	20. d
21. d	22. d	23. c	24. d	25. c	26. a	27. a	28. d	29. a	30. b
31. d	32. d	33. b	34. d	35. d	36. d	37. d	38. b	39. c	40. b